Lost Legion Rediscovered

*To my beloved wife, without whose bemused
diligence this would've been impossible.*

Lost Legion Rediscovered

The Mystery of the Theban Legion

Donald O'Reilly

Pen & Sword
MILITARY

First published in Great Britain in 2011 by
Pen & Sword Military
an imprint of
Pen & Sword Books Ltd
47 Church Street
Barnsley
South Yorkshire
S70 2AS

Copyright © Donald O'Reilly 2011

ISBN 978–1-84884-378-3

Typeset in 11pt Ehrhardt by
Mac Style, Beverley, E. Yorkshire

Printed and bound in the UK by CPI

Pen & Sword Books Ltd incorporates the imprints of Pen & Sword Aviation,
Pen & Sword Maritime, Pen & Sword Military, Wharncliffe Local History,
Pen and Sword Select, Pen and Sword Military Classics and Leo Cooper.

For a complete list of Pen & Sword titles please contact
PEN & SWORD BOOKS LIMITED
47 Church Street, Barnsley, South Yorkshire, S70 2AS, England
E-mail: enquiries@pen-and-sword.co.uk
Website: www.pen-and-sword.co.uk

Contents

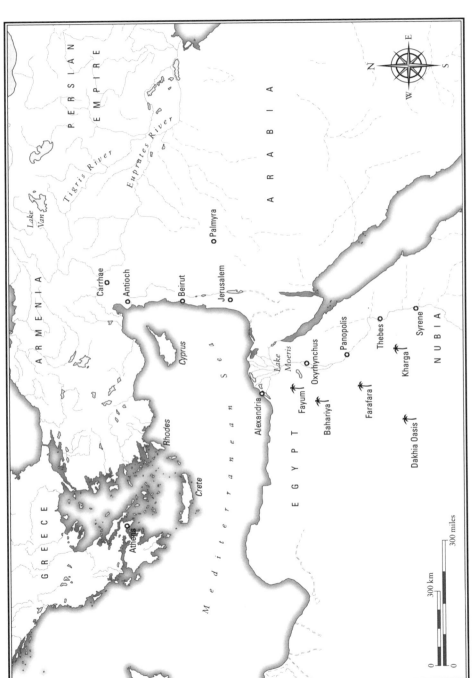

Map 1: Egypt and the Middle East.

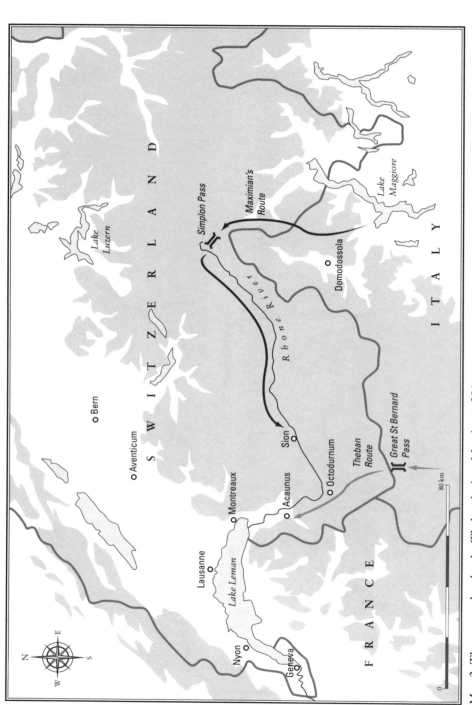

Map 2: The route taken by the Theban legion, March, AD 286.

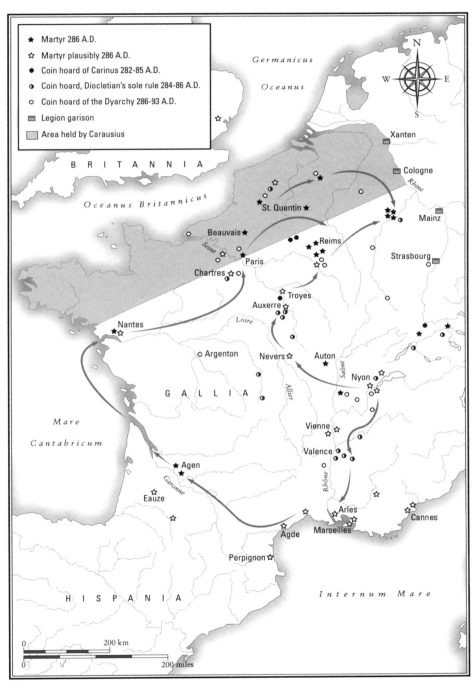

Legend:

★ Martyr 286 A.D.
☆ Martyr plausibly 286 A.D.
● Coin hoard of Carinus 282-85 A.D.
◑ Coin hoard, Diocletian's sole rule 284-86 A.D.
○ Coin hoard of the Dyarchy 286-93 A.D.
▦ Legion garison
▨ Area held by Carausius

Germanicus

Oceanus

B R I T A N N I A

Xanten

Oceanus Britannicus

Cologne

Rhine

St. Quentin ★

Mainz

Beauvais ★

Seine

Reims

Paris

Strasbourg

Chartres ☆

Troyes

Auxerre

Nantes

Loire

Argenton

Nevers ☆

Auton

G A L L I A

Allier

Saône

Nyon

Mare

Cantabricum

Vienne

Valence

Rhône

Agen

Eauze ☆

Garonne

Arles

Cannes

Agde

Marseilles

Perpignon ☆

H I S P A N I A

Internum Mare

0 ___ 200 km

0 ___ 200 miles

Map 3: Maximian's campaign against the Baguadae.

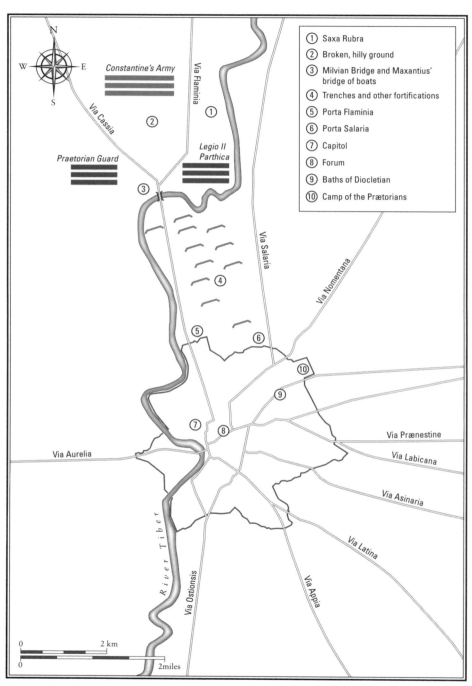

Map 4: The Battle of the Milvian Bridge, 28 October, AD 312.

Foreword

Who knows if the best of man be known?
Or whether there be more remarkable persons forgot?

Thomas Browne

Jesus commanded 'Render to Caesar the things that are Caesar's and to God the things that are God's.'[1] Is military service an obligation to Caesar? The New Testament does not resolve the issue since the first members of the Church were Jews, a people barred from military duty to Rome at their own request to Julius Caesar for religious reasons.[2]

Christians not of Jewish origin in the early Church were mostly Greeks, another people denied access to the army.[3] Auxiliary units were roughly half of the army. Bearing the titles of tribes and nationalities from which they were recruited, none of these units were Greek. This was not the result of requested exemption but discrimination. If Jews disarmed themselves, it suited Rome. Greeks were stereotyped as too clever, ambitious and clannish. Most Christians in the first centuries were pacifists ineligible for army duty.

Religio, to Romans, was literally that which held things together. Cicero in the first century before Christ wrote that 'Philosophy has never touched the mass of mankind except through religions.'[4] As prosecutor in a trial involving a murdered slaveowner,[5] he approved the execution of more than 400 of the master's slaves. Cicero did not believe in a god with personal concern for mankind. He scorned the stoic ideal of human equality.[6] He loathed 'the wretched starving mob, the bloodsucker of the treasury.' While writing of his contempt for superstition, publicly he was the exemplar of religiosity, a priest of the imperial cult as a function of office. This to him was not hypocrisy but necessity, fear of the gods essential to keep the ignorant majority from heinous crime.

Romans were to honour the deities of the imperial cult when required by the government. Those in authority and ordinary people sincerely believed – not necessarily from the same motives – that to deny such rites risked disunity or divine vengeance upon society. To refuse was uncivil, blasphemous and unpatriotic. Jesus had warned that 'the day shall come when they will persecute and kill you honestly believing that they are doing a service to God'.[7]

This religiosity was manifest in the ceremonies of the army. In the Roman era the Judaic religious document called the War Scroll of the Dead Sea Scrolls identified the sons of darkness, the enemies of God and Israel, as those who march about in formation and worship military standards as their idols.[8] In all likelihood these were soldiers of Rome. The rites that marked off the Roman military calendar were routinely religious. Priests of the imperial cult and official fortune tellers accompanied every legion. [9]

The *sacramentum*, the pagan military oath, was not taken individually but by officers acting as representatives. A baptized soldier required to take the oath would be faced with a choice between losing his life or losing his soul as Christians saw it.

The Roman Empire had no military conscription except the rare *dilecta* or draft, which applied only to Italians. Its soldiers were volunteers enlisted for a minimum of twenty-five years. Slaves, city welfare recipients, serfs, criminals and gladiators were barred.[10] As the middle class of free farmers, whether small landowners, hired hands, tenants or share-croppers, was ever decreasing so too was the Empire's pool of recruits. Christians refused to serve as soldiers or officials and were understandably resented by pagans.

The early Church refused baptism to soldiers as well as pimps, prostitutes, slave dealers, gladiators, actors, and teachers.[11] The objection to the latter was not their job but the pagan content of the usual curriculum.

The moral priority of the gospels is the de-escalation of violence. To Mohandas Gandhi, violence was anything dehumanizing. Violence began within a person as self-pity, self-hatred, insult, prejudice, racism, contempt, lies, cowardice, exaggeration and the like. The Stoic Emperor Marcus Aurelius remarked that 'Refusing to imitate is the best revenge.'[12] To turn the other cheek was to refuse to take insult to heart as the insulter desired. It defused escalation of violence. It did not deny the right of self-defence nor the moral obligation to defend those with claim protection.

Roman slaves were set free by their masters in a public rite in which the slave was slapped on one side of the face and then the other.[13] Ages later this *alapsa* became the touch on each shoulder with the flat of a sword, the accolade that made a man a knight. The recipient in not retaliating demonstrated goodwill.

Baptized Christians were excommunicated if they entered the Roman army but soldiers on active duty were attracted to Christianity nonetheless. Catechumens, initiates, not baptized, were allowed to participate only partially in Christian worship. Upon retirement, soldiers, if catechumens, could be baptized.

Soldiers of Christian creed received few guidelines from Church philosophers, remote from the battle zones. In response to situations confronting them they hammered out their own military morality. While the Acts give the impression that they were acting in isolation, comparative analysis shows that they increasingly acted in unison as their numbers grew.

It has been held that the *sacramentum*, the pagan military oath, was the sole reason that soldiers were denied baptism.[14] This implies that obeying orders to kill was no problem in conscience to Christians in the army. Here, emphasis will be on the deeds of the martyrs rather than the philosophy of the Church fathers; events enacted in sweat and blood, not abstract theory.

Violence can be de-escalated but is better not initiated but deterred. Deterrence is best effected by professional military or police. Yet, the worst crimes in history have been committed by normally decent men blindly obedient to military orders.

Introduction

God and the soldier all men adore in time of danger and no more. For when the danger is past and all things righted, God is forgotten and the soldier slighted.

Rudyard Kipling

Most of history is an obscenity, literally off-scene. Most of the reality of events are never recorded. Those in authority may have had motive to suppress it. Nothing remains more obscene than military insubordination, whether in the armed forces of any modern nation or ages ago.

This volume is an adventure in scholarship, a detective quest to reveal the truth of such an event. If the events had occurred in recent memory in Vietnam or Afghanistan, the evidence would be destroyed or concealed. These happened seventeen centuries ago, when Christians of a Roman legion were annihilated for rejecting orders they considered immoral.

Assuming the evidence ever existed, presumably most is lost. The tale is legend.

That every ancient legend contains a grain of truth is an illusion. An old tale may be wrought of imagination, misunderstanding and error hallowed by age and tradition.[1]

In 383, Bishop Eucherius of Lyon recorded that a Roman legion of Christians recruited in the Theban district of Egypt was annihilated in south-western Switzerland at the village known today as St Maurice-en-Valais, for rejecting commands they held immoral.[2] A flood collapsing a bank of the River Rhone revealing a mass grave identified as that of the Thebans had prompted his sermon.

This is cited as occurring under the *caesar* Maximian Herculius, a rank held only briefly in the spring of 286 AD. It relates no miracles but asserts as facts matters elsewhere unrecorded. One might consider it good reason to dismiss it as fiction since Roman authorities never executed an entire legion even in civil wars, yet the monastic accounts all agree that the Theban legionnaires were at least 6,000 in number.

The earliest manuscript of the event was written a century after it supposedly occurred, a time gap that prompts doubts. The story had enemies, both pagan and Christian, with motive to suppress it. Nevertheless, legions do vanish without explanation in Roman histories. Roman rulers forbid bad news to be publicized.[3] No historian mentioned the volcanic destruction of Pompeii and Herculaneum in 79. Only a letter of an eyewitness, Pliny, records it. Plutarch, in his biographies of prominent Greeks and Romans, told quite a different story than the official politically correct versions. He shrewdly arranged his works be publicized only after his death. Tacitus, perhaps the greatest of Roman historians, was beheaded for his blunt honesty about the early imperial rulers.

Christian historians at odds with the story included the bishop Eusebius[4] of Caesarea an Arian Christian who in seeking the favour of Emperor Constantine obscured the insubordination of military martyrs. The Theban Legion has never been recognized by Orthodox churches. Lactantius,[5] a layman, abhorred the thought of Christians in the armed forces. Both writers denied that there were any military martyrs between 252 and 304. Yet scores of records of the deaths of hundreds survive to directly contradict their view.

Martyrs were first honoured only where they fell, usually as mere epitaphs of surname, place of death and the emperor at the time. Family names and career backgrounds were considered worldly and of no concern to a Christian. Years later, the relics might be distributed to several churches, creating an impression that not one but many persons were commemorated. A reverse tendency also existed. Several persons with the same name might be merged by scribes into one super saint, as in the case of St George. Occasionally, the historical details were recorded at some length in documents called Acts or Passions.

Persecutors systematically destroyed whatever evidence of the victims they could find, whether bodily remains or written records. Overall, the pious records convey the impression of a long casualty list with the Acts as occasional citations, with personality, social relationships and politics missing, the complexities and psychological depths of real people reduced to platitude and one dimension.

To delve into the legend of the Theban Legion by relying upon the Acts begs the question. In order to be unbiased, the search must depend upon clues, both official and pagan, such as coinage, chronicles, inscriptions on stone, bureaucratic papyri, imperial army lists and the findings of archaeology.

The Acts used here include previously untapped Church records translated in the twentieth century from the Coptic language of pre-Arab Egypt.[6] That they describe events missing in Greek and Latin accounts suggests that the attitudes of these martyrs disturbed many politically conservative Christians.

In the West, Protestant historians have tended to ignore the martyrs entirely. Hagiographers, largely Catholic, have meticulously assembled and translated the records, but rarely compared them with other sources. This is typical of continental European scholars, specialists in translations, coinage, inscriptions etc., producing a wealth of brilliant but narrow research.

Without the labour of these specialists, this work would have been impossible. The debt to them is total. Nevertheless, only a generalist could have succeeded in this investigation.

Chapter 1

Eavesdropping Yields a Clue

When there are too many coincidences, that aint no coincidence.
                                                        Yogi Berra

History too often is the propaganda of icons of power. How can we ever know the thoughts of ordinary people, the unsung stuff of human nature, lives long forgotten? One way is to read their personal letters.

The first clue that the Theban Legion was a reality emerged in scanning translations of papyri in Greek, unearthed in Egypt by village boys hired by an archaeologist to scour an ancient rubbish dump.[1] His primary motive at the time was to keep them from mischief at his archaeological diggings. These papyri were found at Oxyrynchus, once the Roman headquarters of Egypt's Thebaid district. They were direct sampling of everyday concerns to be placed against the official version of things by censored Roman historians. To read them was to eavesdrop across centuries.

Bills of payment to a mouse-catcher, a reward offered for a runaway slave, shopping lists, loans usually at 12 to 15 per cent interest, marriage contracts threatening loss of the dowry if the bride is mistreated – the papyri weave the tapestry of existence on the Roman Nile.

Questions to a fortune teller ask, 'Am I being poisoned?' 'Will I get a furlough?' 'Should I agree to the contract?' 'Will I be sold?' 'Am I to become a beggar?'

A husband writes to his absent wife that he mourns for her 'weeping by night and lamenting by day'. Spouses usually addressed one another as 'my master' or 'mistress', 'lord' or 'lady', or more typically, 'brother' or 'sister'. Along the Nile, to keep land legally in the family it was not unusual for men to marry their sisters. A wife urges her voyaging husband to return, pleading that a neighbour 'has made a prostitute of me'. A husband on a trip instructs his pregnant wife to abandon her expected infant if a girl. 'How can I forget thee?' he adds.

Another revelation is the apprentice papers for a boy whose mother is not yet of legal adult age. A schoolboy's note tells his father that he has an excellent teacher who has stopped instructing him because he is unpaid. There is no doubt who suggested the letter. Wills dividing slaves among heirs are commonplace. Almost all slaves in Egypt were household servants.

A young woman visiting Syria says that her mother has died on the journey. 'I am an orphan alone in a strange land.' She begs her kin to come to her. Presumably, as a woman she feared to return alone.

Greek was the international language of the East, where it was used routinely by the Roman army. The papyri were usually dictated to a scribe who wrote for a fee.

The importance of the army in Egypt is manifest in the papyri. A civilian intercedes with an officer to be lenient to a soldier who has been AWOL, promising not to intercede again. There are many complaints to officers against their men. The moonlit shearing of sheep to sell the wool, unpaid pub bills and loitering outside the women's public baths are parts of the picture. That the writers expect justice and do not fear to put their names to charges on paper posits that justice was possible.

Only a military court could judge a Roman soldier.[2] In the more than sixty army posts in Egypt, isolation and efficiency gave army officers the status of civilian judges. The army at least had discipline and a clear chain of command. Civil officials too often were like one whom a papyrus letter warns of making the rounds and likely to drink the village dry.

The Roman emperor owned virtually all land in Egypt. The land was rented at reasonable rates as innumerable small farms, in sharp contrast to the plantations leased in huge sections elsewhere in the Empire. Many soldiers in Egypt rented farms by deduction from their pay. They shared peasant interests and attitudes, and had a loyalty to those dependent upon them, unlike soldiers in some provinces – a thuggish race apart, dreaded more than the barbarians. While the majority of the population were Copts, speaking the language of the pharaohs before them, Greeks dominated the economy. The Greeks had conquered all the Middle East five centuries earlier, but their practice of infanticide (especially of females), a practice Egyptian morality rejected, undermined their numbers and political rule.[3]

Forbidden to travel to any other province, the city and seaport of Alexandria legally a separate province, frustrated by hard labour, poverty, monotony and often incestuous village relationships, and smouldering under oppressions against which they were powerless, the Copts could erupt in terrible violence. Exiled to Egypt, the satirist Juvenal related that on one occasion two villages warred in a feud provoked by the killing of a sacred crocodile, a patron deity. A man was supposedly murdered and cannibalized as a result.[4]

The Greeks, in order to unify the region, had invented a new deity, Serapis, the father of the gods, a belief tending towards monotheism.[5] Local temples with their tax and rental revenues were incorporated into the governmental cult. The creed of Serapis was deliberately kept free of myth or doctrine, like that of Jupiter-Highest-and-Best. The temples provided schooling and other social services at a moderate cost. An official religion emphasizing harmony with the state, the worship of Serapis was, nevertheless, genuinely popular, unlike the imperial cult of the Roman gods.

Christianity was expanding rapidly. Serapis tended to be viewed as identical with God the Father. The oldest known fragment of a gospel is Rylands Papyrus 457, dating from about the year 130, found in the Fayoum, west of the Nile delta. By the late third century there were seventy-two communities with bishops in Egypt. The word Copt presently refers to Egypt's Christian minority.

The troops in Egypt were in ancestry from the rest of the Empire, although intermarriage with Copts was usual. One legion, II Traiana, guarded the Nile.[6] The unnumbered Legio Julia Alexandriana was stationed in Alexandria. The other half of the garrisons comprised auxiliary cohorts or cavalry in five hundred or one thousand men complements. In Bar Kochba's revolt, a legion of Greco-Copts, the III Deotariana, had been annihilated. Egyptian troops sent to Armenia in 195 had mutinied.[7] Thereafter, few soldiers from Egypt served anywhere beyond the Nile Valley.

The Empire was faced with a dwindling pool of army recruits. The population was falling, with the class of free citizens dwindling even more rapidly, and fewer willing to volunteer. Slaves, criminals, gladiators, welfare-recipients and serfs were ineligible, considered incapable of good discipline.

Egyptians under Roman rule paid exorbitant taxes, chiefly in grains for export. Farm hands could be temporarily drafted to work on state land. The citizens of towns were exempt from many of these duties, but required to take turns as tax collectors. Collateral for the collection assessment was their confiscated property.[8] As the ruling class dwindled, the burden upon it crushingly increased,[9] motivating many to flee their districts.[10]

An edict of Caracalla (r. 211–217) in response[11] had expanded the number of citizens[12] obliged to do liturgy by granting citizenship to the Greek *peregrini*,[13] legally resident aliens, dominating most towns.

The overwhelming majority of the populace, the Copts, remained *dediticii*,[14] legally prisoners of war, bound to the land with few rights. Most were illiterate and spoke only Coptic.

The papyri reveal widespread abandonment of farms and villages. Plague, revolts and desertion reduced numbers. Reduction of land tax assessments did not keep pace with the lowered crop yields that resulted from neglect of the irrigation system. Emperor Probus, in reaction, put the army to work dredging badly silted irrigation canals.[15]

The dwindling population of the Thebaid had incurred invasion by its barbarian neighbours, the Blemmyes, the bronzed ancestors of the Beja and Somali.[16] Aided by disaffected townspeople, they overran much of the upper Nile Valley until Probus' forces restored Roman rule.[17]

Worsening the Thebaid's vulnerability, its southern frontier south of Syene had been virtually abandoned for a generation. Archaeology reveals its forts to be unoccupied in the period.[18] Encroaching cliffs narrowed the arable lands of the region, which yielded little in taxation.

It was recognized that only a transformation in policy could prevent further invasions. The Nobatae, a negro people that in earlier ages were called Medjay, from Kharga Oasis, some 150 miles due west of Thebes, were invited to resettle in the region.[19] Medjay, originally, was the name of a tribe, but having provided soldiers, police and guards for the pharaohs for long ages, the word came to mean 'a soldier'. The Kharga depression extended for a hundred miles, its water table creating many habitable areas. Paid subsidies by Rome, the Nobatae were neither *dediticii* nor citizens. Presumably, they were *gentili*, tribes friendly to Rome that were brought into the Empire and as recruits promoted to *peregrini*, a status according with facts to be noted later in the Theban Legion's story.

Young Nobatae and people from other oases west of the Nile Valley provided a new source of manpower for the depleted army. They proved to be reliable allies for almost a century. Their non-Roman tribal origins explains the black African predominance in the tradition of the Legion. Only citizens were allowed in the legions.[20] *Peregrini*, however, could join the grain fleet, Legio Julia Alexandrina.[21] The Theban Legion was perhaps intended not as an infantry, but a fleet marine unit.

The present research into the Theban Legion began in browsing through the Oxyrynchus papyri. Perusing the papyri, one in particular caught attention. It was dated about the time the Theban Legion, if it existed, must have left Egypt. It was a receipt penned by a scribe at Panopolis (Akhmim) for bread delivered to the army as shipping-out rations. The requisition dates 13 January 282 and the receipt, dated 21 May 284, states: '…delivered at Panopolis in obedience to the order of his excellency … to the mobilized soldiers and sailors thirty-eight thousand four hundred and ninety-six *modii* of bread, total 38,496.'[22] Sixty *modii*, approximately thirty bushels, was the yearly Roman grain ration for a soldier.[23] For a person relying on no other food, a pound and a half of grain a day is ample ration. A Roman soldier's daily ration was some 3,000 calories.

This, therefore, was an order for some 240,000 daily rations. Bread and hard biscuit, usually of barley, was only disbursed to soldiers going overseas or actively campaigning. The receipt was for enough rations for some 6,000 men, to last a month or more.

Egyptians paid their taxes not in the tetradrachms of the Alexandrian mint but in grain. The government would not accept its own local currency as tax payment. Paper money did not exist. Coins were valued for the quality of their metal. Alexandrian tetradrachms were a cheap alloy of bronze and lead.

The grain demanded in the papyrus was not the normal tax but an addition to it, a portent of things to come. Since the emperor directly owned Egypt's land, unlike that of other provinces, new policies began in Egypt before being attempted elsewhere.

Another papyrus of 284 from the town of Oxyrynchus mentions some of the same officials as the Panopolis receipt. It asks for a special meeting to get supplies immediately aboard the ships at dockside awaiting troops.[24] Neither document mentions any specific unit.

The author as a community college history teacher had as one of his students a professional ancient coin dealer. In conversations with this student, the idea arose that Roman coins might provide objective non-Christian evidence of the Theban Legion. Obtaining a summer grant for study from the Foundation for the Humanities, the coinage of Roman Egypt became the focus of study.

Egypt's coinage denomination was quite unlike that of the rest of the Roman world, and quite inferior, lead substituting for the silver used elsewhere in coinage. The intent was to force anyone leaving Egypt to exchange money lest it be useless outside of Egypt, in effect a tax. Any substantial quantity of Egyptian money outside of Egypt would be an anomaly, something demanding an explanation.

The chief mint in Egypt was that of Alexandria with another at Oxyrynchus, their issues chiefly tetradrachms equal in value to the silver denarius typical elsewhere in the Empire, the day's wages of a semi-skilled worker.

The Alexandrian year began on 30 August. The papyrus receipt from Oxyrynchus in the Thebaid had been officially audited 23 May 8/284 to 9/285, having been written two years earlier.

Roman money bore the portrait of the ruler at the time on one side and a motif on the other. Among Egypt's Alexandrian tetradrachms from 30 August 282 to 30 August 284, the most common motif is that of an eagle standing between cloth banners, *vexilla*.[25] This appeared only in certain years, Roman coins well catalogued by centuries of scholars.

The eagle symbolized the legions of Rome. The cloth banner was carried by *vexillationes*, troop detachments serving away from their home legion or to join a new legion in formative stage.

The meaning of these symbols was well accepted.

Could these coins tell us something important in our quest? The eagle between banners motif appeared from time to time elsewhere in the Empire on denominations other than tetradrachms.

A hypothesis emerged that might explain things, an idea that could be objectively proven or disproven.

A list of every known example of the eagle between banners on Roman coins from throughout the Empire across three centuries was undertaken, in order to compare it with the hunch, the hypothesis, that it appeared only when and where a new legion was being recruited.

Roman historians and inscriptions on stone are the sources for the dates of the inaugurations of new legions.

The motif never appears on the coinage of the twelve emperors who did not create new legions.

Thirty-six matches in time and place of the recruitment of new legions speak for themselves to reinforce the evidence.[26]

Another explanation for the papyrus citing the embarking troops can be posited. Legio II Traiana, long Egypt's only legion, was shipping out to Spain and North Africa under the same rulers as those issuing the eagle between banners, the Emperor Carus and his sons, Carinius and Numerian.[27] Alexandrian tetradrachms of the year beginning 30 August 284 unmistakably bear that legion's name.[28]

None of the coins bearing the name of Legio II Traiana bear the motif of an eagle between banners. The papyrus receipt for bread is dated the sixth Alexandrian year of Emperor Probus, 21 May 284. The troops mobilized from the Thebaid district cited in the papyri had sailed away earlier than Legio II Traiana's embarkation.

To utilize the administration of II Traiana in order to organize the new unit was practical. Recruiting thousands of young men while adding a new tax to a people already sorely exploited in the absence of the legion that had long preserved order could have been an invitation to revolt.

The eagle between banners coins of the year of the shipping-out rations receipt in many cases bear a Greek letter on each banner, a circle on the left and dot on the right, the usual form for omega omicron, the first letters of Oxyrynchus. This suggests that they were issued by an army mint in that city of the Thebaid and not in Alexandria.[29]

Evidently, a Theban Legion had existed but was the legend about it true?

Research revealed that the 1949 collapse of the sheer cliff alongside the church at St Maurice-en-Valais in Switzerland occasioned major renovations. Digging in its foundations, a chamber hidden for centuries was discovered, containing funeral cremation urns. The walls were painted in red and yellow lozenges, the coat of arms of the Egyptian Thebaid.

To discover the life of a little known individual of many centuries ago is obviously difficult, but a legion of 6,000 men is more likely to have left traces. To turn to Christian sources could be held to be prejudicial. Non-Christian and, especially, official Roman governmental sources were to be preferred. Hopefully, mention of the Theban Legion could be found.

This led to an examination of inscriptions catalogued from more than 2,000 Roman legionary gravestones. These recorded the three names that every Roman citizen possessed, age at death and every army unit of service career. Hopefully, mention of a Theban Legion would be found.

It proved to be a blind alley, revealing, however, that every Roman soldier had a Latin name. Many military martyrs were recorded with non-Latin names. That may well indicate that they were baptized.

The Theban Legion was viewed in Jungian fashion by one critic to be a fiction based on archetypical myth. The feast day of the Thebans was the autumnal equinox, 22 September, twelve equal hours of light and darkness. Candidus, an officer of the legion mentioned in its Act, literally meant light. Maurus, the legion's commander, meant dark. That the legend was a pagan myth sprinkled with holy water could be true, or the sort of speculation that emerges in the absence of facts.

Why would the church remain silent for a century after the supposed martyrdom of the legion? Was it possible that church policy itself had changed towards the military in the tumultuous century between the events of the legend and Eucherius' record?

The yearly feast day honouring a saint is usually the day of his death. The Thebans, according to Eucherius, must have fallen in the spring, beginning the military campaign season. Their feast was in the fall. Possibly, the monks in the Valais had sought a different feast day to avoid overlapping with Easter. Candidus, light, and Maurus, dark, may have suggested the equinox, a day later on the liturgical calendar.

Years would occur before the *pièce de résistance* in the coinage was recognized. A Canadian collector published an article noting a peculiarity of a tetradrachm of the year of the papyrus ration receipt beginning 1 September 283. It had the usual emperor's profile on its obverse. The reverse depicted Elpis (hope, in Greek), to pagans not a goddess but an abstraction, to Paul one of the three cardinal virtues.

On the reverse of Alexandrian tetradrachms the symbol L routinely appears, representing not the Latin letter L but 'year of the emperor'. To the right appears a letter of the Greek alphabet. In Greek, letters were also numbers, Alpha A one, Beta B two, etc.

On some Elpis coins of Carinus' second year, LB, the B has a lower lobe, clearly a triangle. This creates a monogram. In three centuries of Alexandrian

Monogram on tetradrachms of Emperor Carinus (283–284) from Alexandria in Egypt.

Roman coin issues, hundreds of designs, this is the only monogram known. The B disassembled, produces:

Greek		Latin
Γ	Gamma	G
Δ	Delta	D
B	Beta	B
P	Rho	R

Placing L before it yields LGDBR.

If this is not an abbreviation for Legio Augusta Thebeorum, what does it represent?

Granted, D is not TH, but can become so in transposing some Greek words into Latin, for example Theos = Deus, Thracian = Dacian.

A critic remarked that this proves nothing except an accident or the curious manner of the engraver in fashioning B. That it was issued the year of papyri indicating a legionary-sized body of 'soldiers and sailors' leaving Egypt was taken as mere coincidence.

It was coincidence that the departure of the Theban Legion in the second year of the reign of Carinus and Numerian gave an alert engraver opportunity to put a monogram on their coins citing the Legion.

Coincidence, luck, chance or destiny? The proverb has it that coincidence comes a lot more easily than miracles and is just as useful.

Carinus, in his second year, issued four motif types in his Alexandrian coinage: Elipis, Nike, Athena and the eagle between banners. His brother Numerian that year issued the same motifs, minus that of Elpis. Initially, it was thought that Carinus' Elpis monogram was a unique and quite rare mintage. Further investigation revealed that all seven types included some coins with the Legio Thebeorum monogram.

The pattern suggests no accident but a policy.

There was a Theban Legion leaving Egypt some two years before the massacre of the legendary Theban legionnaires.

That the reader share the suspense of the pursuit of the reality behind the Theban Legion legend, it is tempting to continue in sequence of the clues, blind alleys, hits, reassessments and clarifications encountered. The evidence was not discovered in the chronological order of the historical events of the story. To present the sequence of discovery necessitates flashbacks not in the order of historical events – a confusing picture. Therefore, the story shall be told in order of historical events, beginning with Mauricius, leader of the Thebans. A professional soldier's life is inexorably caught up in major events of his era. Detective deduction reveals the culture and happenings that helped forge the man.

Chapter 2

What is in a Nickname?

W must be neither murderers nor accomplices in our assassination.
                                                              Albert Camus

Instead of attempting to trace the history of the Theban Legion, it is better to begin with the career of one man. What happens to an individual grips us emotionally more than knowledge of events happening to great numbers. How can we know of the life of Mauricius, the commander of the Thebans given only his name by monastic scribes? Much can be deduced.

Romans had a family name and a first name, the latter known and used only by family and intimates. Christians only recorded a third name, the *cognomina*, given in a ceremony of coming into adulthood at the age of eighteen.[1] This, in effect, was a formalized public nickname that could identify a person either physically or in character. *Crispus* was curly haired, *Paulus* was short, *Genialis* had an amicable personality. *Mauricius* meant a Moor, a North African. *Maurus* as an adjective in Latin meant of swarthy or brownish complexion. *Aethiopus*, as in the name of Aesop, the writer of fables, meant a black.

If it did not create differences within the human race, the vast Sahara long kept them distinct. Transportation across the desert was a dangerous ordeal. Along the thousands of miles of the River Nile, the only river crossing the Sahara, people always in contact, complexions tended to gradually change between north and south.

Prejudice is hardly possible without stereotype. Romans knew people of darker complexions to be of many sorts: in language, tribe and way of life, rich and poor, ignorant and highly educated, herdsmen, farmers, craftsmen, merchants, soldiers, actors, doctors, diplomats, athletes and holy men. No label such as slavery fit them all. Some beyond the Roman desert frontier were *foederati* – allies.

The Moors were chiefly Berbers,[2] but of a wide range of racial and cultural types sharing the same language. The Greeks had referred to them as *Gaetuli*, the robed men, the *melano* or black *gaetuli* being those south of the Sahara.

The double-humped camel introduced by Romans from the Persian Empire had enabled legionnaires to explore across the Sahara to Lake Chad and the River Niger. In return, caravans from south of the desert entered the Empire.

Blacks clad in bright and many coloured robes, herdsmen and horse-traders, metalworkers and healers, they wove their colour into the fabric of Roman Mauritania. Some deduced the laws of genetic heredity and inoculation against disease, discoveries made in raising cattle, unknown to Europe for millennia.

The Roman explanation of race was that cold bleached people's skin as the tropics darkened them.[3] Northerners were sluggish in mind and body, whereas southerners were swift but light minded. They, the Romans, being in the middle, were the best of the lot. That all mankind had common origin was held self-evident. Homer had declared all people more alike than different.

No human difference escaped caustic comment among Romans. 'The absent are always wrong,' as Ovid observed. But Roman prejudice was more a matter of personalities and class than race. With rare exception, the slaves everywhere in the Empire were Caucasian. *Eklavus*, slave, in Greek literally meant blond or fair-haired.

Racial attitudes in the army are revealed by an incident involving the Emperor Septimius Severus, on tour in Britain when a 'black soldier from an auxiliary unit, a popular wit well known for his practical jokes, ran up to him with a wreath of cypress branches'. The soldier quipped 'You have routed the world, you have conquered the world. Now, conqueror, become a god.'[4] Severus, troubled by the wreath, of a type used in funerals, ordered the man removed from his sight.

Emperors after death could be declared gods by the Senate, a rite called *apotheosis*. The auxiliary's remark could have been taken as a veiled warning, joke or omen. There is no mention that the soldier was punished.

That a black man dared publicly taunt an emperor suggests much about the position of blacks in the army. Ability earned respect. Marginal in a sociological sense, a black comedian or soothsayer could effectively bid for more. Colour of itself was not culture to Romans.

Compared with many other ethnic groups within the Empire, Moors were less burdened by slavery and class sensibilities, better educated, more individualistic but family and community oriented, and moralistic yet tolerant of creed. Christianity was widespread among them in contrast to its slower and more sporadic growth in Europe.

Moors such as Mauricius may have out-Romanized Romans in some ways, while ignoring others. Military pride, *brio*, would have motivated one to excel while not giving the appearance of competing, a task building inner tensions. A man would need a positive philosophy of life to pursue a career in a way of life, a culture not of his birth, without becoming bitter or ambiguous.

Without it, he could become acculturated, sharing several cultures, a citizen of the world – the Roman world.

The Moors had little sexual segregation. The family name was that of the mother.[5] With wealth in her own right, a woman's status was not subservient.

Women spoke and voted in tribal council, rejected undesirable suitors or abusive spouses, and could make or break a man's reputation with the praise, wit or slander they sang as troubadours. Dressed in blouses and short skirts, Berber women shocked Latins, who did not realize that in sexual mores the Moors tended to be puritanical compared with other Romans.

St Augustine, a Moor, visiting Italy, complained that Latins had much less respect for privacy than his countrymen.[6] Few could read silently without moving their lips, he complained.

The Empire's influence upon the Moors was so strong that as late as the eleventh century Arabs would refer to Berbers as Roumis, the Romans.[7]

Extensive olive groves, vast wheat fields, aqueducts and unwalled cities north of the Aures mountains evidenced the peace and prosperity of most of Roman rule. Only in the extreme west of North Africa were towns walled, Volubilis being the best-known example. Every summer, desert tribes ventured northwards into Roman domain, grazing their herds of sheep, goats and camels and working as harvest hands, putting up straw huts amidst the fields. Their numbers were probably less than 100,000 in the entire region.[8]

North Africa's landlords were largely absentees residing in Italy. After the first century BC slave revolts in Italy and Sicily, Roman authorities avoided concentrating large slave populations. North Africa's land holdings were leased and sublet as in Egypt, but the farms were much larger and the leasers were *equites*, upper middle class. Ironically, Roman law protected the rights of tenants in the provinces but not in Italy.[9]

The Berbers called themselves *amzgyah*, the 'free people'.[10] They had never been conquered nor did they enslave others. By treaty they had been annexed to the Empire.

The Moorish King Juba II in the first century BC had been the author of fifty works of history and science and had sent explorers to find the Canary Islands. The last ruler of semi-independent North Africa, King Ptolemy, was executed by Emperor Caligula (r. 37–41) while visiting Gaul when the populace openly demonstrated its preference for him.

Many Roman high offices were obtained by North Africans. The sculptured bust of Lucius Quietus[11] reveals negroid features and cheeks scarred in tribal rituals like those of the Senegalese and Gambians. Quietus, a tribal chief 'from the unknown desert', had joined the Roman army as an ally, *foederatus*. Given equestrian rank by the Emperor Domitian, cashiered for insubordination, then reinstated and promoted by Trajan, he led his cavalry on the Danube and versus Persia. He became a senator, governor of Palestine and one of Rome's two consuls, within reach of the throne at Trajan's death. But Rome was not yet ready for a barbarian militarist as emperor. Trajan made a fellow Spaniard, Hadrian, his heir. Quietus revolted and was killed.

Septimius Severus had been a North African, so too was the Emperor Piscennius Niger of Moorish visage.[12] In the 270s, the admiral of the Atlantic fleet, the Moor Bonosus, had proclaimed himself ruler of Britain. Another Moor, Victorinus, sent by Probus, successfully ousted him.

North Africa's only legion, the III Augusta, dominated from the Atlantic to Libya for four centuries. It policed the coastal plain. In the interior it guarded against raiders, explored across the desert and created farmland from semi-arid wilderness. Some 2,400 cities and towns dotted the legion's territory.[13] (Four hundred would survive two millennia later; the results of climate change and political neglect.)

The III Augusta waged an unceasing warfare against the desert. It dug countless *foggara*, deep gravity-fed wells connected by tunnels, and built aqueducts, drains for the rare rain and covered cisterns. Veterans farming on the desert's edge were granted lower taxes in appreciation of their vital task in holding back the desert. The climate was growing much drier as wind patterns shifted. The predecessors of the Romans, the Carthaginians, had brought lasting ecological havoc by cutting down mountain forests in order to build their war fleets. Goats, tearing up roots, completed the ruin as the desert expanded.

All the Abrahamic faiths, Judaism, Christianity and Islam, were born in the desert. Much as the Israelites had regarded Canaan civilization, Berbers living in tents regarded the civilization of the coast.

Berber hospitality was proverbial. Yet there was a strong streak of moral righteousness and revolt beneath the traditional civility of Berber values.

Christianity had grown much faster in North Africa than in Europe. In North Africa, Tertullian preached deeds, not Greek theologies. 'What has Athens to do with Jerusalem?'[14] he demanded. He emphasized that faith was not provable and condemned whoever held those who disagreed with Christianity to be of ill-will. 'It is the law of mankind and the natural right of every individual to worship what he thinks proper, nor does the religion of one man either harm or help another. It is not proper for religion to compel men to religion, which should be accepted of one's own accord, not by force,' he insisted.[15] The individual was spiritually alone save for God, he taught. His was a teaching, not a church. Expecting the end of the world, he made no provision to pass on his ideas. His puritanism was tainted with the Montanist ideology, a heresy to many Christians because it despised all worldly matters. Tertullian courted martyrdom boldly yet never attained it, fortunate to live in a generation without persecution. He despised Greek philosophy but also condemned the Judaic Bible, holding it not as the roots of the New Testament but in opposition to it. Tertullian was uninterested in organized charitable works or evangelization.

Cyprian, a bishop of Carthage, a lifetime later than Tertullian and contemporary with Mauricius' youth, differed from Tertullian in his social consciousness. When Cornelius, the first Latin in ancestry to be bishop of Rome, successor of Peter, his predecessors Jews or Greeks, was challenged by Novatian and a minority of the congregation in Rome, Cyprian spoke eloquently in Cornelius' defence. To Cyprian, Cornelius' authority took precedence over that of all other bishops but was interdependent with them. He was their leader, first among equals, not their lord. During persecution, Cyprian sharply criticized the lax attitudes formed in years of security that had made many betray the faith.[16] Nevertheless, he readmitted *lapsi* (Christians who worshipped the gods under the threat of persecution) to the church despite opposition by many of proven courage.

Both Cornelius and Cyprian were confronted by clergy defying their authority. Pope Cornelius accepted people baptized by such schismatics but Cyprian summoned a council of eighty-seven bishops who unanimously rejected this tolerance. His martyrdom in 258 saved him from being a schismatic condemning schismatics. A touch of fierce independence was part of the character of North African Christianity.

Many North African Christians referred to God as *senex*, the 'old man', their ancestors' term for Baal-Saturn – a view of God as stern despot rather than loving father.[17] The cult of martyrs replaced that of human sacrifice.

Cornelius, Novatian and Cyprian: all were martyred.

In 238, a Balkan peasant, a thuggish soldier of quite unRoman traditions, Maximinus Thrax, succeeded where Lucius Quietus had failed. He became emperor. He doubled army pay by outrageously raising taxes and seizing municipal and temple funds. In Mauritania, North Africa, his procurator confiscated land. A number of young aristocrats, raising their farm workers in revolt, killed the procurator. Realizing that there was no turning back, they hailed an elderly senator, Gordian I, as governor and emperor. Their envoys to Italy swiftly won the support of the Senate and slew Maximinus Thrax's Praetorian prefect.

Capellianus, commander of Legio III Augusta, moved his troops against Carthage. The Gordians, defended only by a hastily recruited citizen's militia, were crushed in battle, their reign only twenty-two days. Legio III Augusta ran riot: rape and arson, and slaughtering and looting[18] exposed the powerlessness of civilians against the army's avarice. The aftermath was becoming typical; the Emperor Maximinus Thrax was slain by his soldiers with his two senatorial successors (Galbinus and Pupienus) within the space of three months. The grandson of Gordian, a boy of thirteen, was made emperor by the Praetorians. He was killed by the troops of Philip the Arab, who then asked the Senate to hail his victim as a god.

There was long a tension between many military and the civilians they supposedly protected. 'Wolves set to guard fat sheep,' as a Roman writer put it.

The lack of anyone in the army on terms of duty of less than twenty-five years except *tribunes,* six to each of the Empire's thirty-two or more legions, split society. Some soldiers, increasingly recruited from barbarian tribes on the frontiers, scorned civilians with a repressed resentment capable of fuelling an astonishing rage.

Gordian's followers were *equites,* the upper middle class and tribal chieftains supplying *tribunes* to the army, usually for four years of service. They led the farm labourers, free but humble folk who accepted the *equites* as their tribal leaders. Tribe was family expanded to include hundreds and even thousands of kinsmen. As in many cultures then, and the Middle East and Africa in the present, tribal loyalty often superseded any loyalty determined by lines drawn from maps by dominating foreigners.

The revolt in North Africa was not a class warfare, nor anti-Roman, but the people in arms defending their rights as Romans. Civilians, however, were no match for disciplined soldiers clad in iron and marching in shieldwall, mowing down any foolhardy civilian in their path. Renegade troops were at war against the people of the Empire's richest province.

Mauricius must have been about ten years of age when these events, unlike anything previous in North Africa's history, peaceful for centuries, erupted to shock the populace. Many in the towns fled to the temples for sanctuary, only to discover them becoming slaughterhouses. In retrospect, soldiers would be astonished at their own bloodthirsty rage. Normally in Roman warfare, prisoners would be taken in order to be enslaved, the profits divided, the chief incentive to wage war in the minds of many military. This was different. No one was spared.

The actions and rank of Mauricius' father amidst this carnage is not known except that he would not be ousted from the army but sent to another province, unlike comrades regarded as criminal or cowardly. To remain in camp as smoke arose on the horizon and wailing refugees pounded on the gates to enter might have seemed safe and neutral to some soldiers but, in effect, was taking sides with the predators.

To order men to defend the local populace could have put a soldier against former comrades. It might have been asking a man to defend tribal folk, old enemies of his kinsmen, while his own tribe was under attack miles away. In times of crisis, conscience is most deeply needed and values taken for granted would have been badly shaken, re-evaluated or evolved.

Roman forces from other provinces restored order. The aggressors were executed or cashiered. Many fled to the interior and became bandits, the alternative career for misfits. The populace fundamentally distrusted them and had no illusions that they were guerrilla heroes fighting for the oppressed of society. The army had good intelligence to counteract the scattered rebels.

Legio III Augusta was disbanded in disgrace in 238.[19] Those of its soldiers not thrown out of the army were sent to the Rhineland and Austrian legions.

Mauricius, probably a boy in North Africa when it was plundered by Legio III Augusta, had been an impressionable eyewitness to soldiers terrorizing those who expected their protection. His father, handicapped in promotion, exemplified that army authority could be unjust and fickle and that soldiers could commit atrocious crimes against civilians.

Deduction can posit much concerning the career of Mauricius. Romans had a nickname, *cognomina*, made formal in a ceremony on becoming an adult about the age of eighteen. *Felix* meant happy or lucky, *Severus* meant harsh, *Innocentius* one who ignored unpleasantness. Character label as lifelong name demonstrated Roman fatalism, the view that personal character was unchangeable. A primary appeal of Christianity was its belief that old ways could be cast off and temperament could find new ways of expression.

To call a Moor in North Africa Mauricius would be redundant. It would be reasonable if Mauricius received that name when living outside Africa as a kin of a soldier sent to Europe from III Legio Augusta struck from the army list. Since many Moors were hardly distinguishable from other Mediterranean peoples, Mauricius may have been darker than most and from the interior.

In the reign of Augustus, the first Roman emperor, there were seventy-seven hereditary members of the Senate of Rome. A century later there were only four. The rulers of the Empire may have been immoral compared with their ancestors in the Republic, but worse was a growing amorality, a shaking off of all responsibility. The *cursus honorum* (the career of honour), serving for some four years as an army officer before entering rank in civil service and government, withered along with the desire to continue family.

The people of the Republic had possessed a strong sense of shame. *Dignitas* was similar to the idea of saving face and public reputation found in cultures worldwide. The first century biographers Plutarch and Seutonius depicted a world largely determined for good or evil by men with flawed but wilful character. Later historians avoid mention of the moral faults of the emperors, men depicted attempting to rule a world increasingly out of control.

The reaction of many to epidemic diseases, wild inflation, underpopulation, family collapse, banditry and invasion was a renunciation of worldly values. Pagans, sceptics and Montanist Christians were among those washing their hands of obligation. They seemed to lose their virtues with their vices, overcome by pessimism and loss of confidence.

There seemed to be a centrifugal force in Roman values. As the leading classes living in the safest interior regions of the Empire grew increasingly self-indulgent to the point of excluding *pietas*, social duty, those on the embattled frontiers cherished the old virtues more so. To Romans, *virtutatis* made a man –

vir a person who merited and gave respect. This attitude influenced Christian attitudes. Faith was not simply creed but action.

Jesus repeatedly told persons healed of illness that their own faith had healed them. Some could hardly have known Jesus. Not all claiming to believe in God were healed. This faith that healed seemed a trust in goodness of itself, an acceptance of self and life. The pampered slave-owning and exploitative ruling classes might grow anxious and contemptuous of social inferiors, but men like Mauricius on the margins between civilization and chaos lived in a psychological world with dimensions of feeling and sentiment that the more smugly secure scarcely recognized, becoming morally colour-blind.

Christians in their writings showed an awareness of decline not found elsewhere in Roman literature. Men like Mauricius, or the future Emperor Probus, did not despair of creating a better society. Unlike many others, they trusted that reform was most effectively carried out within the institutions needing it, not by quitting them.

Valerian reinstated Legio III Augusta in 253.[20] A new legion would have taken several years to organize before it entered the army list. Mauricius' early career probably involved service in the newly reinstated Legio III Augusta.

A man entered the Roman army between the ages of eighteen and twenty-two. He had to be at least five feet ten inches in height and have letters of reference that he was of good family, *disciplina* regarded as best learned not in barracks but at home. All were volunteers for twenty-five years of service.

Mauricius, future leader of the Theban Legion, would be baptized by Zabdas, Bishop of Jerusalem according to the medieval church historian Gratian. Eusebius, a Roman bishop, cites Zabdas as bishop in 279. Since twenty-five years was a soldier's term of service and two or three years' preparation required for baptism, he must have entered the army about 251.

There were three ways to become a Roman officer.[21] Most rose from the ranks of enlistees with the approval of the centurions. Centurions ranked the equivalent of lieutenant to colonel and might retire as *equites*, hereditary upper middle class, literally those who rode horses. Probus had been directly appointed a tribune by the Senate, his father of senatorial rank. This method was abolished by the Emperor Gallienus because it too often ranked political hacks serving short terms in the army above professional officers[22] but without it, the door to militarism opened wider.

A third way was entering the army as an *equites* given centurion rank directly with the approval of the Senate. If he was the son of an officer, Mauricius may have entered the army as an *equites*.

A legionnaire, especially an officer, would have many duty stations in his career. The sixth century Christian poet Venatus Fortunatus wrote that Mauricius had belonged to a *legio felix*, a 'happy legion'.[23] This was perhaps poetic usage. One legion in the East bore the title Felix, III Gallica Felix, stationed at Beirut.[24] If Mauricius had served both in III August and III Gallica Felix, the only two legions in Roman history disbanded for insubordination and later reinstated, it could help explain his eventual dissent. He would be following a virtual tradition.

In his choice of career Mauricius revealed a respect for his father's example. His father may have been insubordinate to immediate superiors in being loyal to the citizens he was supposed to protect.

St. Maurice's head on the shield of Corsica (and Savoy).

Chapter 3

The New Testament Tradition

If the excesses perpetuated by persons of unlimited and frenzied avarice could be checked by some self-restraint ... But the only desire of these uncontrolled madmen is to have no thoughts for the common need.

Diocletian's Edict on Maximum Prices

No Christian ever recorded the history of his fellows in the army. Only by analysis of the isolated records of the military martyrs can it be reconstructed. In the first two centuries, records of martyrs in the military are few. In context, they were not killed for their creed but for insubordination. Some refused to execute prisoners, others refused to return to service after retiring and probably having accepted baptism, while others refused to take the pagan military oath.

Greek tradition records two martyrs named Longinus,[1] one the enlisted man who lanced the side of Jesus at the crucifixion, the other a centurion baptized by Peter who was killed after retirement when he had become bishop in his homeland of Cappadocia.[2] A third Longinus, with Megistus and Acestus, was a guard killed with St Paul.[3]

Initially, Romans knew of Christianity only as another Jewish sect. The humorist Juvenal confused people of the two creeds[4] and despised both. Nero (r. 54–68) began persecution[5] of Christians and set the pattern that, regardless of imperial law, Christians might be subject to the whim of the emperor.

By 90 tax collectors were complaining of *professi* living a 'Jewish life', i.e., Christians who refused to pay the tax on Jews for exemption from worshipping the gods.[6] To make up the loss government added another tax to those paid by Jews.[7] This hardly endeared Christians to Jews. A few years later, the Emperor Nerva abolished the new law.[8] Christians claiming tax exemption had, meanwhile, made themselves known to the authorities.

The pagan historian Tacitus mentions Flavius Clemens,[9] a cousin of the Emperor Domitian (r. 81–96), appointed in 95 to be one of the two consuls in the Empire for the year.[10] Clemens, whose name meant merciful, was executed for 'atheistic Jewish practices' and '*inertia*', his refusal to preside at the pagan rites intrinsic to his office. Two other ex-consuls and a senator died with him. Clemens was quite plausibly a Christian. His family villa became Rome's first Christian cemetery and his niece Flavia Domatilla, a Christian martyr.

Two Praetorians, Nereus and Achilleus, guards of Clemens' family in exile, were martyrs, their surviving tomb inscription declaring that they had 'fled the impious camp'.[11]

Under the Emperor Trajan (r. 87–117) the number of martyrs, still few, nevertheless increased, particularly in Italy. Almost all were soldiers, retired and apparently baptized, but thereafter recalled to service. Rome's bishop Alexander I, jailed south of Rome near Tivoli in an area where many officers had retired, evangelized the tribune and martyr Quirinus. A soldier, Herculanus,[12] was executed with him and the officer Eustace.[13] All refused to sacrifice and were killed with members of their families. Getulius, the priest Maro, Eutyches and Victorinus, all retired baptized officers, living in the same district as Quirinus, were killed for rejecting the recall to active duty.[14] Ten enlistees, including Amantius, the brother of Getulius, fell with them. Inasmuch as every Roman soldier was required to have a Latin name and Zoticus,[15] Irenaeus and Hyacinth were Greek, it can be posited that they had changed their names at baptism.

Secundus,[16] a minor officer, is described receiving baptism at Milan, burying the martyred bishop of Tortona and fleeing the army to be killed at Asti. Three former soldiers, Maurus[17], a bishop, Pantaleon, a deacon, and Sergius, a *lector* (literally, a reader at ceremonies), were executed on 27 July 117 in Apulia. Many veterans were attracted to the Christian clergy as a new career.

Outside of Italy, Romulus,[18] a high ranking officer at Melitene, Cappadocia (Malaytya, Turkey), headquarters of Legio XII Fulminata, the one unit known to have included many men of Christian sympathy, died protesting the persecution of Christians.

About this time Pliny the Younger, governor of Bythnyia, wrote to the Emperor Trajan regarding Christians. He held the Christians accused by the populace of lacking respect for the gods to be otherwise law-abiding.[19] Trajan responded that they were not to be sought out, but, if accused, must sacrifice or die.[20] Christianity had thus become a *religio licita*.[21] The faith was not illegal but individuals unpopular with the mob could be killed if they chose not to worship the gods. Freedom from persecution became dependent on public tolerance, which differed with locale and time.

The martyrs were fanning the issue of freedom of conscience first ignited by Judaism. The choice to refuse or toss a few grains of incense into the fire before the idols was that of life or death.

Hadrian (r. 117–138) placed the weight of evidence upon the accusers in cases of Christian '*inertia*'.[22] False accusations could bring penalties upon the accusers. This paradoxic policy lessened accusations. If a Christian tossed the incense, his accuser had broken the law.

Men of Christian sympathies gathered in one army unit were revealed by an incident in a campaign of Marcus Aurelius (r. 161–180) on the Rhine.[23] The emperor's army was saved from barbarian attack by a furious thunderstorm depicted as a miracle on Aurelius' arch of triumph. The pagan Dio Cassius attributed this to an Egyptian magician in army employ. Flavius Vopiscus credited it to the emperor's prayers.[24] The bishop and historian Eusebius[25] claimed it happened in answer to prayers of a detachment of Christian soldiers of the 'Melitene' legion, the XII Fulminata with headquarters at Melitene. Surviving inscriptions reveal a detachment from it on the Rhine in 165. Tertullian, a Christian North African of the era, praised the event.[26]

Three emperors minted coins honouring the individual legions. In each case the same two legions were uniquely omitted. One was the IX on Hadrian's Wall in Scotland, the other the XII Fulminata,[27] each guarding a northernmost corner of the Empire. Presumably, they were taken for granted because they were non-political, too strategically vital to be risked in the army coups making and unmaking emperors.

Tertullian boasted:

We are but of yesterday, and we have filled everything of yours – cities, islands, forts, towns, marketplaces, the army itself, tribes, councils, the palace, Senate, forum. We have left you the temples only! For what war were we not fit and ready if not equal in forces, we who are willing to be slaughtered, since by our doctrine greater permission is given to be killed than to kill.[28]

Tertullian undoubtedly exaggerated the number of Christians in the army. Evidence of them north of the Alps is minimal. He evidences that they must have been fairly numerous in North Africa's forces. Rome, Melitene, Carthage, and Alexandria seem to have been the centres of faith within the army.

About 180 imperial policies changed in a manner favourable to *professi*. *Immunitas*,[29] special assignment status for enlistees, was made permanent duty. This had already been the practice in Egypt. Clerks, blacksmiths, medics, military police, scouts, spies, engineers etc. were *immunes*. A soldier henceforth could spend his career in the army without being called upon to kill.

Julius, an enlistee about 304, refusing to worship the gods, declared that he had served twenty-seven years in the army. 'I went on seven military campaigns and never hid behind anyone, nor was I inferior to any man in battle.'[30] His comrades were astonished to discover his faith. He may have been a scout or engineer, an *immunes*. He called his re-enlistment 'an error'. Presumably he had been baptized after retirement.

Churchmen regarded the pagan gods as diabolical entities. They gave lapses of unbaptized catechumens more leniency than those of persons baptized.

Since the twice-yearly military oath was sworn by officers as representatives of their men, it was primarily of danger to Christian officers. Accordingly, *professi* avoided rank.

Permanent *immunes* clarifies the Apostolic Tradition of Hippolytus written in the early third century affirming earlier Church laws.

> A soldier in power must not kill anyone. If he should be ordered to do it, he shall not do it. He must not take the military oath. If he will not agree, let him be rejected (from baptism). A military governor or magistrate of a city who wears the purple, either let him desist or let him be rejected. If a catechumen or a baptized Christian wishes to become a soldier, let him be cast out (of the Church). For he has despised God.[31]

Hippolytus clearly opposed both killing and the military oath. Judging from the Apostolic Tradition and the Acts, soldiers who were *professi* avoided baptism until retirement. If some were on active duty and baptized, they were *immunes*.

Tertullian was to reverse his approval of *professi* serving under the brass eagles. He cited an unnamed martyr in North Africa who, handed a wreath at a pagan army celebration, refused to wear it. He was executed for insubordination.[32] Influenced by the heresy of Montanism, which scorned secular authority and Judaism, Tertullian declared the episode proof that a Christian could not serve God and *caesar*. He acknowledged that his view was unpopular with many North African Christians who regarded the martyr as an extremist violating the 'long peace' between pagans and Christians.[33]

In the secret cult of the war god Mithra within the army, which admitted only high-ranking persons as members, a crown of flowers on the end of a sword was offered the initiate to one of its highest grades. He rejected it, stating 'I have no crown but Mithra,'[34] a symbolic pledge not to take power by coup.

Montanism paralleled the sinking fortunes of the Empire. Under Marcus Aurelius, about 165, the first of many foreign-born epidemics had devastated the Roman world.[35] As plagues from Asia and Africa came across the trade routes, precious metal in coinage flowed out of the Empire, never to return as the mines within it became exhausted. While the ruling class had an insatiable craving for silks, perfumes, spices and the like, their faraway sources were disinterested in Roman products except gold and silver.[36] In reaction, Roman mints grossly lessened the percentage of precious metal in coinage, provoking inflation.

Epidemics, inflation, higher taxes, crime and army coups made Montanism's denial of the world a 'sour grapes' reaction tainting Christian and pagan alike. Four Church authors wrote to Marcus Aurelius between 176 and 177 to disassociate the Church from Montanism's contempt for society.[37] Many pagans regarded Montanism as typical of Christianity nevertheless.

Alexander Severus (r. 222–235) granted Christians permission to own churches and cemeteries.[38] Previously, private homes had sufficed for worship. Significantly, the earliest known Christian church is the archaeological find of a chapel on the Persian frontier at Duro-Europos attended by soldiers, judging from its wall murals.[39]

However tolerant the emperor, the army remained governed by its own laws. About 230 Quiricus (the Bishop of Ostia, the port of Rome) and eighteen soldiers evangelized by a woman, Aurea, were executed.[40] Probably, these enlistees were members of Legio Julia Alexandrina, the newly created police and grain fleet marines with headquarters in Alexandria, Egypt.

Bishops had leeway to adjust general policy to suit the local situation. Clement of Alexandria (r. 217) would proclaim:

> ... if you be a farm worker, we tell you cultivate the earth, but cultivating the earth, mind God. Again, you that be held in a love of seafaring, sail but adhere to the Heavenly Pilot. You who the knowledge of Christ has reached employed in the army, hear you the Emperor who commands you to just deeds ...[41]

He is the only bishop of the era known to have actively encouraged soldiers to remain in the army. Christians could *militare*, do military service.[42] They were forbidden to *bellare*, to do violence to people.

Philip the Arab, (r. 244–249), formerly the Praetorian prefect of Emperor Gordian, was the first Roman sovereign openly favourable to Christianity. Several Christian writers[43] repeat the story that the Bishop of Antioch denied Philip permission to attend Christian ceremonies. The earliest states that it was demanded that he place himself among the penitents, a public sinner. A later version says he was excommunicated for being party to the assassination of his predecessor's young son. As a public official, he could not have been baptized. Nevertheless, he may have asked to attend Christian rites.

That Philip was adverse to paganism is manifest in his coinage, which utterly lacks the usual images of pagan deities.[44] Some sixty years after the anti-Christian diatribe of the pagan author Celsus, Philip's wife asked the Christian writer Origen to write a reply.

A Montanist in convictions, Origen was to write that when Jesus told Peter at Gethsamene to sheath his sword, he forbade all military service,[45] a view quoted many times since. Origen, an Egyptian, was a brilliant and courageous idealist but his extreme views were not balanced. Interpreting the analogy of Jesus that if your eye causes you to sin, pluck it out, Origen had castrated himself.[46] His absolute pacifism must have disturbed Philip, his patron.

Until Philip's reign, no known Christian enlisted man had ever applied for officer's rank. Marinus,[47] probably an *immunes* and apparently long known as a Christian to his comrades, asked for promotion at Caesarea in Israel. Tertullian had written that *professi* served as *milites caligati* or enlistees, 'boots', without obstacle.[48] Marinus was denounced by a rival for the promotion who said that customarily Christians did not apply for commissioned rank. Marinus was executed, presumably after refusing to participate in pagan rites he previously had been able to avoid.

Marinus was either violating Church strictures or the local bishop or the *ecclesia* itself had changed its policy towards men of the faith in the military and allowed them to be officers. It is unclear if Marinus was a catechumen or baptized.

Marinus is celebrated in the calendar of the saints, an unlikely honour if he had been violating Church law. The time had arrived that pagans were alarmed that Christians were seeking secular office, an irony considering that the pagan complaint for two centuries had been that Christians shunned public service. *Professi* were damned if they did not and damned if they did.

Bishop Dionysus of Alexandria anticipated that Philip's open partiality would provoke a violent pagan reaction when he was removed.[49] A horrendous plague entering the Empire in 252 endured for fifteen years, and reduced the population of the city of Alexandria by two-thirds. Lacking explanation, defence or cure, feeling despairingly helpless, the mob had the illusion of power in destroying someone as scapegoat. Alexandrian Christians warned that the end of the world was fast approaching with Rome's one thousandth anniversary and the anti-Christ near. They described the anti-Christian riots in Alexandria after Philip was murdered as a 'holy war'.[50]

According to pious accounts, Mauricius, leader of the Theban Legion, was baptized by Zabdas, bishop of Jerusalem, about 279. Since twenty-five years was a soldier's term of service, and two to three years' preparation were required for baptism, he must have entered the army about 251, not long after Philip's reign.

History is continuity and change.

The times were changing, both the dangers and the opportunities for the faithful accelerating, a crisis fast approaching both the Empire and Christians.

Chapter 4

Civilization's Collapse and Recovery

Greater love hath no man than that he lay down his life for his friends.
Jesus of Nazareth

Mauricius' career would span the most tumultuous years the Empire had ever endured as it was for the first time in its history assaulted by invaders on every frontier, yet recovered. In those years Christian influence accelerated as it provided aid to countless refugees ignored by the Roman state as persecution also gained powerful momentum.

Because a soldier's career is inseparable from the military history of his era, Mauricius' years in service can be placed amidst that chaotic age of the near collapse of the badly shaken Empire.

In the world of the third century, the Persians and Roman Empires rivalled and menaced one another as civilized areas witnessed birthrate decline and barbarian populations increased. Decay infested cities with crime and riot. The ruling class was growing fantastically wealthy as the middle class withered away, neither providing leadership. Former slaves of the state gained power, bringing with them a bureaucratic scorn towards civil rights. Crushing taxes weakened society as the military expanded.

Roman philosophy lacked vision of a better society. Roman values were profoundly conservative. In Latin, *res novi* (new things) was the idiom for social revolution. Everything new was viewed as potentially dangerous. Democracy was seen as ancient history, a rule by the mob that had destroyed Greek civilization. The early Roman Republic had been composed of free citizenry, farming their own land without slaves. That, too, was ancient history.

With the outbreak of epidemics, the Empire (with a third less people) was by the third century struggling to hold on to the same huge area. Epitaphs in a Christian catacomb reveal that of 127 people, fifty-three died before the age of ten and another twenty-three in their second decade.[1] Most soldiers, as revealed by their gravestones, died before reaching retirement, yet they lived longer than most civilians. The archaeological evidence of decline is manifest in datable abandoned villas and constricted town walls.

Felix, 'happy' Dacia, the region presently known as Rumania, was evacuated in 265, a first step backwards. Rich in agriculture, its grasslands lacked natural defences.

Romans were advanced enough in technology to have had an Industrial Revolution, but these advances were forbidden by authority lest they increase unemployment or make slavery unnecessary, a transformation unthinkable to those in power, a pattern typical of slave societies.

Except for Italy, the Empire had no military reserves. Rome's troops directly confronted their enemies across the Danube and Rhine, the moors of Scotland and the Sahara and Syrian deserts. The North Sea was becoming less a defence than a highway for raiders as Saxons took to their longships.

As Mauricius entered the army, the tolerance towards Christianity, sporadically broken in the past, was fast moving towards confrontation. The Emperor Philip's sympathies had touched a raw nerve in pagan sensibilities. Increasingly, pagans accepted all gods to be expressions of the one, a view that Christians and Jews opposed. Jews at least worshipped the God of their ancestors. To pagans, Christians were traitors to their gods and ancestral cultures, yet arrogantly intolerant, angering heaven.

To worship the God of Christians seemed to some a perverse atheism. Was not Jesus of Nazareth an executed rebel, King of the Jews? It could no longer be tolerated.

It was a time of apprehension among pagans and Christians alike. There was increasing preoccupation with the supernatural, dreams, prophecies, omens, and a morbid fear of demoniac powers. The cultural mood fed upon a sense of powerlessness. Individuals tended to retreat into self, neglecting worldly concerns. Family life deteriorated. Single life to many seemed increasingly attractive. Fatalism grew as human cordiality and ethics eroded. Extremes met. Montanism and pagan fanaticism reinforced one another. They both required enemies. They had one another.

The army general Decius, with Senate support, had Philip murdered while returning from a campaign against the Scythians. An inscription survives hailing Decius as *restitutor sacrorum*, restorer of the sacred.[2] Decius (r. 250–253), unlike any emperor before him, was determined to destroy Christianity. Previous persecutors had attacked individuals, the oppressions local, unsystematic and usually initiated by the pagan public. The priority of the authorities had been to preserve order, not to destroy the Church. Decius attacked not simply the faith of individuals, but the Church organization collectively.

The emperor's first decree of persecution arrested Christian clergy throughout the Empire as the provinces were swept by popular terror. Months later, assured of public support and having won the approval of the Senate, he commanded all suspected of Christian creed to publicly worship the gods.[3] The threat or use of torture, paid informers and angry citizens revealed many. Those who honoured the idols were issued certificates, *libelli*, protecting them from future harassment. Those who did not were killed. Pagan clergy suspected of Christian sympathies were among those harassed, judging from *libelli* surviving from Egypt.[4]

The peace of many generations, broken sporadically and briefly, leaving many provinces virtually undisturbed, had poorly prepared Christians for the ordeal. In some areas entire villages were annihilated. Elsewhere, Christians fled or hid, resorted to bribery or forgery, or called upon pagan friendships. Judging by Church laws opposing it, some magistrates directed that the fists of the faithful be pried open, incense inserted and their palms placed over the burner while the *professi* shouted denial. The official signed the certificate and gestured for the next would-be victim.

Many Christians yielded and honoured the gods only to ask to be restored to the Church. This was a sign of weakness but also of the continuing attraction of the faith, *lapsi* having escaped torture and death again risking it.

The number of Christian military who fell under Decius reveals the crisis. They were more than in all previous persecutions combined. Probably most Christians by this time were neither Greeks nor Jews in ancestry and therefore eligible for military service.

Many were *immunes*, men on non-combatant special duty. Four men led by Severus[5] who died at Albanum, south of Rome, were *cornicularii*, officers detached from their unit. Mercurius[6] who fell at Caesarea in Cappadocia was a *primicerius*, a senior acting officer not formally on regular status. Another Mercurius[7] and nineteen of his comrades killed at Lentini, in Sicily, were escorting Christian prisoners.

An increasingly aggressive zeal among Christian soldiers, at least in Italy, can be detected from the Acts. Minias,[8] an Armenian, was beheaded at Florence for openly preaching the gospel in the barracks. He perhaps made the error of thinking the situation to be the same as that among Legio XII Fulminata, the legion of his homeland. Felinus and Gratianus[9] were baptized officers killed at Perugia for openly preaching the faith.

Some martyrs must have been of Alexandria's fleet marine. Ammon,[10] Zeno, Ptolemaeus, Ingenes and Theophilus were guards caught signalling a wavering Christian not to sacrifice. Their Greek and Egyptian names when every Roman soldier was required to have a Latin name suggest that they were baptized. They were apparently *immunes*. Agatho[11] fell after attempting to protect the corpses of victims from the mob. Besas[12] was discovered signalling encouragement to a victim who was burned alive with his slave. Isiodorus[13] was an *immunes*, a grain officer of the fleet who refused to sacrifice and was slain on the isle of Chios. The tribunes Theodorus[14] and sixteen other soldiers and a senator converted by the woman Aurea were killed under Decius at Ostia, the port of Rome and grain fleet base. At Corinth, another major seaport, the soldier Adrianus[15] set fire to a pagan temple.

Basilides,[16] an enlistee at Alexandria, defended the young woman martyr Potamiana from the mob. This caused no frictions with his superiors. He was doing his job. Not long afterwards he was asked by his colleagues to take a pagan oath. Apparently, this was not the military oath but a password for the day. His comrades at first thought his refusal a joke. Revealed, he would not honour the gods and was beheaded.

The local persecutions that encouraged Decius in his actions had begun at Caesarea in Palestine where Asturius,[17] a civilian, had exposed a fraudulent miracle at a celebration worshipping the god Pan. His friend, Marinus,[18] was the first Christian enlistee known to have applied for promotion to centurion. This unprecedented Christian bid for army rank must have fuelled pagan apprehensions and antagonized rivals for promotion.

Decius had hardly left Rome to stop an invasion by the Goths when bishops gathered in the city to choose the successor to the martyred Pope Fabian. A contemporary quoted Decius: 'I much prefer news of a rival to the throne than that of another bishop of Rome.'[19] The common folk of the eternal city could be fickle and brutal but there is no record that they ever rioted against Christians or Jews. In the emperor's absence the persecution rapidly abated.

Lured into a swampy area where his legions could not manoeuvre or properly form up, Decius was killed in battle, the first emperor ever slain by the Empire's foes. Pagans were alarmed but Christians must have had difficulty concealing their relief and joy. This fired public hatred against them. Unable or unwilling to reform the Empire's ills, leaders took satisfaction in blaming the Christians. Another epidemic swept the Empire, prompting in Alexandria an hysteria against the *professi* who uniquely were willing to tend the ill.[20] Rumours flew that Christians were poisoners and robbers of the dead.

Fabian, the first bishop of Rome who was neither Jew nor Greek in ancestry, took the name Cornelius,[21] that of the officer baptized by Peter, the first of the gentiles he accepted. With the next emperor, Trebonianius Gallus (r. 251–253) the persecution revived. Cornelius was exiled south of Rome where he died in prison.[22] Two soldiers instructed by him, Cornelius and Cerealis, were martyred.

Pagan guards converted by the example of their prisoners appear repeatedly in the Acts. Justus,[23] Maurus and Heraclius were such examples, killed under Decius at Rome.

Gallus[24] was murdered by the followers of Volusian who a few months later was cut down by his own troops who hailed Valerian (r. 253–260) emperor.

The coups destabilizing the army gave opportunity to Rome's enemies. For the first time in four centuries a barbarian horde crossed the Alps and raided northern Italy. A new and vigorous Persian dynasty seized Roman cities on its frontier. Goths entered the Mediterranean in squadrons of undecked ships pouring forth from the great rivers of eastern Europe into the Black Sea.[25] Since Rome had faced no foe on the Mediterranean in ages, it had few warships on the inner seas. Goths raided the ports of Greece with impunity. Nature itself seemed to have become an enemy of Rome. In 256, a devastating earthquake shattered a wide area of northern Iraq and Syria while a prolonged drought and famine gripped much of the East. The cry of enraged despair arose in cities throughout the Empire. 'If the Tiber rises too high or the Nile too low, the cry is "Christians to the lion!" What, all to a single lion?' Tertullian had wisecracked.[26]

The tribune Olympius,[27] influenced by his wife and servants, was baptized by Pope Stephen and martyred in 256. The Emperor Valerian was an aristocratic soldier indecisive in power, gullible and fatalistic. His unlucky reign was beset by problems worse than any in centuries. Initially quite friendly to Christians, his anxieties eroded his patience. At a formal ceremony of his *haruspice*, the official fortune teller, he was told that it was impossible to discover what fate held because the presence of Christians drove away the spirits. Valerian's tolerance metamorphosized into a persecutory rage.[28]

Decius had demanded worship of the gods but had not killed people for Christian worship of itself.

In 257, Valerian confiscated all Christian meeting places, churches and cemeteries and placed the clergy in supervised exile.[29] Attendance at church services was to be punished by death. His second decree, approved by the Senate, ordered all arrested church leaders to be executed.

This was a radical transformation of policy. No longer was the faith tolerated if its *lapsi* honoured the gods. The pagan writers Celsus, Porphyry and Plotinus had argued versus Christian belief but none had advocated persecution. They had urged Christians to participate in civil and military service. Valerian, in contrast, was determined to rid the forums and camps of them. This suggests that believers within public service had become numerous enough to worry pagans. Valerian's second decree removed all Christian senators and *equites*, the local gentry, from office and seized their property. They were to sacrifice to the gods or die. One of these was the martyr Cornelius Domitius Philippus, ex-prefect of the Praetorian guards.[30] That office, army chief of staff, was a stepping-stone for many soldiers to mount the throne. A Christian had been a heartbeat away from being emperor. Pagans saw good reason for anxiety.

In Carthage, Tunisia, a fifty-year-old soldier, Aemelianus,[31] was killed about 258. In 259 Polyeuctus,[32] an officer at Melitene, smashed several idols, probably after being recalled for campaign against Persia. He was executed.

The Persian (Iranian) Empire was Rome's most civilized, populous and dangerous foe. Valerian was persuaded by the tribunes, the short-term Senate appointees to the legions, that he should negotiate directly with the Persian Shah-I-Shah. Prompted by the plague ravaging his army, under a flag of truce, Valerian met the Persian king in 260. Perhaps his trust was encouraged by the secret cult of the Persian wargod Mithra, that of many Roman officers, officials and business leaders, a sort of international freemasonry, with Persian its sacred language.

Under a flag of truce the rival emperors met. Valerian was seized, the first Roman emperor ever captured by a foe.[33] Made literally a footstool unto his enemies, he was forced to kneel so that the Shah might use him as a step to mount his horse. His corpse was flayed and his skin stuffed with straw to be exhibited as a trophy of war.

It had long been Rome's good fortune that her foes were of many cultures more often fighting one another than Rome. Simultaneous assault against every frontier had never occurred until the Emperor Valerian's fall.

News of the Emperor's capture raced along the borderlands, triggering attacks by all of Rome's enemies. Persian forces occupied Syria. Every frontier from Britain to Egypt was overrun. The usual dispatch of Roman troops from peaceful areas to those under attack was impossible. Valerian's son Gallienus (r. 260–268) as emperor dared not leave Italy. For ten years the Empire was in chaos as local generals and satellite royalty fought back against the invaders while proclaiming themselves Roman emperors.

In 259, there were eighteen claimants to the Roman throne. Valerian's fall a year later prompted more. Many were bandits, others were officials caught with their hands in the public treasury, their superiors not objecting to graft but without mercy towards subordinates denying them their share. There were leaders forced to seize power by the urgings of troops and civilians loyal to them. Some were contenders sincerely believing their firm hand upon power was essential if law and the Roman order was to prevail amidst economic collapse, anarchy and invasions.

Mauricius was an eyewitness. He could no longer view authority without question, idolizing it, if he ever had. The faith of the public that the army was genuinely their protector needed to be confirmed.

It seemed the end of the Roman world.

Christians rejoiced as pagans were stunned. The God of the Christians seemed to hear their prayers. First, Decius, now Valerian. The God of the Christians hardly seemed a Roman patriot.

Bishop Dionysius of Alexandria[34] wrote to a friend that the imminent end of the world that he had expected was cancelled. Instead, Valerian's son, the Emperor Gallienus, was ushering in a new age of tolerance and peace. Gallienus was a man of civilian talents, open minded and practical, who freed the army of the Senate's tribunes whose bad advice had caused Valerian's capture. This, however, lessened whatever remained of civil control of the army.

Gallienus rescinded the edicts of persecution, sending the announcements as personal letters to various bishops.[35] He exempted all Christians in public service from pagan rites and oaths as Mauricius began his career. Thus, Mauricius may have begun his army career openly as a Christian, in sympathies if not baptized.

If the sole objection of the church to military service was the pagan rites and oaths it entailed and not an objection to shedding blood, nothing now stood in the way of Christians entering the service.

Gallienus remained in Italy as the army struggled to restore overrun frontiers on every side.

The invaders, unprepared for unexpected success, failed to consolidate their gains. In innumerable battles the foot-slogging Roman infantry pressed forward and recovered the borders, only to deal with hordes of runaway slaves, wandering barbarian bands, refugees turned looters, army deserters and local chiefs resorting to banditry to escape oppressive taxes and heartless punishments. Liberation became reconquest. City after city, ravaged repeatedly by invaders, was plundered anew by unpaid soldiers. Finally, venturing to restore order in Gaul, Gallienus was killed by legionnaires.

In his career Mauricius probably moved from posts in North Africa to Syria where he would have been engaged in ousting the Persian invaders. Many of the leaders of auxiliary units in Egypt were Moors. That rank was prelude to a legionary command, likely to be the highest he would attain before retirement.

Officers were allowed to live in camp with their families. Septimius Severus (r. 192–211) had allowed soldiers to marry and live outside the camp, loosening discipline. It was hoped this would increase enlistment of soldiers' sons. Under the previous policy, with family life handicapped, military birthrates were too low to maintain the original idea that the army should be virtually an hereditary caste.

In army tradition, Mauricius probably maintained a family of kin, veterans and *calli*, soldier's slaves who could be armed in an emergency.

Increasingly, it was difficult to distinguish slave from freeman. Most slaves wore a broad leather belt. Freemen wore *bulla*, a semi-precious stone or small ball of gold or silver around their neck, signifying that they had certain legal rights. Slaves serving as stewards or slave managers as depicted in the gospels were wealthy. Most free folk were poor. Among Christians the line between slave and free was held to be essentially an accident, every individual of equal importance in the eyes of God.

The concept of equality in rights was also a Stoic faith but Stoicism discouraged emotional attachment to any idea or person. Mauricius probably found Stoicism reasonable and admirable, but to be utterly dispassionate was alien to his Moorish cultural values. Jesus was no mere philosopher, but an angry man, as Stocis held, to discount him. Stoic values, nevertheless, moved many towards Christian integration of emotion and reason.

Claudius II (r. 268–270) was an elderly senator given the throne by the army as an interim ruler rather than yield to the general Aurelian, notorious for his severe discipline. Learning that the Senate was purging Gallienus' associates, many of them Christians, Claudius sent a dispatch urging clemency.[36]

It was too late to save many.

The Senate was the most conservative institution in the Empire and quite pagan. Senators were ministers of the imperial cults. Most were egregiously wealthy, their unearned prosperity increasing as rapidly as the poverty of the majority. Everywhere, senators were the major landholders. Although Italians comprised less than a fifth of the Empire's populace, the Senate remained overwhelmingly Italian. Senators saw the Church as a threat in its egalitarianism and organization surpassing imperial frontiers. Increasingly powerless before the military, in attacking Christian soldiers the Senate was moving against the two things it feared most, the faith and the army. Since Christians would not defend themselves, attacking them gave the Senate an illusion of power.

In and around Rome, an accelerating wave of persecution struck the army. Twenty-five soldiers led by Secundus[37] were beheaded on the Via Lavicana. In 269, forty-six soldiers, including Theodosius,[38] baptized by Bishop Dionysius,[39] fell at Rome while others led by Herculanus died at Ostia. A year later at Ostia thirty-eight soldiers instructed by the woman Bonosa[40] were executed, like those evangelized by the woman Aurea at Ostia a generation earlier. Five more of her converts, baptized by Felix I, were beheaded in Rome.

Outside of Italy there were no military martyrs in these years.

More martyrs fell during Claudius' brief reign than the total in the previous two centuries. Gallienus' bid to attract Christians to the standards by exempting them from pagan practices was no guarantee of their safety.

After twenty-one months in office, Claudius died of a new plague brought into the Empire by invaders. Aurelian (r. 270–275) took command amidst virtual collapse. The Rhine and Danube were crossed by invaders. The East was partially recovered with the aid of the Roman satellite kingdom of Palmyra, which then claimed to rule it. Gaul was in the hands of rebellious generals.

Aurelian's coins bore the motto 'Restorer of the world'. He promptly marched from the Danube to save Italy, smashing barbarian raiders. In Rome, he ordered the city to be walled, a frank admission of increasing imperial vulnerability and deterioration. Following Claudius' policy, he recruited troops from the Goths and other invaders defeated by the legions. In 271, the emperor led his forces against Palmyra while sending Probus to recover Egypt.

A devotee of the sun god, Aurelian as a monotheist recognized that the imperial cult of many gods no longer inspired popular confidence. He formally replaced it with that of the god Sol.[41] Given hierarchal office in the new worship and generous pay for it, the senators accepted the religious revolution without complaint. It was no threat to their power. That so fundamental a change in religious policy could be carried out with virtually no opposition from the public speaks for itself as regards the appeal of the imperial cult.

In and around Rome, in 270 fifty soldiers were martyred,[42] and in 272 the officer Sabas and seventy of his men were executed.[43] He apparently was one of the Goths recently conscripted by Rome from its defeated foes. As a *doctor*, a training officer, Sabas was an *immunes*. In 275 in Rome[44] 165 Christian soldiers were beheaded. Persecution within the army was accelerating but restricted to the Empire's capital.

In the summer of 275, Aurelian was assassinated by an official who had been warned that the emperor, a man furious towards deceivers, was aware of his thieving from the Treasury. Believing that he had to kill Aurelian or face his vengeance, the assassin was then killed by those who had warned him, a repeated Roman scenario.

Proof that Aurelian's death was not part of a coup was that his legions took the unheard of step of asking the Senate to choose the next emperor. The most experienced of these legionnaires were of the generation after the catastrophe of Valerian's capture. They had seen the danger of coups dividing the Empire in the face of enemies on every frontier. The Senate had a window of opportunity opened to it and appointed Tacitus, a man in his seventies, one of their own. It was a rare moment when positive decisions by authority seemed to meet with an army and public ready to accept them.

Tacitus was an able leader but many professional military had expected the Senate to have chosen a soldier, not a civilian. That a Roman emperor had to rule not from a throne but on horseback was the common opinion.

The army placed upon the throne a civilian, Tacitus, who realized that the Senate was powerless before the army. Within six months he was murdered as emperors usually were, by a soldier. His brother, Florianus, in charge of the Praetorian Guard on campaign, assumed the throne. On the march in the Middle East he halted at Tarsus, today in southern Turkey, the birthplace of St Paul. There, his plague-stricken forces met those of his rival Probus, raised as candidate of the desert armies from North Africa to Syria. Probus' army was undermanned. He bided his time, refusing combat.

At this point in time the Empire could have moved towards a restored Republican democracy with a reinvigorated Senate recruited empirewide or yield to militarism, a vast array of soldiers and officials exploiting the population and an emperor honoured as nothing less than a living god. The results would determine society for centuries to come. A key element in this crisis would be the Christians in the army, a small minority with influence beyond their numbers.

The earliest event in the Theban epic was discovered midway in the research. Ronald Bainton, a major scholar on Christian attitude towards the military, cited a large group of soldiers in the Roman army in 276 whom he regarded as

Christians. Curious, and suspecting an error, examination of the third century document quoted proved the date correct.

Eucherius' account cites Mauricius as a *campidoctor*, a retiree on recall and another record mentions his baptism about 280. Baptism required several years' preparation. Thus, 276 may well have been the year of his discharge after twenty-six years of service.

The document begins with an otherwise unknown event occurring that year one night in what is today northern Iran. It was an event that would have scarred the psyche of a soldier with conscience for years to come.

Chapter 5

An Error of War

War is the unfolding of miscalculations.

Barbara Tuchman

Persia's temporary overrunning of much of the East had made it vital that Romans be alert to any future attack. This was accomplished by preemptive reconnaissance probes deep into Persian territory, a dangerous task complicated by the formerly Roman areas on the frontier still held by Persia.

The year was 276, the season late autumn, the time of planting before the winter rains. The region was the Roman province of Mesopotamia (northern Iraq), claimed also by Persia, a killing field where empires contended. It was a no-man's land, three times within the century changing hands between Romans and Persians.

The Roman expeditionary force was returning at night from the river Hibero (Nahr Khabour).[1] The proud and warlike Persians (Iranians) had evaded battle despite every effort to goad them into action. Their failure to respond was uncanny.

To strike when the foe was weary and off-guard en route to home was a Persian tactic. The night march escaped the heat of the day and, hopefully, the enemy's notice. Their path was off the usual and most travelled route but through a labyrinth of hills bordering the vast desert stretching to Syria.

It was a region where agriculture had been born and science and magic commingled in seeking to dominate nature. Fertility of the fields was undertaken by careful observations of sun and stars to determine the calendar, by fasts and masochistic penances, ceremonial dances around bonfires, sexual couplings and human sacrifice. Sin, Baal and Mammon were fertility gods deemed devils by the writers of the Bible. Faiths had come, gone or endured. Judaism and Christianity absorbed the ancient calendar and many agriculture customs celebrating planting and harvesting.

The goal of the troops was safety behind the stone battlements of Carrhae (Kasr Karh), several days' westwards.[2]

In 43 BC,[3] a Roman army in the region had suffered the worst disaster a Roman army would suffer in the East. Crassus, a civilian millionaire, a supporter of Mark Antony and Octavian in their rival hopes of becoming the first emperor, had won approval to lead an army invading Persia. He dreamt of being another Alexander. His colleagues knew his incompetence. No matter, following the advice of good officers he might be victorious. If he lost, they had one less rival for the throne.

Crassus proposed marching with legionnaires and additional auxiliary cohorts across the Syrian desert eastwards to Carrhae. His allies, Armenians and Arab tribesman, urged him to reconsider. A campaign in spring by way of the hill country would escape the summer heat and the cavalry that was Persia's fame and Rome's weakest arm. Crassus disregarded the advice. Sensing the outcome, the Armenian and Arab light infantry and superb horsemen never arrived.

In lockstep across a vast void of sand without a patch of greenery, each man carrying fifty pounds of armour and equipment, Crassus' army had moved onwards. Near Carrhae, they were met by the Shah-I-Shah's cavalry. Some 20,000 of Crassus' soldiers were killed and 10,000 captured.

The night marchers were nearing Carrhae, returning from the east while Crassus had been approaching from the west. They would reach the desert the next day. Far deeper into enemy territory than Crassus' force had ever ventured, they were also far fewer in number.

Strangely, scouts reported the villages in the area to be deserted, with the livestock unattended.

Officers spoke in low voices, the men forbidden to speak or light a torch.

Perhaps an auxiliary with a pebble in his shoe brooded that the official soothsayers who used dice, horoscopes, palms of hands, dreams and the guts of chickens to predict the fortune of army campaigns might better examine the calluses on infantrymen's feet. That better determined the fate of empires. The soldiers were tired and anxious. The red dragon banners of the cavalry writhed as if alive in the night breeze.

Scouts reported a large camp of unidentified people on a hillcrest overlooking the route.

The Romans had no idea of the enemy's strength or the whereabouts of the foe's cavalry. Within minutes they might be detected, if they had not been already. It seemed vital to attack immediately.

Trumpeters blared the *buriti*, the Roman call to battle, the word mimicking its sound.

A survivor described what followed.

My lord Marcellus, we believe in the living God alone. And we have a custom of such a nature as I shall now describe, which has descended to us by the tradition of our brethren in the faith and has been regularly observed by us up to the present day. The practice is that every year we go beyond the bounds of the city, in company with our wives and children and offer up supplications to the only and invisible God, praying Him to send us rains for our fields and crops. Now when we were celebrating this observance at this usual time and in the wanted manner, evening surprised us as we lingered there and were still fasting, thus we were feeling the pressure of two of the most trying things men have to endure – namely, fasting and wont of sleep. But about midnight sleep enviously and inopportunely crept upon us ...[4]

Accordingly at that hour a multitude of soldiers suddenly surrounded us, supposing us, as I judge, to have lodged ourselves in ambush there and to be persons with full experience and skill in fighting battles. And without making any exact inquiry into the cause of our gathering there, they threatened us with war, not in word, but at once by the sword. Though we were men who had never learned to do injury to anyone, they wounded us pitilessly with their missiles, and thrust us through with their swords. Thus they slew, indeed, about one thousand and three hundred men of our number and wounded another five hundred.[5]

It was an accident of war.

The captives numbered about 8,000,[6] every one a civilian and most women and children.

And when the day broke clearly, they carried off the survivors amongst us as prisoners here, and that, too, in a way showing their utter lack of mercy towards us. They drove us before their horses, spurring us on by blows from their spears and impelling us forward by making the horses' heads press upon us. And those who had sufficient powers of endurance did indeed hold out; but very many fell down before the face of their cruel masters and breathed out their life there ... All of those whom on old age had come were sinking, one after the other, to the earth, overcome with their toils and exhausted by want of food.[7]

The proud soldiers nevertheless enjoyed this bloody spectacle of men continually perishing, as if it had been a kind of entertainment. They saw some stretched on the soil in hopeless prostration. Others, worn out by the fierce fires of thirst, the bonds of their tongues utterly parched, lost the power of speech. They beheld others with eyes ever glancing backwards, groaning over the fate of their dying little ones who were constantly appealing to their most unhappy mothers with their cries. The mothers themselves, driven frantic by the severities of the robbers, responded with wailing, which indeed was the only thing they could do freely. Those of them whose hearts were most tenderly bound up with their offspring chose voluntarily to meet the same premature death as their children. Those, on the other hand, who had some endurance were carried off as prisoners with us. Thus, after the lapse of three days, during which time we had never been allowed to have any rest, even in the night, we were conveyed to this place ...[8]

The Romans bivouacked. Interrogation revealed the prisoners were farmers from villages several miles from the dry riverbed, the soldiers' path. They were Christians following Jewish customs, people viewed as heretics or non-conformists by Jews and Christians alike, known as Ebionites or Jacobites, the followers of St James, although the document does not identify them.

It can be deduced that they had gathered to celebrate the feast of the planting, Succoth, when workers lived in the fields. That year the feast coincided with the beginning of the Sabbath at sundown. The festivities were joyous and prolonged. Forbidden by ritual law to walk more than a thousand paces on the Sabbath, they had spent the night outdoors, the men separated from the women. In accordance with tradition, on the last night of the feast all fires had been extinguished.

Their captors regarded the prisoners with bitterness. Roman soldiers, unless officers, scarcely had a private life. The Empire had reluctantly granted the privilege of legal marriage to auxiliaries after several centuries of denying it. Most had families. Indeed many had several. The army provided no funds for transfer of kin when a soldier was posted to a far distant region. Wives and children were left behind for ever and new households created.

The captive men were kept separated from the women and children, hostages to one another. The decision was made that the column would march by day to Carrhae, stealing more distance and time from any Persian force tracking them. In daylight the Romans could use cavalry and archers properly. Hopefully, the Persians were not ahead of them.

Prisoners stirred, pleading, surging against the guards, demanding information. Horsemen cantering their mounts pressed in upon the crowd and menaced with their lances.

A Roman soldier obeyed orders. Ordered to slit the gullets of the captives, he was supposed to do so without remorse. Ordered to aid them he was to do that, begrudgingly or otherwise. An officer solemnly warned that every prisoner lost would be that much less prize money from the sale of the slaves.

The dead were left unburied.

At dawn the troops struck tents and assembled in marching formation.

Officers trotted their mounts. Right arm extended, one saluted the *praepositus* and enquired loudly as daily morning ritual demanded, 'Are the army and the Emperor well?'

'The army and the Emperor are well!' was the shouted reply. Drawing weapons and rattling them against their shields, the troops gave three cheers. The commander signalled, an officer gave the command to march and the column advanced.

Months earlier, rival contenders for the imperial crown, Florianus and Probus, had been confronting one another at Tarsus where an epidemic disease was ravaging Florianus' troops and the population. Roman desert forces from North Africa to Syria supported Probus, an Illyrian (Albanian) born in Egypt. Probus, in keeping with his name (cautious), had waited until his enemy's forces weakened and ultimately yielded with little bloodshed.

While the auxiliaries were defending the Empire, legionnaires were as usual playing politics to decide who became emperor. Half the army was composed of auxiliaries, the rest legionnaires. The auxiliaries were paid less, yet worked harder.

The captives plodded forwards. Riders harassed them, lance point and lashes of knotted rope persuading. The villagers had little food or water and had not been allowed to venture home to get any. The ordeal of the march continued.

Roman law forbid the enslavement of Roman citizens. The prisoners were Romans. Roman citizenship could not be lost by conquest by foreigners. A mistake had been made. It would be set right when they reached Carrhae. It was a hope or a mirage in the minds of the prisoners.

A trumpet blast announced a halt for midday.

Resumption of the march brought a sharper awareness of thirst and fatigue.

From level horizon to level horizon was silence and emptiness. The awesome isolation of the desert and its dazzling night sky made humans feel insignificant. Lightning could strike from a clear sky. Dust devils swirled and disappeared. Mirages distorted reality. The desert inspired introspection. It had left a profound mark upon Judaism and Christianity. It also made individuals more keenly aware of their dependence upon one another.

Messengers brought news of the death of the Persian Shah-I-Shah. Powerful lords were contending to succeed him, explaining the Persian failure to respond to the Romans.

On the third day, Carrhae stood before them, stone walls built on a bedrock terrace set back several hundred paces from Balikh tributary of the northern Euphrates. Smoke-blackened and cracked walls testified to the earthquake that had helped the Persians to take the town after the Emperor Valerian's fall two decades earlier. Behind the town were green fields and higher ground.

Carrhae was also known as Caschar, Castra Carra, the biblical Harran. Abraham had sojourned there on his way from Ur to the promised land. Carrhae had been a mingling place for ages of many peoples. It was one of the few regions in the Empire that was predominantly Christian.

Alexander the Great had travelled this royal road, adding Greek to the region's stew of languages and races. Romans, recognizing Carrhae's strategic importance, had added to the town's fortifications. In 217 AD, the Emperor Caracalla, halting near Carrhae to relieve himself, was assassinated by his bodyguards, an ugly end to a murderous man. The assassin was killed shortly thereafter by those whose order he had obeyed.

Revived by water and a brief pause, the column filed between legionnaires saluting them, the grizzled campaigners contrasting with the polish of the garrison troops. They marched through the main gate to enter the plaza adjoining the many stepped hall of Marcellus, military-governor of the Roman province of Mesopotamia.

Clasping arms with the governor, the commander announced the expedition victorious. Considering that the victims were citizens of his province, the military-governor considered that was hardly the appropriate word.

In war, the unexpected is to be expected. The worse cruelties to prisoners of war often result not from calculated malice, but lack of foresight in planning for the number of captives – a task perhaps best handled by civilian government.

The fate of the prisoners was in the hands of the military-governor.

Chapter 6

Law, Order and Compassion

Hell is where there is no possibility of reason.
Prologue to the film *Platoon*

The sole record of these events appears in a document written in the fourth century in four different languages, 'The Dialogue of Archelaus with Mani'.[1] This document presented the philosophy of Mani, a Persian firebrand who sought to create a new universal religion. He had requested a debate with Bishop Archelaus of Carrhae, with Marcellus as mediator. A generation later the pagan emperor Diocletian would declare Manicheanism illegal in a decree displaying an extensive knowledge of it, perhaps utilizing the Dialogue as his source.

The episode of the massacre introduces the Dialogue without explaining why these events should be recorded in a theological document. No specific army unit is cited. No Christian soldier or official is specifically mentioned. Presumably, the prisoners were Christians as Archelaus and his congregation became their hosts.[2] The region was predominately Ebionite,[3] sects retaining Jewish customs while accepting Jesus as the Christ.

The various language versions of the document had different commentaries, one of which declares that the debate occurred when Probus was emperor.[4] Since Probus took power in the summer of 276 and Mani was executed in Persia in 277, the time can be roughly placed.[5]

Marcellus' family name and background, nationality, career and title are unstated. Christians in the era consistently ignored these matters in recording the dead.

Marcellus is depicted as a rich man in command of both army and civil affairs, on excellent terms with a Christian bishop and sought out by a foreign religious zealot as protector and open-minded listener. Marcellus was a person obviously well known at the time, judging from the Dialogue, yet no Marcellus is known to history by that name who could fit his description.

The military-governor of Mesopotamia in 275 was a Marcellinus[6] who was also one of the two consuls of the Empire that year, his partner the emperor. As consul, Marcellinus was the most honoured Roman in the eastern regions of the Empire. Marcellinus in Latin signified little Marcellus – Marcellus junior. In

Semitic languages it could be put as Marcellus Bar (son of) Marcellus. In translation and in omitting the governor's parentage along with other biography, could Marcellinus have become Marcellus? Christians routinely ignored family in identifying people in the era.

If he were governor, Marcellus was not a baptized Christian as he would have had to preside at pagan rites. An enlisted man or minor civil servant might circumvent these rites, an official or officer could not and refusal was punishable by death.

A few years earlier, the Emperor Aurelian in 272 had besieged the oasis of Tadmore, capital of Palmyra. The Palmyrenes, led by King Odenathus, had stemmed the tide of Persian invasion, acting independently yet never formally rejecting Roman authority. Odenathus' widow, Zenobia, defied Aurelian and was defeated. Aurelian dealt with the Palmyrenes leniently. The town was placed under the protection of a garrison of archers. Zenobia, courageous, cunning and overreaching, revolted. The Roman garrison of five hundred bowmen was virtually annihilated.

Marcellinus was offered leadership of the East if he joined the insurrection.

Marcellinus warned repeatedly that the revolt was a gamble against the odds, treachery in exchange for mercy – unforgivable in the eyes of Aurelian. Admitting that the offer was attractive, he repeatedly advised the conspirators to abandon the revolt. Secretly, he informed Aurelian. The emperor, en route to Europe, reversed his march and hastened to Palmyra, renewing the siege of its capital. In the effort he was wounded in the leg by an arrow. Having stormed the town, resplendent with colonnaded temples atop its steep hills, Aurelian demonstrated as much severity as he had mildness previously. The city was razed and the entire population killed or enslaved.

With the caravan town destroyed, trade between Rome and Persia collapsed.

The *Historia Augusta* says Zenobia was paraded in gold chains in a triumph through the city of Rome, peacefully ending her days in a comfortable villa.[7] The historian Zosimus states that Zenobia was murdered by drowning while crossing the Dardanelles, the woman in gold chains presumably an official deceit.[8]

Aurelian rewarded the governor Marcellinus with the consulship in 275.

Was Marcellinus identical with Marcellus? The name Marcellinus was not a Christian usage. He would have been Marcellus to the Christians.

When Marcellus, the man of consummate piety, had heard this recital, he burst into a flood of tears, touched with pity for misfortunes so great and so varied. But making no delay he at once prepared victuals for the sufferers and did service with his own hand for the wearied; in this imitating our father Abraham the patriarch...[9]

In the chaos of the generation past, the churches had effectively ministered to refugees whom Roman bureaucracy callously ignored. The Government had motive to be grateful. A decade earlier, Christian leaders had asked the Emperor Aurelian to settle a dispute between two claimants to a bishopric. The Church no longer avoided those in power. In the Middle East it sought them out.

The Bishop Archelaus asked permission for the local church to care for the prisoners. Marcellus readily agreed. The soldiers demanded of the Bishop a ransom price for each captive. Archelaus could not meet the sum.

A green branch hung in a marketplace announced a slave auction.[10] Slave dealers were *mangones*, scorned by even the corrupt, forbidden baptism; their money respected but not their presence. Roman law held the buyer at fault if cheated. *Caveat emptor.* Let the buyer beware. Slaves were an exception. A *mangone* could be sued or jailed for fraud.[11]

Slaves for sale were stripped, signs stating their origins and skills placed around their necks. Many adopted a shamelessness as psychological self-defence. A slave had no legal family. A female slave could accuse her master of abuse if she dared. Court judges were usually slave owners.

Cato the elder in the second century BC had written the classic manual on slave maintenance. Warning that the most dangerous slaves were those who finished labouring and did not immediately sleep, he advised they be worked until exhausted, even if the work was unneeded.[12] He recommended that the sick, elderly and disabled slaves be set free because they were useless and none would buy them.

On the feast of the *Saturnalia*,[13] the winter solstice, about 25 December to Romans, traditionally, master and family departed or locked themselves in an upper floor, handing over the villa to the slaves. In some households it was a pleasant feast respecting human equality, an occasion for gift giving. Elsewhere, it was an occasion for drunken rages, rapes and stabbings. *Libertas* in Latin was something to be dreaded: anarchy, an anomie, a freedom without direction or discipline but violence.

The aristocratic Roman poet Horace wrote that civilization was based on the use of tools, namely dumb tools, semi-communicative tools ... cattle, and speaking tools ... slaves.[14]

Matrimonium meant that a man recognized legally only one mother of his children, a convenience to slave owners. Often the most cruel oppressor a slave encountered was the owner's jealous wife or a master suspicious of his wife's infidelity.

Romans who worked for wages did so on a daily basis without job security. The Church did not dogmatically condemn slavery. To free a slave unable to earn a decent living was not a kindness. St Paul in his letter to Philemon said of slaves that it was better to be free but did not insist upon it. He urged Philemon to treat the runaway slave returned to him as a brother in Christ.[15] That slave, Onesimus, eventually became a free man and Christian bishop.

Slavery corrupted victim as well as victimizer. Survival under oppression necessitated duplicity. To *cavile* was the Latin term for playing one role to one person and another to another. It pervaded society. To escape responsibility by assuming a passive stolidity was a common survival mechanism. Masters might condemn slaves as stupid, lazy, dishonest and thieving, while motivating them to be so. Resentments a slave repressed could be unleashed in terrible violence, usually against another slave. Many slaves dared not hope lest it produce despair.

For free people, enslavement and being torn from family was a shock for which they were not prepared.

The average Roman infantryman in the era could barely afford to buy a new tunic in a year.[16] The overrunning of the frontiers at Valerian's fall had crippled the government's tax incomes at the same time that gold and silver lost in trade beyond the Empire was becoming irreplaceable as mines exhausted. Coins were issued with ever lower quantity of precious metal, triggering a wild inflation. Soldiers might not strike. They did riot and overthrow emperors.

Auxiliaries were paid less than men in the legions.[17] About half the army comprised auxiliaries in units of five hundred or a thousand men, the rest legions of some six thousand men each. The intent was that auxiliary units, recruited from a particular tribal or ethnic group unlike the well integrated legions, would be too small and independent to cooperate in coups against the state. To counteract the grievous inflation in the era the legions enjoyed the simple solution of ransacking Roman cities. The auxiliaries, underpaid and employed to do the most dangerous and harshest tasks of the army and stationed far from the towns, lacked the option of robbing the public treasury.

If the captives could be sold as slaves the campaigners could hope for undreamed of rewards. An adult skilled male could bring a price at auction equivalent to several years of an auxiliary's wages. Officers would receive the lion's share.

Infants, children and mothers would bring a poor price at the auction block. The Roman preference was to buy adult male slaves rather than to encourage the slave population to reproduce. At least a third of the Empire's population were slaves.

Marcellinus paid the soldiers the price demanded for the prisoners.[18] He then, astonishingly, ordered that all were to be set free and returned home. 'He at once distributed the gifts of duty among the soldiers without any strict consideration of number or distinction.'[19] He urged many soldiers to leave the army. Some took scarcely a fourth of the ransom and the rest made their departure without receiving even so much as would pay the expenses of the journey.[20] No explanation is given. Plausibly, some were Christians following John the Baptist's advice to be content with their usual pay.

Since Marcellinus is described urging soldiers to leave the army, he must have been speaking to men eligible for discharge. A man quitting the army before twenty-five years of service lost his retirement bonus and could be executed unless he had permission for disability.

The soldiers discharged were eligible for the usual salary or *stipendum* paid three times a year, the retirement bonus or *praemia* given at least to legionnaires, as well as the forced savings given at discharge and a donative, a bonus award from the emperor as substitute for campaign loot.[21] *Viaticum* was the travel money given to retiring veterans. Romans had seized the booty Persians had taken in overrunning the Middle East a few years earlier.[22] The governor would have been in charge of it. *Donatives* were given to cement the loyalty of the troops.

Looking upon the riches surrounding him – art in stone, gold, silver, bronze and ivory – Marcellus perhaps was reminded of an Egyptian proverb. A flood was disaster but the same water in ten thousand channels a great blessing. He had paid off the troops generously, even as many refused to take all their due.

Outside the walls of Marcellus' palace people lived crowded together, bringing forth children as if forging weapons against their enemies, each group's gods arrayed against the next.

He was weary of imposing peace as if people were incapable of it of themselves.

He had shown mercy. That would be taken as weakness by some. It was time for him, like many of the soldiers he had paid, to retire. By 277 he was no longer consul.

In the Middle Ages Vincent of Beauvais wrote that an unnamed 'old book' (Gratian's?) recorded the Theban legionnaires baptized at Jerusalem and confirmed in Syria by a bishop Marcellus.[23]

Could this have been the same Marcellus as the *Dialogue*, retired and become a church leader? In this era the Church was remarkably open to swift promotion of leaders from secular life becoming higher clergy over the heads of men long in the priesthood.

As a governor, Marcellus chose his bodyguard and administrators from soldiers of the two legions found in most provinces and their auxiliary forces. Christians, presumably, were among them. Unlike other soldiers, they were not in the habit of assassinating their host. Mauricius may have been among them.

If Christians were among the soldiers at Carrhae, they would remember the brutality against civilians in the campaign of 276. Confronted with a situation threatening civilians in the future, they would be psychologically and morally prepared.

This would be all the more likely if in the interim they had been free of army routine and in an environment conducive to reflections in conscience, i.e., as retired veterans at Jerusalem.

Gratian in the eleventh century would write that Mauricius was baptized by Zabdas, Bishop of Jerusalem during the reign of Probus. The two or three years of preparation then required for baptism and the fact that only veterans, not soldiers on active duty, were allowed baptism matches well with the time and region of the troops retiring at Carrhae, future officers and men of the Theban Legion.

In the Roman Republic soldiers had been discharged individually after fulfilling their service. On active duty they had been forbidden to marry. Alone in civilian life, unaccustomed to freedom from authority, a senator described many 'as orphans' in their behaviour. Augustus, the first emperor, desired that the army be virtually a hereditary military caste, a goal contradicted by the continued prohibition against soldiers on active duty marrying.

In reaction, a policy emerged of discharging veterans in groups every two years to be sent to veterans' *colonias*, of which there were scores throughout the Empire. These enclaves were expected to provide a loyal and stable population in times of upheaval and a recruiting ground since soldiers' marriages were made legal at the beginning of the third century.

Jerusalem, ravaged and depopulated in two disastrous attempts at revolt versus Rome, was the *Colonia Aelia Capitolina*, one of many in Israel established to displace the Jewish population. Mauricius chose it as his retirement home, accompanied by comrades of many years. He was retiring as the pressures upon the Empire were reaching a window of opportunity that if neglected might never emerge again in the Roman era. It is in crisis that a society, like an individual, is most likely and able to change.

Chapter 7

The Church as New Creation

You've got to have something to eat and a little love in your life before you can hold still for any damn body's sermon on how to behave.

Billie Holiday

If they had been in Carrhae that year, troops of Christian sentiment retiring to Jerusalem in 276 would have arrived with that accident of war fresh in their memories. In Jerusalem, Mauricius would have lived a life with leisure to meditate upon Christian attitudes towards war and the army.

Living in Israel, he must have reflected on his experience of civilians in North Africa opposing a brutal emperor as did the Jews of Israel in 66 and 132. Whatever the ideals for which they fought, civilians were no match for the legions; revolt was virtually suicidal. Under Roman brutal administration, Jews had, nevertheless, enjoyed considerable self-rule until the revolts. Israel thereafter lost its autonomy.

The first revolt was recorded at length by Flavius Josephus – Pharisee, rebel and turncoat joining the Romans. Lack of any other record leaves his version of events questionable in his facts and possible omissions.

The second revolt left scarcely any record, Roman or Jewish, which is an intriguing gap in history. Enough is known that the leader of the second revolt, Bar Kochba, was feared by compatriots as a tyrant. Israeli archaeologists would discover a letter with his signature threatening anyone sheltering 'The Galileans.' Who these Galileans were, people of that region of northern Israel or Christians often referred to by that name, remains unclear.

Whatever the case, the revolts split Christianity and Judaism apart. The Church was loyal to the most harsh emperors and under persecution remained non-violent. The pacifism of most church leaders while the Empire had almost perished from invasions must have disturbed Mauricius as a veteran with *brio*, pride as a professional military man. To reject violence to defend one's self was one thing. To reject violence if it was essential to save others, was something quite different.

What then was he to believe? The three years of preparation usually required for baptism encouraged him to consider the origins of Church policy towards the military, a policy that was evolving.

Most great writers of the early Church were pacifists. Justin,[1] Tatian,[2] Athenogoras,[3] Origen[4] and Lactantius[5] and many others firmly opposed baptized Christians in armed service.

In the Torah, the first five books of the Bible, the book of Deuteronomy declared that the conscript who was '*yareyverach halevav*', fearful and fainthearted, was to be sent home.[6] Rabbi Akiva (c.50–135 AD) interpreted this to be the 'hero among heroes', powerful among the most powerful, who is at the same time merciful,[7] the conscientious objector, not the fearful but the compassionate. His view opposed that of the leader of the second revolt versus Rome, Bar Kochba. Akiva died heroically under torture as a rebel against Rome. His perspective seems a reinterpretation. Deuteronomy[8] gave the recruit excuses from service if he had built a house and not yet dedicated it, planted a vineyard and not yet enjoyed its fruit, or become engaged and not yet married. Bar Kochba probably forced men to join the revolt.

The Jewish community of Alexandria, Egypt, had successfully asked Julius Caesar to exempt Jews from military conscription,[9] pleading that a devout observer of the laws of Moses could not serve with pagans. Forbidden to dine with the uncircumcized or to be in the presence of idols, restricted in diet, repelled by meat consecrated to pagan divinities by the butchers, prohibited from marching or fighting on the Sabbath and holy days or to be cremated in accordance with Roman army regulations, the devout Jew found military service with gentiles impossible. Morever, Judaism gave a high priority to married life, while Roman enlisted men in the era could not legally marry. If religion disarmed Jews, Roman authorities were pleased with the fact.

While religion disarmed some believers, it encouraged others to violent revolution. The unnamed author of the secret War Scroll of the Dead Sea Scrolls apparently regarded the Roman legionnaires as the enemies of God, to be destroyed by the Sons of Light led by the Messiah.[10] The inept instructions for war in the War Scroll seem of a mindset removed from realities. Neither devotees of the War Scroll nor pacifist Church fathers were open to questions posited in goodwill by soldiers striving decently to pursue their profession. The danger then as now was a public conscience polarized between militarists and the irresponsibly naive, ideological extremes ousting the balance of facts and ideals.

Military conscription, *dilectus*[11] was rare in the Empire until the time of Diocletian. Jesus and his apostles as Jews were never liable to *dilectus*.

In 129 BC, conversion and circumcision were forced upon the conquered Idumeans[12] of the Negeb and in 103 BC similarly imposed upon the Ituraeans[13] east of the Jordan and Galilee.

Their descendants tended to be lax observers. The city of Pella was destroyed because its populace was not adhering to Jewish customs.[14] Herod the Great, of

Idumean ancestry, was called a 'half-Jew'.[15] Nevertheless, uncircumcized converts[16] by the first century AD were allowed to attend synagogue in concession to resistance to ritual law of persons not ethnically Jewish.

The Herodian Kings of Galilee had troops including five cohorts of 'Jewish', i.e. Ituraean archers.[17] The troops of the Roman military governor of Judea were largely Syrians[18] with a tradition of animosity towards Jews. The Ituraeans had a reputation for rioting over arrears in pay, as did the Idumeans serving in Judea as temple police.[19] The population preferred them to pagan soldiers nonetheless. These Ituraean cohorts centuries later probably provided troops for the Theban Legion as shall be seen.

The New Testament mentions five Roman centurions: the one meeting Jesus at Capernaum; Cornelius, baptized with his household by Peter at Joppa; the officer rescuing Paul from a mob at Ephesus; the one escorting him as a prisoner to Rome and the soldier at the crucifixion who called Jesus 'Indeed the Son of God'. All are portrayed favourably.

Is this a pro-Roman presentation made to placate reprisals by the imperial government? Or does it express a sincere bias in favour of some military? The usual stereotype was that of X Ferrata, the 'Ironclad' Legion, stationed in Israel, composed of anti-semitic thugs, mostly Hellenistic Syrians – long enemies of the Jews. The emperor had been repeatedly petitioned to replace them but never did. This set the scene for Israel's ill-fated revolt in the year 66.

Jews had been mercenaries for many centuries.[20] Five hundred Jewish horse-archers who had fled from the Persian Empire became the bodyguard of Saturninus, Governor of Syria, at Valatha near Antioch and were granted a veterans' colony at Batanea, Ituraea.[21] This same duplicitous Saturninus in 19 AD persuaded the Emperor Tiberius to banish all Jews from the city of Rome. Four thousand were conscripted in violation of Julius Caesar's decree and sent to unhealthy regions of Sardinia. Those too old or too young to serve were threatened with enslavement if they defied the order.[22] Josephus relates that many were punished for refusing to serve.[23] Later, these conscripts were made non-citizen freedman, *generis libertini*, employees of the state.[24]

Only Luke mentions soldiers present as John baptized at the Jordan, more accurately, guards or police.

> The tax-collectors too came to be baptized. 'Master', they said to him, 'What are we to do?' He told them 'Do not go beyond the salary appointed to you.' Even the soldiers on guard asked of him 'What of us? What are we to do?' 'Do not use men brutally, do not lay false information against them. Be satisfied with your pay.'[25]

John declared baptism a prerequisite for salvation. 'What are we to do?' seems appropriate if these people were refused baptism.

The centurion at Capernaum, his servant healed by Jesus, was probably a *sebomenos*, a 'God fearer' in Greek, a convert to Judaism not practising every detail of Mozaic law. He was introduced as a 'friend of the people' who had contributed to the building of the local synagogue. A devout Jew was forbidden to enter the home of the uncircumcized. The centurion's protest against Jesus entering under his roof may have been in part his desire to save Jesus from the violation of ritual law. Jesus did not ask him to quit the military. As this centurion is not named in the gospels, it is uncertain if he is in the Church calendar of saints.

Jesus' response was unique and extraordinary. To the soldier's knowledge he declared, 'Amen. Amen. I say to you I have not seen such faith in all Israel.'

There were many official Roman military veterans' colonies in Israel. Originally, army soldiers were retired individually whenever their term of twenty-five years expired. They were described entering civilian life 'like orphans alone'. Roman military life made it quite difficult for a soldier to maintain a family. Only officers were allowed to have wives within the camp. Then the law was changed early in Jesus' lifetime to discharge veterans in groups every two years, arranging that they be settled together in colonies throughout the Empire as they chose.

Typically, Romans referred to household slaves as *familia*. Retired officers included enlisted veterans as members of their household. Peter's baptism of Cornelius thus was not baptism of a man on active military service. Similarly, John the Baptist had apparently refused baptism to temple guards on active duty.

In driving the cattle sellers and money changers from the temple,[26] Jesus used violence against property. Loss of their money seems to influence many in power much more than loss of human life.

On the night of his arrest Jesus told his apostles to sell their cloaks in order to purchase swords.[27] Yet, a moment later, shown a sword by one of the twelve, he declared 'Enough.' This apparent change of mind is never explained in the gospels and seems to conceal a gap in the narrative.

What did Jesus seek to defend? Twelve civilians each armed with a sword were hardly a match for the Temple Guard or Roman troops.

Since this episode concerns Jesus' betrayal it plausibly involves the traitor, Judas Iscariot, not to be confused with the Apostle Jude or Judas.

The word Iscariot is meaningless in Aramaic, Hebrew and Greek. In Latin, *sicarius* means an assassin or terrorist, literally a 'dagger-man'.[28] Jesus wished to die as the prophecies of the Messiah had foretold.[29] If he feared being murdered by an assassin, the arming of the apostles makes sense. If Jesus saw the Iscariot alone as essentially the danger and if Judas, the treasurer of the apostles, had been the one handing over his sword, one sword was enough.

When seized in the garden at Gethsamene, Jesus was defended by Peter who slashed with the sword a member of the arresting party. Jesus abruptly told him to sheath his weapon, declaring that 'He who draws the sword dies by the sword.'[30] This statement has been broadly interpreted to condemn all military service. Surely many men use weapons in war and do survive to live in peace. Without self-defence they might not. Jesus' statement referred to the immediate situation. Peter's violence in the face of a large group of military could have triggered a massacre. That is the paradox of deterrence. The threat of force can be effective in keeping peace. Its use can rapidly escalate violence.

Before Pilate, the only gentile Jesus ever addressed in the gospels, Jesus stated that 'I am a king but my kingdom is not of this world. If it were of this world my followers even now would be fighting in the streets to set me free.'[31] Jesus was certainly a Jewish patriot. He wept over the destruction of Jerusalem, which he expected if his commands were not followed.[32] The last question asked of him by his apostles was 'When shall Israel be a free nation?'[33] Jesus' death can be seen as sacrifice, symbol and scapegoat forestalling a suicidal national rebellion against Rome for more than a generation.

In the Jewish revolt of 66–70 the Ituraean forces under Herod remained loyal to Rome but defended Jews against the pagans in Galilee, attacking them amidst the chaos unleashed. Herod's forces quite probably became thereafter the six Ituraean auxiliary infantrymen and cavalry units on the Roman army list.[34] About 56 AD, the Jewish horse-archers at Batanaea became Cohors I Augusta[35] These Judaic units in the Roman army must have compromised religious practices if they retained Judaic beliefs. Christianity could have been attractive to them.

In contrast to the satellite Judaic forces in Galilee, Judea and Samaria, the forces of Roman citizens (the legions), generally remained in Syria[36] although non-citizen auxiliary infantry and cavalry units were stationed at cities in Palestine.[37] Cornelius, the centurion of the 'Italian cohort' at Caesarea Maritima[38] from archaeological evidence was probably in Cohors II Italica Civium Romanorum Voluntariorum,[39] unusual as an auxiliary unit in that it was composed of Roman citizens.

Cornelius was apparently a *Sebomenos*, 'God fearer', a convert to Judaism since Peter as a strict observer of Mozaic law would not have willingly entered a pagan household. Cornelius was baptized in his home. As an officer he would have been allowed to live outside the camp if on special duty status, *beneficiarius*, or semi-retired after twenty years' service.

In 13 BC Emperor Augustus had allowed soldiers to leave barracks life after sixteen years of service provided that they served four more years semi-retired[40] in special cohorts under a *curator veteranorum*. By 15 AD,[41] these semi-retirees trained recruits and dealt with administrative matters in return for various privileges, including living outside camp with their families. Presumably, Cornelius was one of these personnel.

Paul recorded a centurion saving him from a flogging,[42] another stopping a plot to kill him,[43] and Julius,[44] probably of Cohors I Augusta at Batanea, taking him as prisoner to Rome.

By the third century the aforementioned Ituraean cohorts were stationed in Egypt.[45] All were archers. These units disappeared from the army list in the third century. The Theban Legion must have incorporated some experienced troops of old units. This suggests a link between Judaic Roman military and the Theban Legion.

Another army unit of significance to Mauricius would have been Legio XII Fulminata, the 'thunderstruck' legion with veterans retired to colonies in Israel.

Josephus described Legio XII Fulminata as one of the finest units in the Roman army. However, a Roman contemporary, Tacitus, described it as lax and poorly outfitted for war. In the first revolt it was called from Syria to the siege of Jerusalem, chosen among five legions to lead the assault to enter the city. The Fulminata rapidly gained access over the outer city wall to the rooftops within as Jews at the gates fought against rebel countrymen in order to allow the legion into the city. With victory within sight, the Roman commander ordered the Fulminata to withdraw.

Josephus gives no explanation for this puzzling happening. The Fulminata was subsequently sent to northern Israel, not to crush rebels as much as defend Jews against the Greek-speaking populace rioting versus them that had sparked the revolt. With defeat of the revolt, the legion was sent to Melitene in the Roman satellite kingdom of Armenia with many thousands of Jewish captives to resettle them as useful contributors to a kingdom in need of workers.

Possibly the reason for the Fulminata's order to withdraw was that it was regarded as too friendly to Jews seeking no violence versus Rome. If it had readily seized the city, the opportunity for plunder for the other legions might have been cancelled. Intermarriage between the Legio XII Fulminata's personnel and Jewish women could explain this to some degree . The Legio XII Fulminata was to become known as the unique Christian legion.

The Empire was no longer an aggressive power menacing its neighbours. It had been on the defensive for a century, although its policy conducted sweeps beyond its frontiers from time to time. The Fulminata's strategic role was defensive. The change in the army's function lessened Christian objections to military service, the more so considering the near collapse of the Empire at Valerian's fall.

The essence of morality is caring. To be a Christian and scorn the defence of others must have seemed hypocritical to Mauricius, a man with *brio*, a soldier's pride in his profession.

The Moors among the veterans practised old routines, such as a stave dance that was a military drill put to music and jousts of two horsemen racing at one another to fling short poles blunted at one end by cloth wrappings, the Moorish style of cavalry attack with javelins. Typically, the Moors wore no helmets and displayed thick mats of crinkled hair. The thought occurred that their efforts would have been better used training new troops instead of entertaining themselves. Mauricius was restless out of service in what had been a turbulently active career.

Rumours abounded of great changes to take place in order to secure the shaken Empire. There were veterans jealous of the opportunity to undertake such reforms; they missed being part of a larger institution. To be a Christian was to be a member of a universal community. Religious conversion had a strong appeal to some soldiers. To be intelligently honest a person needs be a cynic, but ultimately there is need to be cynical even of cynicism. That is where faith enters.

Chapter 8

To Find Oneself in Jerusalem

One is not born a Christian, one becomes a Christian.

Tertullian

The Gospels affirmed that one found oneself by losing oneself in something greater than self alone. A good cause or movement, an institution such as the army, a project, ambition, or goal, gave purpose and discipline. Having left the army, veterans felt a loss but also a freedom new to them. Profession may help define what we are but who we are is determined by our relationships with other people.

Because of their status and pay, relatively few soldiers were able to maintain a family life. Neither did the wealthy in power reproduce themselves as a class. The third or more of the populace who were slaves did not reproduce their numbers. The effect of epidemics on this already fragile population structure was devastating.

Soldiers turned to religious groups for support. The secret cult of the war god Mithra, ironically a Persian deity of Rome's most dangerous foe, bonded many officers, officials and important merchants in fraternity. Hundreds of its shrines have been brought to light by archaeologists. All are small as befit an exclusive society. Persian violation of its international fraternity with Valerian's fall occasioned the near cessation of building of new Mithraic shrines.

Christianity, too, offered a support network but was open to all ranks. It also offered a much better opportunity to meet women.

Romans pressed by circumstances redefined family. Soldiers without sons often adopted slaves they made their heirs; the centurion at Capernaum who asked Jesus to heal his servant was perhaps an example. *Familia* in Latin included household slaves. The Roman historian Tacitus wrote that Germanic chiefs physically struck household servants, an act unthinkable to a proper Roman. A master's children commonly called adult household slaves Uncle or Aunty.

Widows were socially pressured to soon remarry so that their children would not have to support them.

Originally, all property had been inherited by the eldest son, ensuring family solidarity in the Roman Republic. In the Empire, property was equally divided among all heirs in the absence of a will. Individualism and economic competition were promoted, a new freedom to some, anti-social egotism to others. Meanwhile, many plantation owners denied slaves a family life and regarded the children of the farm workers as useless expenses, preferring to buy adult slaves. As plantations grew larger, consuming smaller farms, families withered.

Abandonment of infants, especially girls, was quite common. *Alumnus* meant an abandoned child adopted and raised to be sold by a slave dealer. The parental drowning or strangulation of infants was entirely legal. Yet policy was contradictory; parents of three or more children were given privileges and at times governmental bonuses. The death rate among children was devastating.

Under Augustus there were seventy-seven senators who had inherited office. Some seventy years later there were only four. The meek inherited the earth however poorly society prepared them to maintain it.

Many factors combined to weaken the Empire but the dwindling population was probably the most erosive. Death by disease would become too common for historians to notice.

Marriage to Romans of the Empire was neither a religious institution nor a romantic one. Lucretius the atheist, Seneca the Stoic and Plutarch, the priest of Eleusis, similarly viewed passion in marriage as 'inappropriate' and advised brides to be grateful if their husband was unfaithful. Legally, wives remained under the guardianship not of their spouse but their father or his appointee. A wife could have her own property, although her husband took possession of her dowry.

Sex was blatant and confrontational. Images of male genitalia hung from shop doorways. Prostitutes' prices were written on the walls of wine shops. In the city of Rome, metal tokens for free admission to the brothels were handed out by the government, along with bread and wine to the fathers of families on welfare.

The impact of Roman law discouraged having large families lest the heirs had less to inherit. The government heavily taxed unmarried men between twenty-five and sixty years of age and unmarried women between twenty and fifty years of age and forbid them from attending the public games. They could not inherit from outside their family. Divorcees had to remarry within six months, widows within twelve. Bachelors and spinsters were rare. Indeed, there was no Latin word for an unmarried woman.

Retired military officers invited other veterans to join their households; men who had served them as staff, bodyguards or well regarded subordinates and their families. When Peter baptized the centurion Cornelius and 'all his household' there can be little doubt that this was the situation.

The officers retired to Jerusalem would have brought with them an entourage of kin, servants, comrades, trusted and familiar veterans, their familiars and friends.

Roman Jerusalem was the military veteran's colony of Aelia Capitolina. The city was destroyed in the revolt against Rome of 66–70 AD, its population killed or enslaved and deported. Nevertheless, by 132 imperial decree, Jews had largely resettled the city. That year, the Emperor Hadrian ordered a temple of Jupiter built in the city to prepare it to become an army colony. Once again, Israel arose in revolt, this time led by Bar Kochba, who claimed to be the Messiah.[1] He attacked anyone opposing his absolute leadership. The result was further tragedy for the Jewish people.

Hadrian forbid circumcision of converts to Judaism[2] and renewed the prohibition of Jewish settlement in the city. Judaism turned in upon itself, its missionary impetus of the first century greatly diminished. By the third century Jerusalem was again largely Jewish in population, with Roman prohibitions unenforced, but only one synagogue existed where there had been hundreds.

Before the first revolt Christians had attended the temple and synagogues as one among many Jewish sects. Between the two revolts a daily prayer, the Twelfth Benediction or Birkat ha-Minim, 'May the Nazarenes and the heretics be suddenly destroyed and removed from the Book of Life,' was added to synagogue ritual.[3] Nazarene was the word for Christian used by the high priest Ananias in the Acts of the Apostles. Thereafter, Christians no longer attended Judaic ceremonies.

Legionary badges on coinage with images of the god Serapis or the sphinx reveal that most of the city's veterans were from Egypt's Legio II Traiana or Alexandrianae fleet marine.[4] The emblem of a wheel, rumblings identified with thunder, suggest the presence also of retirees of the Legio XII Fulminata, the 'thunderstruck' legion, unique as Christian in sympathies.

Aelia Capitolina was reduced in area and population like cities throughout the Empire by the third century. Between its ruined outer walls, colonnaded tile-roofed streets crossed the city from the Jaffa and from the Damascus gates.[5] Confined by the south-western wall was the old camp of Legio X Ferrata. The temple of Jupiter, an 'abomination of desolation' to believers, stood upon the Jewish-built Temple Mount, the largest manmade platform in the world. A great temple of Aphrodite, the patroness of whores, faced it from the west. A theatre, public baths and a racetrack were additional Roman constructions.

The whereabouts of the churches in the city at the time awaits the archaeologist's trowel. Probably, the veterans' colony was near the headquarters of Legio X Ferrata, today a parking lot next to Jerusalem's National Auditorium. The retirees were free to live in other districts. What would become the churches of St Sabas, a military martyr, and that of St James were probably somewhere between the south-western wall and the military camp.[6]

The city's population was quite poor. Jerusalem's Christians were a minority divided into minorities. Some were Ebionites[7] who demanded that every detail of kosher law, circumcision, Jewish holidays and customs be obeyed by Christians of gentile origin. In contrast, Greeks developed Monophytism, propounding that Christ was a vision, never flesh and blood, and, therefore, never a Jew. Both sects drifted away from the rest of Christians. The Nazarenes[8] or Jacobites followed the Ebionites in their own lives but made no such demands upon gentile Christians. Approved by Peter and Paul, they held themselves to be truly Jews and truly Christians. In the first revolt most had died rather than abandon their countrymen, although convinced that the revolt was doomed.

Judaism and Christianity had entered upon separate paths. Christ's teachings were the expansion of Judaic ideas. Christianity moved from its Judaic roots at peril. Much in the Gospels assumed a Jewish sense of values. Jesus' admonition to 'Love thy neighbour as thyself' presumed a healthy self-respect. Some gentiles 'loved' neighbours as themselves, despising both.

Jesus broke with paganism's unity of church and state and ethnic or class exclusiveness. He refused worldly power. Instead of physical and social coercion, he demanded a free choice to reject evil. He asserted the equal importance of every soul. His answer as to why God allows suffering was his own suffering, an example where words might not have moved souls.

In Hebrew, *nepes*, soul, literally meant breath – spirit intrinsically related to the body. The earthiness of Judaic belief enabled it to soar spiritually without losing balance. Greek philosophy, despite athletics and nakedness in art, despised the flesh, the 'corruptible clay' entrapping human spirit. The *psyche* was literally a butterfly, free of its decaying bodily cocoon.

In Jewish life education in a craft and biblical study were both demanded. Learning was all the more essential to Jewish devotion after the destruction of the temple and its rituals. That Jews scattered throughout the Empire did not lose their identity after the temple's destruction was an extraordinary achievement.

A Roman might be Italian, Celt, Moor, Greek, Semite, Aethiopus, German, Egyptian, Slav or any one of dozens of tribes. A Christian was a citizen of a universal institution, *catholicos*, also but by choice, not birth. The 'Mother Church' as even the hostile pagan Celsus described it emphasized doctrine not only because truth was one but because keeping a lot as ethnically diverse as the faithful together demanded unity of belief. Judaism could tolerate sectarianism since most Jews shared a common ancestry. Christians did not.

To some degree, both religion and politics tend to reflect family values writ large.

God as *Abba*, father in Hebrew, remained unique to Judaic and Christian creed, a term of intimacy and affection perhaps better translated as Daddy. Psychology can be applied to both religious believers and atheists. A survey of modern philosophers hostile to religion reveals that most lacked a father in childhood or had one who was dysfunctional.[9] Christians who risked their lives to hide Jews in World War II typically spoke with admiration of their parents.

All Roman public assemblies were illegal unless licensed. Permission was hard to obtain. Many towns were denied volunteer fire companies or athletic clubs from fear that any association might cover a plot to revolt. As family life withered, so did private organizations, with the exception of the Christian Church.

The members of that strange cult named for an executed carpenter hid from public scrutiny. Like Jews, they avoided gladiatorial games, the theatre, official ceremonies and the restaurants where the meat was from animals slaughtered with pagan prayers. To pagans this prompted the accusation first flung at Jews, that Christians 'hated life'. They admitted to drinking the blood of their god and eating his flesh. Some Christian heretical sects had bizarre sexual practices as churchmen acknowledged.[10] 'You can find them in the morning amidst the haze of the garbage dumps, scurrying away like rats with some poor wailing babe carried off to who knows what awful fate,' a pagan wrote. Infants were commonly abandoned by pagans in the garbage dumps and adopted by Christians. Others were seized to be raised and sold as orphan slaves, *alumni* by businessmen.

Christians, in abandoning the gods of their forebears, seemed unstable. Divisive religious and ethnic rivalries strengthened and necessitated Roman rule as policeman. An international creed was feared as undermining it.

When creed was from birth, reflection could be minimal. Converts often confronted persecution with more courage than people raised in faith from childhood. They had already made a considered and stressful decision in breaking away from their upbringing.

Rebellion without awareness of one's own limitations readily becomes arrogance even as faith without doubt can become delusional. A personal morality without community could become a contempt for humanity. *Consciencia* was ideas shared.

Humilitas in Latin was to know oneself, to be aware of one's limitations, virtues, likes and dislikes. The centurion at Capernaum had told Jesus:

> I am not worthy to receive you under my roof. That is why I did not presume to come to thee myself. My servant will be healed if you will only command it. I too know what it is to obey authority; I have soldiers under me and I say go to one man and he goes or come to another and he comes.[11]

Humilitas was not false modesty. Conversion required *humilitas* to find one's identity. To acknowledge one's own guilt if lacking in self-esteem is crushing if no one is forgiving. Mercy, forgiveness, in Hebrew *hesed*, was what Christ above all else demanded.[12]

Without forgiveness, fearing retaliation, a person might continue in evil. Forgiveness, however, requires an admission of guilt. To forgive those with no remorse and in denial could encourage evil. The cycle of victim becomes victimizer was to be broken; truth, acceptance of responsibility, trust in self-worth and mercy, repentance and forgiveness were key to the healing process. Forgiveness was to be granted 'seven times seventy', according to Jesus' answer to Peter.[13]

Stoic philosophy, pantheistic and abstract, scorned all emotions. Recognizing neither tragedy nor comedy, it sought to elevate the mind to ignore the body.[14] Many pagan religions, in contrast, demanded masochistic orgies of torture and mutilation in expiration for sin. Manichaeanism,[15] like the heresies of Gnosticism and Montanism, viewed everything material to be irretrievably of the realm of evil, whether sex, family, business, politics or society. None of these creeds had organizations involved in charitable activities.

Research among twentieth century religious converts reveals that most people are not strongly attached to a new creed's beliefs until after their conversion.[16] Few are originally members of any denomination, but few also are from a family with no religious identity. Typically, the potential convert feels powerless, lonely and vulnerable and is critical of society's injustices. He or she may seek a more liberal creed than that of strict parents or, if emotionally troubled, one more severe. It is the network of personal relationships with believers and their practical assistance that usually bring the convert within the religious group. Exceptions to these patterns presumably mark converts of especially intellectual or individual character.

Sacrifice of some personal desires can have rewards for community.

Amidst epidemics, Christians treated the sick regardless of creed. The famed pagan Roman medical doctor, Galen, who admitted abandoning his patients amidst plague and fleeing Rome, called Christians tending the ill 'naturally courageous'.[17] Most people stricken by epidemic recovered if given continued aid in their weakened condition. While some Christians tending the sick died, others acquired immunities, which, unknowingly, they spread in their community.[18]

Paganism seemed helpless to console in such disasters. Its religion had no doctrine to urge benevolence towards strangers. Its loyalties were exclusive. Bereft of loved ones and enabled to recover by Christians, some pagans were probably attracted to their community.

The faith spread most quickly in cities because of the ease of communicating with large audiences, but also because the Church provided a network of sorely needed social welfare amidst people uprooted and confused. The homeless, unemployed, orphans, widows, ill and aged received concrete aid as well as spiritual.

The early Christians followed Jewish principles in opposing abortions and infanticides, increasing their numbers. The Roman historian Tacitus wrote that Jewish condemnation of the killing of unwanted infants was an example of their 'sinister and revolting' practices.[19] Most victims of infanticide were girls, causing a disproportionate male majority in pagan society.[20] Women were the majority of Church members. Intermarriage usually resulted in children being raised in the faith.

Pagans regarded unmarried women with contempt even if they were their daughters, according to the poet Catullus.[21] Widows were pressured to remarry although they would lose their inheritance. The fewer heirs, the better for the rest, was the mentality of many upper class Romans.

Early Christianity was sexually revolutionary in encouraging people to marry for love, regardless of slavery, class, parental arraignments or ethnic origin. The Church also gave both men and women an option frowned upon in paganism, the freedom to remain celibate.

Women in the Church frequently remained single rather than marry men chosen by pagan parents. Many took active leadership as deaconesses. The marriage of a free person with a slave or ex-slave or an aristocrat with a commoner was illegal under Roman law. The Church permitted it, leaving the legal inheritance in confusion. Slaves could not legally marry, yet the Church insisted that their union was sacrosanct, setting slaves against their masters.

Paul, following Jewish law, allowed converts to divorce hostile spouses whose bitterness thereafter can be well imagined.[22] In mixed marriages partners might love one other, but could barely tolerate one another's beliefs. Husband and wife, parents and children, siblings and in-laws might be religiously divided. Death did not bury the discord. Christians were buried in Church cemeteries, not with their pagan families. Children became bones of contention between parents of different beliefs.

Women greatly influenced men to enter the community of believers. Army wives, living far from their families, needed wits and independence of spirit. A soldier depended upon his wife's fidelity and good judgment. With the social network of the *ecclesia* to aid her, he could feel more secure. For many the Church was, in effect, family.

'Who is grateful would be generous had he the means' was the proverb of the North African slave and playwright Terence. Gratitude is perhaps the purest of all religious motives.

A person had to be introduced to the *ecclesia* by a trusted member. The catechumen or novice was not allowed to attend the sacred meal nor receive any other sacrament until baptism. Fearing official informers and cultic thrill seekers, the *ecclesia* was so secretive that persecutors were shocked to discover Christians among family and close friends. Increasingly, knowledge of the faith was more than hearsay and held by someone familiar.

In Roman society the exploited unleashed their rage upon those worse exploited, the conquered aided in conquest of others, and slaves and citizens clashed in hatred, while Christianity preached that 'Among us there is neither slave nor freeman, Greek or Jew, male or female...'[23]

Linus, the second Bishop of Rome, was a slave. Slaves generally lived lives not only physically harsh but psychologically barren, character and talent ignored unless profitable to the master. The Church offered opportunity to affirm ability, its ranks many: priests, scribes, healers, prophets, the deacons who handled all Church finances, teachers, singers and what might be termed volunteer social workers.

Quite likely, the veterans retired to Jerusalem because they were already of Christian persuasion. Denied baptism while on active duty, they were eligible when retired.

Belief in a hereafter was an essential of Christian faith, a belief that by the third century few pagan creeds but those of Egypt held and stoics despised. Plutarch described a priestess of Alexandria who strode through the streets with a flaming torch in one hand and a jug of water in the other, shouting that she would burn heaven and douse Hades so that people could act in pure moral freedom without expectation of reward or punishment.[24] Virgil had written 'Happy the man who has trodden under his feet fears and inexorable fate and the roar of greedy hell.' Virtue to the stoic was its own reward, a dubious consolation to the victimized.

Plutarch's priestess had admirable intent but ignored justice, an oversight in keeping with aristocratic values.

To many Romans, there was no responsibility, achievement, justice or freedom – only fate. Jesus insisted that although evil will happen, one must not be its agent. To some Romans this may have seemed egotism but to Christians one had a duly to save one's own soul. Baptism was a heightened awareness rejecting evil. It was a free choice, a finding of self, not alone but as a member of a community of belief, *consciencia*.

Early Christians had a sober attitude towards 'magical thinking'. The acts of the martyrs show that they expected no miracles to save them. In the church people prayed for healing but organized to care for the ill. Imprisoned martyrs not infrequently were visited by believers ready to use bribery and political pull to aid them.

The ruling class considered religion a necessity to keep the losers of society in their place. Why then object to Christianity? If it taught human equality, so did Stoicism. The faith was in accord with most Stoic morality, including that regarding slavery and rights of women.

Stoicism aspired to philanthropy but remained individualistic and unorganized. It was no threat to Empire. The Church was organized to deal with social problems the government ignored. The Church, not Christianity, seemed a threat to those in power.

The Roman upper class was profoundly conservative and authoritarian. It respected ancient creeds because their origins were beyond memory and criticism. Christianity was new, its potential unpredictable and immeasurable.

There were several forms of baptism. Martyrs were regarded as baptized 'in blood' if not in water: 'red' martyrs. Baptism by desire was to seek God according to one's circumstances, even if unaware directly of Jesus' teachings. Who obtained it was not for man to judge considering that, without the goodwill of many non-believers, Christians would have suffered much worse persecution.

The Church, to a convert like Mauricius, would not have seemed alien in culture. Its seven sacraments were comparable to the seven ranks of initiation of the pagan mystery cults. There were many cultural borrowings within the Church, including the Easter egg reminiscent of Osiris, the Egyptian god of resurrection, and the bowtie pretzel in the form of the hieroglyph for prayer baked for religious holidays. The wedding ring, holy water and Christmas tree were borrowings. The Church had no desire to crush native culture but adopted many of their usages.

As Paul clearly took for granted in his first letter to Timothy, most priests were married, ordained after the congregation approved. Priests elected the bishops with approval of the *ecclesia*. That word adopted from Greek originally meant not church but town meeting. Most centurions were chosen in much the same way. Bishops were expected to be celibate, separating from their wives if married. The administration of the Church closely paralleled Roman imperial organization. Curiously, in Gaul, where only the Celtic word *garçon* for servant or boy survived amidst Latin, administrative regions within each diocese would bear the names of the dozens of pre-Roman tribes.

Conversion, religious or otherwise, is rarely a one-way street. The stronger the religious imprint before Christianity, the more deeply it influenced the new faith. To win over a pagan priest or priestess to Christianity generally incorporated many of their followers. Like light through a stained glass window, every culture encountered to some degree coloured the new creed, not diminishing but enriching it. Most heresies were carry-overs from paganism rejected by the church.

A two or three-year period of probation was required before baptism, depending upon the bishop.[25] The veterans had probably asked for baptism soon after arriving at Jerusalem, their convictions reinforced by their numbers. Usually, people were baptized in a group, once a year on Easter Sunday. About 279 or 280, clad in white, after spending the entire night in ceremony, some of the veterans received the sacrament in the light of early morning from the city's bishop, Zabdas.

To violate their baptismal vows would be to them to lose their innermost being. Their faith did not make them selflessly mindless, but the more stubborn when crossed in conscience.

Mauricius and those with him probably never anticipated that they would return to army duty amidst the violent transformation of the Roman world.

To pagans ready to give honour to any creed demanded, seeing all as names for one, this was an arrogant independence. They saw themselves as tolerant, Christians and Jews were seen as exclusive but at least Jews honoured the religion of their ancestors as all should. Christians betrayed their own traditions and thus caused the distrust and resentment that conservative folk might feel toward them.

So those in governmental authority believed. They had the power to crush such dissonance.

Chapter 9

From an Imperial Perspective

To those who may have to pay again for the new blunders – nevertheless always the same – of the big shots who don't want to consider the errors of the past.

Pierre Closterman

The historian Polybius, a Greek writing in the second century before Christ, acknowledging the virtues of the democratic Roman Republic conquering his homeland, sought the cause.

The most important superiority the Roman Commonwealth displays, in my opinion, is their religious beliefs, for I think what in other nations is looked upon as a reproach, I mean a scrupulous fear of gods, is the very thing which keeps the Roman commonwealth together. To such a degree is this prevalent among them both in private and public business that nothing could exceed it. Many people think this unaccountable, but in my opinion their object is to use it as a check upon common people. If a state wholly of philosophers were possible, such a custom perhaps would be unnecessary. But since every multitude is fickle and full of lawless desire, unreasoning anger and violent passion, the only resource is to keep them in check by mysterious terrors and scenic effects of this sort. Thus, in my opinion, the ancients were not acting without purpose or at random when they brought among the vulgar those opinions about the gods and punishments in Hades: much rather do I think that men nowadays are acting rashly and foolishly in rejecting them. This is the reason why, apart from anything else, Greek statesmen, if entrusted with a single talent, though protected by ten checking-clerks, as many seals and twice as many witnesses, yet cannot be induced to keep faith, whereas among the Romans, in their magistracies and embassies, men have the handling of a great amount of money and yet from pure respect to their oath keep their faith intact.[1]

Two centuries later, officials of the Roman Empire had a reputation for brutal greed.

Success, unchecked or balanced, like power, tended to corrupt. Polybius' contempt for the masses prompted his endorsing Plato's view in Book Three of the *Republic* that recommended 'noble lies' as a means of ruling.[2] To some upper class Romans, religion was the noblest lie of all, essential for social unity in a world coming apart. Archaeology reveals by absence of evidence that, by the third century, virtually no one prayed in private to the imperial cult, the Romanized Greek deities.

Many Romans lived existentially, in anomie, unsure of any guidelines or commitment. Greek philosophy had long since largely demolished belief in the many gods among the educated. Socrates and Plato had pointed the way to monotheism, without suggesting any specific morality or supportive community.

Democritus had attacked belief in the gods without denying providence. To Greeks, an atheist might be either one attacking false ideas about the divine or denying any supernatural. Christians were, rightly, in the first sense regarded as atheists.

Three centuries later, the Roman Lucretius had proposed a much darker cosmology than Democritus, a universe without a moral centre. He derided romantic love and denied that death was an evil. One account has it that he died of the effects of a love potion, others that he committed suicide.[3] Fawning praise for his patron, Caius Menius, 'a thoroughly evil man' in the opinion of Catullus, a self-proclaimed womanizer, was the price he paid for favours.[4]

Paganism was struggling to survive through syncreticism, all the gods' names for the one. Rulers could thus claim tolerance even as they persecuted. The Roman world was filled with spiritual shoppers, wandering from one philosophy or cult to another.

Fortune tellers and interpreters of dreams abounded. With political and social freedom vanished, helpless before natural disasters, feelings of powerlessness encouraged fatalism. Astrology's popularity grew as personal options withered. No other field demanded such knowledge and skill. The astrologer was astronomer, geometrician and mathematician. Every legion in the army had a birth date, its inauguration, its horoscope cast daily thereafter by priests assigned to the task. Death was the penalty for casting the horoscope of the emperor, lest he be caught at a vulnerable moment.[5]

In the countryside, *pagani*, the villagers, still worshiped tribal deities. In the cities, many traditions had evaporated. Mystery religions emerged to fill the void. They were secretive and exclusive, usually involving seven ranks of initiation, their morality an arch loyalty to their clique.

In the Apocalypse, Jesus condemned *pharmaticopaia*, generally translated as magic but specifically the use of narcotics by mystery cults. Sexual orgy and torture were practised in some. Every bodily organ seemed to have had its cultists: the worshippers of Bacchus relishing alcohol and the belly; Aphrodite the genitals; Orpheus an ear for music; the Pythagoreans and Elusians the elevation of the brain through mathematics and philosophy. The mystery religions concentrated upon recruiting the rich and powerful.

The Stoics stood aloof from exclusiveness and sensuality. Unhappiness to them was not the result of the outer environment but one's response to it. In appealing to the universal morality and equality of the golden rule, they had much in accord with Christians. Stoicism was especially appealing to educated men of action in the military, government and imperial trade. Yet in denying the emotions, Stoicism left many people unmoved.

The chief pagan critic of Christianity was Celsus, a Greek writer about 178 who viewed Judaism and Christianity as likewise wrong in holding man made in the image and likeness of God. 'In no way is man better in God's sight than ants and bees,'[6] was his view. To him, Jews and Christians were 'like a swarm of bats – or ants creeping out of their nest – or frogs holding a symposium round a swamp – or worms in congress in a patch of mud – debating which of them is the more sinful.'[7] To Celsus, moral character was inborn and unchangeable, human freedom nil, the social status quo sacred.[8] It was proper that 'each people worship its own traditional usages, living by ancestral traditions.' Jews at least did that. Celsus wrote: 'I think it makes no difference whether you call Zeus the most high or Zeus, or Adonai, or Sabaoth, or Amun like the Egyptians, or Papaios like the Scythians.'[9]

Celsus spoke of angels and demons and the efficacy of various pagan shrines in foretelling the future, healing the ill and averting catastrophes. Why the gods should answer prayers considering his conviction that they had no fondness towards humans he did not explain.

Human wrongdoing to pagans was *hubris*, the arrogance of reaching out for that which belonged to the gods. Prometheus, stealing fire from heaven that humans could live as more than wild beasts, was condemned to eternal torment. Asklepios, the god of healing, and Hephaistos, patron of metallurgy, were cast out of heaven for revealing their arts to benefit mankind.

To Jews and Christians, wrong was viewed more often as *hamartia*, falling short, missing the target. Since man was made in the image and likeness of God, wrong was being less than what one should be.

Celsus described Christians.

We see them in our own houses, cloth and shoemakers and clothes cleaners, the most uneducated and vulgar persons, not daring to say a word in the presence of their masters who are older and wiser; but when they get hold of the children in private, and silly women with them, they are wonderfully eloquent … But if, while they are speaking, they see some of the children's teachers, some wiser person or their father coming, the more cautious of them will be gone in a moment, and the more impudent will urge on the children to throw off the reins – whispering to them that while their father or their teachers are about, they will not and cannot teach them anything good ... they must come with the women and the little children that play with them to the women's quarters or the shoemakers' shop or to the cleaners' to receive perfect knowledge. And that is how they persuade them.[10]

To Celsus, the Christian God was a 'most unnatural father' in allowing his son to be crucified.[11]

Celsus appealed to an upper class audience learned in Greek literature rather than Roman history or Jewish culture. He despised Christians for their poverty. He attempted to persuade the convinced while ignoring the masses. He offered nothing as a substitute ideal nor did he criticize societies' injustices.

The first two centuries had produced Rome's unique moralists, neither religious prophets nor philosophers but comic satirists.

Juvenal, Ovid, Catullus, Martial, Petronius and Apulius – all were scathingly critical of the excesses of the rich and their parasitic hangers-on. They made no claim to being any better than those they savaged. They acknowledged being part of what they condemned. The moral sense they expressed emerged neither from the faith of Jews nor the reason of Greeks, but perhaps some echo of the *honestas* and *aequitas* (honesty and fairness) of their Italian peasant ancestors. Ovid described the pessimistic alienation of these comic writers concisely. 'I hate what I do yet I can do no other.'[12]

By the third century, satire had disappeared. The gross behaviour lampooned had grown too common. Satire was considered subversive by the government.

The upper classes were paranoid about the slaves surrounding them. Seneca, Nero's Stoic tutor and victim, had written:

In every slave is a foe. No. We don't find slaves our foes, we make them so. They are slaves, people say. No, they are human beings. 'They're slaves.' But they share the same roof as ourselves. 'They're slaves.' No. They're friends, humble friends. 'They're slaves.' Strictly speaking they are our fellow slaves, if you once reflect that fate has as much power over us as over them.[13]

The pagan physician Galen witnessed a master gouging out the eye of a slave in a fit of rage.[14] 'Our spoilt child existence drives us into tantrums,' Seneca observed.[15] Slaves had virtually no protection in the legal system. Whatever the laws, the judges were usually slave owners. Runaways were returned with the letter F for *fugitivius* branded on their forehead.

Nero's accomplice and victim Petronius gloated that 'Nothing is evil if your master commands it.'[16]

In Latin fashion, few trusted the laws. What mattered was personal influence. An individual's power was measured by the number of people dependent upon him as a *patrone*. Important folk began their day attending to the *clientalia*, their hangers-on. A *patrone* guarded by gladiators might dispense from the vestibule of his home money, jobs for the day, letters of recommendation, judgment in quarrels, errands, purchases, bribes and political advice in return for the toadying of a host of semi-employed opportunists dealing in gossip and blackmail for advancement. Termites who would be tyrants, Juvenal called them.[17]

Shrewdly intelligent slaves placed as stewards managing private estates bought freedom with the wealth they manipulated and became a major element in Roman commerce. The parables in the Gospels speak of similar stewards. Men of similar status as slaves of the government exerted enormous influence. Freedman who had risen to the top of society brought with them contempt towards former superiors once flattered and used. If no worse than their former masters, they lacked their civility.

Gurus of exotic learning and supposed virtue were hired as household exemplars, their speech lofty, their table manners like 'gulls swooping upon garbage.'[18] They fasted, rubbing ashes into their faces to give the semblance of austerity, their private morals ribaldly ridiculed. Great store was given to their interpretation of dreams and rationalizations of employers' behaviour.

The cities represented Roman civilization yet the vast majority of the populace lived in the countryside, with the weather unpredictable and crop failures common. Galen described rural folk, most of whose wheat and barley was sold to inland cities. They relied chiefly on lentils, peas and beans for food.

The country people during the winter finished the pulses and so during the spring had to fall back upon unhealthy foods. They ate twigs and shoots of trees and bushes, bulbs and roots of indigestible plants, they even filled themselves with weeds or cooked fresh grass. You could see some of them at the end of the spring and practically all at the beginning of summer attacked by various ulcers springing up on the skin ...[19]

The absentee landlord was usually in a city miles away as stewards and bullyboys kept farm labourers in line.

The traditional elite dwindled in numbers, birthrate low and ambition satiated. Ex-slaves or their descendants rose to dominate civil life as half-barbarian soldiers rose through the ranks to imperial command. Those who had the wisdom to realize how perilously thin was the layer of civilization covering egoistic impulse considered religion to be much of that veneer.

Freedmen whose parents had been slaves were rarely found in an army career until the manpower shortage of the third century loosened recruitment standards. Traditional prejudices held them servile, duplicitous and arrogant. The time had arrived that such men were within reach of political and military control of the Empire. They had a ready solution for Roman problems, a totalitarian state eliminating all pretences of private power. Bureaucracy and militarism were idolized beyond any criticism, the emperor to be worshipped as a living god, the Roman people, in effect, enslaved.

The Emperor Probus, as an Illyrian raised in Egypt, was of an ethnic minority long of service yet neglected in promotion in the army. Aurelian was the first Illyrian emperor. Diocletian, another compatriot, would later follow to the throne. Ethnic minorities long denied rank offered an alternative to the avaricious climbers within the system.

The Illyrians, long snubbed for promotion, could relate to other minorities in the Empire whose talents had long been overlooked. Some might respond by outdoing their suppressors. Probus responded with a willingness to expend good fortune to those without it.

Some would detest his attitude.

Chapter 10

A Dream for Betterment

Unless the youth have dreams and the elders the wisdom of experience, the people perish.

Isaiah

Probus sought to revive the democratic values of Rome's early Republic. He had faith in a better future, while many Romans had no vision but to survive amidst worsening hardships and oppression.

Except for Seneca, no pagan Roman cried for justice for the oppressed anywhere in Latin literature. Greek culture had had a strong sense of tragedy, its cult of Asklepios, the god of healing, honouring physicians and philanthropy, but Roman culture had no sympathy for losers. Those Romans admiring the philosophy of Stoicism denied their own suffering.

The Roman world was in decline, yet, again, no Roman writer noted it. Official censorship helps explain this but more influential was the upper classes' insulation from the stresses upon society. The writing of Roman history deteriorated sharply after the first century. Like a frog in water slowly brought to the boil adapting its temperature to its environment and thus unaware of change, a society without honest historical memory is unaware of its need to act rather than passively react.

Many of the ruling class were Epicureans, a group criticized by the Stoic Epictectus:

I ask you to imagine a nation filled with people having your Epicurean principles, in which no one would marry, no one would have children, and no one's family or property would be safe. Where could you find decent, loyal citizens to be farmers, soldiers, administrators and doctors? Where could you find teachers to educate people in their duties?[1]

Mani, the Persian debated by Archelaus, had similarly taught that marriage, sex, politics, business and the like were evils, all matter and worldly affairs the domain of devils.[2] He held renunciation of the world a religious virtue, while announcing the impending violent destruction of the world in a war between the holy ones and the wicked. Heretical Christian sects such as the Montanists held to much the same ethos, so too the Gnostic monks fleeing public life. 'If someone commits murder he regards it as a crime; if the murder is carried out in the name of the state, it is considered virtuous,' wrote Cyprian, convert and Bishop of Carthage, an outspoken challenger of the abuses of Roman society. 'The laws are written on the twelve tablets and in the public edict but the judge sells his decision to the highest bidder, wills are falsified, law is in league with crime,'[3] he continued.

Writing to a pagan, Demetrianus, Cyprian expressed a frank pessimism towards the Empire.

> Even if we Christians did not speak and give expression to the warnings of Holy Scriptures and divine prophecies, the world itself is already announcing its decay, events themselves the evidence of its decline and fall. In winter there is no longer plenty of water for the seed, in summer no longer the accustomed heat to mature them; nor is spring weather happy nor autumn fertile in harvest. The production of silver and gold has gone down in the exhausted mines as well as the production of marble; the worked out veins give less and less from day to day. The cultivator is no longer in the fields, the sailor on the seas, soldier in the barracks, honesty in the marketplace, justice in the law court, solidarity in friendship, skill in the arts, discipline in manners ... As for the greater frequency of wars, the even more grievous preoccupation with famines and sterility, the raging of diseases which ruin health, the devastation wreaked by the plague in the midst of men – this too, make no mistake, was foretold: That in the last times ills are multiplied, misfortunes are diversified and the approach of the day of judgement, God's angry punishment moves towards the ruin of men. You are mistaken, in your foolish ignorance of the truth, when you protest that these things happen because we do not worship the gods; they happen because you do no worship God.[4]

Epidemics ravaging the population do not alone explain its continual reduction. A world weariness united the atheist philosopher Lucretius, Cyprian the saint and people of every class. Inflation and ever higher taxes discouraged marriage. The widespread use of lead cooking utensils and water pipes caused sterility, birth defects, mental retardation, paralysis and fits of rage.[5] *Garum*, the fish paste Romans were exceedingly fond of, was so salty that modern efforts to use the Roman recipe are virtually inedible. A symptom of lead poisoning is the loss of the ability to taste saltiness.[6]

Upward social mobility, common in the first century, had stagnated except where former slaves of the state rose to leadership. Meanwhile, poor free folk were reduced to virtual slavery, the middle class of craftsmen and entrepreneurs taxed into fleeing cities and towns.

Removed from an active career, the veterans could more easily be critical of society. Few invest twenty-five years of life in a profession only to totally reject it. To scorn public responsibility and claim to directly honour God was appealing yet ambiguous. Christ had condemned those who buried their talents. Christian soldiers could sympathize with pagan criticism of Christian avoidance of public duty.

It was bad enough that many civilians scorned the men at arms who defended them from barbarism. That was understandable. Many soldiers were oppressors. But rejection of public service by these same critics must have seemed hypocrisy. The Empire was in peril.

The highest award for gallantry bestowed by Rome was for soldiers who risked their lives to save a citizen.

The gravestones of thousands of Roman soldiers survive.[7] The minority who did retire died within a few years, perhaps felled psychosomatically, no longer feeling empowered or of use. Like warhorses put to pasture, some were restless at the sound of distant trumpets.

Probus, emperor while Mauricius was in Jerusalem, was neither a Christian nor a persecutor. His sister Claudia, a cognomen meaning 'the cripple', was praised for her virtue by the pagan Vopiscus. His brother Calocerus would be bishop of Byzance, his son Adrianus and nephew Demetrius military martyrs.[8]

Probus was 'a man of every virtue' as the Senate proclaimed, declaring him a god after his death when it had no need to flatter nor fear him.

Probus wrote that '... it is no longer in my power to lay down a title so full of envy and danger. I must continue to play the part which the soldiers have imposed upon me.'[9]

He was quoted in an extraordinary statement. 'Soon,' he said, 'we shall have no need of soldiers.' What else is this than saying 'Soon there will be no Roman soldier?'

Everywhere the commonwealth will reign and will rule all in security. The entire world will forge no arms and will furnish no rations, the ox will be kept for the plough and the horse will be bred for peace, there will be no wars and no captivity, in all places peace will reign, in all places the laws of Rome, and in all places our judges.[10]

Perhaps Probus' intent was a citizens' militia working family farms and paying its own way, requiring little tax support – a system like that of the early Roman Republic. This might have provided the defence in depth that the frontiers lacked and the moral incentive for patriotism. Dream or not, the Empire needed some vision of a better future to survive, let alone progress.

How much if any of the above statement was genuinely Probus' and how much the non-Christian historian Vopiscus' is anyone's guess. The statement could be the dream of a biblical prophet. That oxen would be kept only for the plough – and not for pagan sacrifice – suggests a Christian's views.

Probus was an able soldier, a ramrod of a man, popular but strong willed, not a militarist. He antagonized part of the army by ruling that soldiers in peacetime should earn their keep by building public works, dredging the canal system of Egypt and planting vineyards on the Pannonian Danube.

The Emperor was an Illyrian (Albanian) in ancestry, born and raised in Egypt.[11] He was a professional career man. In speaking of having no need of soldiers, he presumably intended to return to the democratic values of the early Roman Republic, when every able citizen served in the army reserve. The ruling classes for centuries had long ago opposed a democratic army from fear that an armed citizenry would revolt.

Probus was far more respectful of the Senate than his predecessors. Yet the Senate, composed of the wealthiest land owners in the Empire, could hardly have been enthusiastic toward his program.

The Empire was at a turning point. It had reached a crisis. The decisions made would mark the western world for ages to come. *Kairos*, as the Greeks called it, the opportune moment, had arrived. To recognize and act upon it was viewed as a grace of God by Christians.

Early in his career in the 250s, Probus had been given command of a task force of 'six cohorts of Saracens and entrusting to him besides the Gallic irregulars [auxiliaries?] along with that company of Persians which Artebessis the Syrian delivered over to us'. These Saracens were in all likelihood Ituraeans and the Persian Armenians. Quite probably, this task force, in size a legion, would provide the veterans on recall leading the Theban Legion. Cohorts of Ituraean archers had long been stationed in Egypt. Ituraea was southern Israel, the Saracens the Arabs of the Negeb and its borders. In the late third century these Ituraean units disappeared from record without explanation.

Long before the Romans the pharaohs of Egypt had recruited Nubian archers from the Kharga oasis tribe known as Medjay, a term that came to mean soldier or policeman.

Probus ordered the creation of a new legion, to be recruited largely from men long denied citizenship and permission to serve in the legions, the people of southern Egypt, the Thebaid. In the dwindling population of the Empire, they were an untapped resource. Probus asked veterans to return to serve as *campidoctores*,[12] training officers, *evocati*, veterans on recall, forming up the new legion. Their task was not combat and perhaps did not necessitate the usual rituals and oaths. They would be in charge until the new unit was inaugurated. Especially, he sought veterans of the desert army who understood Egyptian sensibilities, for the inhabitants of the valley of the Nile were regarded as an explosive lot when badly led.

Roman law pressed upon the veterans for decision. Veterans were free of most taxes for the first five years of retirement, after which they were subject to impositions rapidly eroding their income.[13] They could be drafted to become tax collectors and given a quota which, if unachieved, had to be made up from personal finances. These liturgies, as they were called, devastated the middle class. Neighbour was set against neighbour, destroying the community. Collections over the quota could be legally personally pocketed. The designers of the system presumed everyone as avaricious as themselves.

To remain in retirement and refuse recall was not attractive when threatened with liturgies.

The tugs of responsibility to the Emperor and those of protecting colleagues in faith pulled for once in the same direction.

Egypt was the most Christian province in the Empire. Unbaptized Christian recruits would benefit by having officers of their faith. If Bishop Zabdas opposed the veterans responding to recall there is no record of it.

Since the veterans would be confirmed by Bishop Marcellus in Syria, they must have ventured from Jerusalem to that province, perhaps travelling the road to Caesarea Maritima on the coast to take voyage from there to Antioch, Syria's chief port. Caesarea was the Roman capital of the holy land. Its breakwaters, quays, temples, aqueduct and government buildings, surrounded by a wall, had been accomplished under Herod the Great. The population was almost evenly divided between Jews and gentiles. The writer Origen and the Church historian Eusebius, an archbishop of the city, would be among its celebrated writers.

From Caesarea they may have embarked for Antioch. The trip by sea could be made in leisurely fashion with nights at anchor at Sidon, Beirut or Tripolis.

It was in Antioch that believers were first called Christian. The gospel writer Luke, in tradition a physician and artist, was probably from Antioch. It was in Antioch that the faith first grew in an environment not entirely Jewish.

The team of officers and men assembled to organize and train the new legion for the most part probably did not take part in its recruitment. The task before the headquarters cadre demanded plans, schedules and decisions. A legion was a unit integrating men of many ethnic backgrounds, all citizens. Egypt's II Traiana could provide some experienced men, its Legio Alexandriana, the grain fleet marines could provide others. Only the fleet accepted *peregrini*, in legal status non-citizen resident aliens, as soldiers.[14] Auxiliary units along the Nile could provide other soldiers or be directly incorporated into the new unit. The priority, however, was to find a new source of recruits. Most native Egyptians, being *deditici*, legally prisoners of war, would not be eligible. Presumably, the new legion recruited tribal peoples bordering Egypt to fill out its ranks, especially Medjay of the oases west of the Nile.

The new unit's duty station would be Britain, as shall be demonstrated, guarding its coast from invasion, by definition a defensive task. They would provide fortress garrisons and fleet marine, their tactics chiefly those of bowsmen.

That the Theban Legion's leaders were all *campidoctors*, veterans on recall as training officers, can be deduced from their Acts. '*Tunc Exsuperius quem ante princepem vel campidoctorum superius memoravi…,*' i.e. then Exsuperius who in front of the executive officer of the *campidoctos* above mentioned.[15] Since only Mauricius, Exsuperius and Candidus were previously mentioned by name, they were *campidoctors*.

This was a special case, as the cadre planning the new fighting force saw it. Its Christian members saw it as proof to pagans of their patriotism.

The veterans were eager to again be of service. They did not realize that their apparent good fortune was the eye of the hurricane, Probus' hopeful reign.

Chapter 11

Recall and Recruitment

Feed the enemy if he is hungry, give him drink if he is thirsty. By doing this you will heap coals of fire on his head. Do not be disarmed by malice. Disarm malice with good.

Romans 12:20–21

Until the reign of Caracalla (r. 211–217), half the imperial army had been not the legions of citizens but auxiliary units, usually of 500 men recruited from non-citizen tribes long friendly to Rome. Upon finishing their twenty-five years of service they were granted citizenship.

Paul mentions this when he was saved at Ephesus from a mob of image-makers who feared he would destroy their market for idols. The officer rescuing him was astonished that Paul was a Jew not only fluent in Greek but a Roman citizen as a citizen of Tarsus, a city granted hereditary privilege as reward for being a loyal ally when it had been an independent city-state. The centurion explained that he had won citizenship after much hardship and expense. Presumably, he had been an auxiliary who had to pay a bribe to finally gain his goal.

Caracalla extended citizenship widely for the sake of increasing the tax rolls.[1] This lessened the motivation to enter the army for some within the Empire and pressured the state to recruit from tribes beyond the frontiers. The army was becoming virtually a *Legion Etrangeres*, an army of foreigners increasingly alien to Roman culture and values. What continued among the auxiliaries was their units smaller than the legions and their segregation by tribal or ethnic group under citizen officers.

Egypt had remained a special case, the labouring population *deditici* (literally prisoners), the townspeople largely *peregrini* with the status of resident aliens. Those Egyptians who were Roman citizens, generally descendants of Alexander the Great's Greeks, had been eligible to enrol in the Legio Deotariana destroyed in the second revolt of Israel versus Rome.

For many centuries a Roman citizen marrying a non-citizen could not transmit citizenship to his heirs. The Empire was a class society. Citizens legally could not marry non-citizens, slaves or freedmen ex-slaves. *Equites*, literally horsemen, were the hereditary local upper middle-class, originally the source of many officers. Their privileges were many, with seats at the public arenas reserved for them and their identity marked by a special ring. They were expected to marry within their class.

Probus, in drafting barbarian prisoners of war, revealed the desperation of authorities confronted with a population that was steadily dwindling amidst diseases, ever-increasing taxes and a world weariness–eroding family life. Gallienus, in abolishing the Senate-approved tribunes staffing the legions, had intended to end leadership by four-year term non-professionals who usually continued as high civil servants. An unforeseen result was to end the *cursus honorum*, the career of honour serving the state.

Raised in Egypt, Probus saw its people without the stereotypical viewpoint of too many imperialist officials. He was well aware of the Empire's need for new sources of recruits other than the dubious employment of uncivilized hirelings. Soldiers, by experience and necessity, tended to be less prejudiced than civilian authorities. In the legions they mixed with men from all over the Roman world. In the auxiliaries their lives might depend upon men of another culture and language.

An undated papyrus from the third century may refer to the Theban Legion, since no other large scale recruitment in Egypt from this period is known. It was sent by a woman to kin in the Fayoum, the western oasis.

Isis to Thermouthion her mother very many greetings. I pray for you every day before the lord Serapis and his fellow gods. I wish you to know that I have arrived in Alexandria safe and sound in four days. I send salutations to my sister and the children and if Aion wishes to join the army, let him come for everyone is in the army. I pray for the health of your household.[2]

Candidates for the new legion clad in their best white robes, apprehensive but buoyed by camaraderie, gathered at the army depots of the Thebaid. Clutching credentials, they assured recruiters that they were of 'good family', a matter the army insisted upon.

Military service was an opportunity forbidden to Copts,[3] the peasantry still speaking the language of the pharaohs. Every occupation in Egypt was virtually hereditary and chances for a poor freeman to improve his lot rare. Christian influences upon the Thebans must have been largely Coptic. The faith had its greatest numbers among them. The Gospels had been translated into Coptic in that era.[4] The Copts had proved loyal during the invasions after Valerian's fall. Intermarriage may have won some the status of *peregrini*.

The recruiters understood that the attitudes of the fledglings had to be taken in context. They tended to tell authorities, if there was no means to have the answer checked, anything they thought the questioner wanted to hear. First and family names were so few that officials had to delineate a man's lineage for generations.

However cheerful, hardworking and devoted to good patrons Copts might be, they could be as stubborn as mules and play obtusely dim-witted. These were admired virtues in villages where scars of the tax-collector's lash and thumb noose were badges of honour. These values, nevertheless, reinforced army prejudices against them.

Some of the Thebans may have been Blemmyes from the coasts of the Red Sea who had overrun the Thebaid after Valerian's fall to be thrust back by Aurelian and Probus' forces.[5]

Probus had recruited 16,000 young Germanic tribesmen into the army from defeated enemy tribes, scattering them in groups of thirty or forty 'so that their strength might be felt but not noticed'.[6] He may have used a similar policy in Egypt.

As a general, Probus had organized a task force of Saraceni and Gauls, the Saraceni probably Ituraeans, many of units usually stationed in Egypt in the Thebaid.[7] According to Flavius Josephus in the first century, many Ituraeans had been 'half-Jews' converted to Judaism. Such Sebomenoi or 'God-fearers', were a significant element among the earliest Christians.

The recruits were athletic in build, no less than five feet ten inches in height, identifying scars or blemishes carefully recorded. Accustomed to discomfort and hard labour, recruits, nevertheless, were seldom in good shape medically by modern standards. Bad teeth were common from gritty flour milled in stone churns. Virtually everyone suffered from intestinal parasites in several varieties from polluted water. Accepted, the recruit began the *probatio*,[8] the four to six months' basic training intended to weed out all but the fittest. Training was intended to be more arduous than war, with drill incessant.

In slang, the common soldier was called boots, porridge-eater, copper and Marius' mule. Only soldiers wore the studded sole footgear. The diet was almost exclusively grain, with meat rations usually half-rotten and resented. Copper was a misnomer, armour of iron, bronze and copper a decoration. Marius' mule was also the wooden T-bar or cross on which the soldier carried his belongings. It could be dropped instantly, unlike a backpack. Three marches a month were the infantry's norm. Armour for enlistees was forty pounds of iron bands encircling the torso, padded with sponges and worn over a net shirt of thick cord. In addition, there was a helmet and a shield of wood of five thicknesses of belt leather. Every soldier bought his gear, preferably from a veteran no longer needing it. The shield in colour and design distinguished the unit. Only the colours red, yellow, blue, black and white were employed. Hollywood may prefer Roman soldiers in bright red cloaks, but permanent colour dyes were non-existent until the nineteenth century except for purple, derived from Murex shellfish and very expensive. Soldiers' cloaks were usually of dull, dark blue, green, grey or brown.

Probatio accomplished, those selected took the military oath, the *sacramentum*, considered the most serious vow a Roman could take. Anyone breaking it was an outlaw who could be victimized with impunity, no longer under legal protection. The oath was not taken individually but through representation by officers. The recruits, *tiros*, were then tattooed to discourage desertion.

Those lacking Latin names were given them at a ceremony similar to the coming of age rites at which *cognomina* were given. Among the Theban legionnaires, or at least their officers, were: Longinus the tall one; Ursus the bear, perhaps resembling one; Victor the winner; and Carpophorus the shining light or example. Alexander meant defender of others, Bessus was the ancient Egyptian wargod, Thyrsus the rod or whip, and Innocentius, unbothered. Defendens was one defended by God, Solotur the sun-bull, and the Egyptian god Apis. It was not uncommon that Christians bore the names of pagan gods. Adventor was the visitor or guest, probably a comment upon some personal quirk.

Once enlisted, a recruit received three gold coins. As much as two-thirds of his pay went to buy his arms, armour, tent and the like. Army pay scale reflected the gross inequalities of the society. In the era a corporal (*principal*) earned half again as much as the lowest enlistee, a sergeant (*senior principal*) three times as much, a lieutenant (*optio centurio*) sixteen, colonel (*tribunus or primus ordino*) thirty-two and generals (*primus pilus*) sixty-six times as much or more. The ranks only roughly compare with modern military titles.

Riots had once been so frequent when quarterly pay was in arrears after officers lost it gambling that the tradition evolved that the *signiferius* or standard-bearer was appointed only with the approval of the rank and file. He was officer and treasurer for enlistees, a popular and well trusted man. To rally to the tall metal standards decorated by badges in battle was motivated not only by loyalty but to defend the account books that determined pay and life savings.

Standard-bearers were impressive figures, the skin of a lion, leopard, wolf or bear draped over their military garb, the upper jaw serving as a skullcap. They carried neither shield nor weapon, both hands needing to carry the heavy ensign. The standard-bearer of the Theban Legion, according to its Acts, was Exsuperius, the name meaning of the tallest, best or oldest. It was a common name among the Galatians, a Celtic people living in central Anatolia (Turkey) speaking the same Gaelic spoken in Western Europe.

In villages of whitewashed houses, palm trees and domed pigeon coops, the noise lasted late into the night as *tiros* attended going-away parties. In all the Middle East women were publicly veiled and segregated from men except among the Copts. Recruits fixed in mind faces they knew they would never see again.

Life in Egypt responded to the Nile. Between January and April, waters and river traffic were at their lowest. Officials were anxious to empty silos to receive the harvests of April and May. Grain was two years old before it reached Alexandria to be shipped to Rome and other cities. The river surged in full flood between spring and midsummer as river traffic diminished to resume from October to December.[9] The Thebans probably left for northern Egypt in the spring about 283. Few ships sailed the Mediterranean in winter.

On 5 March the ceremony launching the ship of the goddess Isis at Alexandria began the sailing season. The soldiers embarking downstream were leaving their very gods. Each village had its divinity. What was a man to believe when family, friends, ancestral soil and local gods were gone? The oldest known Christian inscriptions on stone in Egypt date from the decade.

Two thousand years earlier, the world's oldest known moral code had emerged on the Nile written in the Book of the Dead buried with the nobility. Eternal life awaited the good: 'he who does what is loved', 'the peaceful man', 'he whose heart is pure and cheerful, light as a feather'. Tried before the gods, the dead were imagined uttering forty-two disavowals. Regard a few: 'I allowed no one to hunger. I caused no one to weep. I did not murder. I did not command anyone be murdered. My fortune was not great but justifiably mine. I did no violence to a woman. I did not speak lies. I was not deaf to truthful words. I did not insult anyone in instructing him. My heart was not envious. I took part in no harmful gossip.'[10] Eight of the ten commandments are in the Book of the Dead.

This code had yielded over centuries to magical incantations to bribe and threaten the gods, the supernatural jury. The old morality lived on, nonetheless, in proverb and folktales, the ethos of people who longed for an afterlife because they loved this one and sought justice.

While the Thebans were training, the Emperor Probus went to Illyria (Yugoslavia and Albania), the homeland of his forebears, on his way to a new campaign against Persia. In keeping with his policy of putting the army to useful civil projects, he supervised soldiers terracing and planting vineyards on Balkan hillsides. The government had forbidden the raising of grapes in many areas outside of Italy. Probus considered his action generous in allowing vineyards in the Balkans, Gaul, Spain and Britain, where previously forbidden. Malcontents grumbled that it would be years before wine would be produced from their labour. A web of intrigue was in the making.

From 182 to 284, of twenty-eight emperors, twenty-two had been murdered by their soldiers, usually by their bodyguards.

In Raetia (Austria), the commander of the Praetorian Guard, Carus, declared himself emperor. The Praetorians were officer candidates garrisoning the city of Rome and providing the emperor's bodyguard – in effect, the Empire's military academy. They were the centre of militarism and the Mithraic cult. Carus may have been as much a tool as instigator. If a general nominated emperor by his men refused, he gained enemies on every side.

Probus announced that he would march against Carus. Some of his troops joined Carus. Invited to inspect a moveable siege tower shielded by iron plates, Probus went within the structure where he was cut down like a bull in a slaughterhouse by men he had trusted.[11]

Mauricius and his comrades must have heard the news with dismay. Probus had been their patron, sympathetic to their values. Christians were among his in-laws and his blood relatives.

They resolved that to honour their patron best would be to complete what he had started, the training and posting of the Theban Legion at its distant overseas station.

Chapter 12

Shipping Out

I don't aim at the puck. I aim at where it will be.

Wayne Gretzky

From the southern apex of the Nile delta, within sight of the pyramids, the Thebans must have travelled along its western stream to Alexandria, the greatest port in the Empire. In population it had been the largest Jewish, largest Greek, and largest Coptic metropolis. Temples, stadiums, theatres, libraries and bazaars flanked its wide avenues. The first residential city ever built according to a unifying plan, with Alexander the Great its founder, its university would be the prototype for all.

Egypt was the breadbasket of the Mediterranean and Alexandria its chief port. The city was richer than Rome, its populace more free and better educated. Greeks were the butchers and bakers, Jews the glaziers and metal-workers, and Copts the stevedores and porters. Syrians, Arabs, Armenians, Persians, Ethiopians, Moors, Thracians (Bulgarians), Illyrians, Sarmatians (Ukrainians) and Italians added to the mosaic. The slightest slur, real or imagined, against one group's honour or gods provoked strikes paralyzing the entire economy, as well as riots and massacres. The threat of ruthless intervention by the army kept peace. The Empire was united not by patriotism but mutual fear of what would happen without Rome's firm grip on affairs.

Let the Roman Vopiscus describe the situation, keeping in mind his imperialist biases:

... the Egyptians, as you know well enough, are puffed up, madmen, boastful, doers of injury, and in fact liars and without restraint, always craving something new, even in their popular songs, writers of verse, wisecrackers, astrologers, soothsayers, quack healers. Among them indeed are Christians and Samaritans and those who [are] always ill-pleased with the present though enjoying unbounded liberty ... wholly light minded, unstable and blown about by every breath of rumour. There those who worship Serapis are in fact Christians and those who call themselves bishops of Christ are in fact devotees of Serapis. There is no chief of the Jewish synagogue, no Samaritan, no Christian priest who is not an astrologer, soothsayer or anointer…They are a most seditious folk, most deceitful, most given to luxury. But their city (Alexandria) is luxurious, rich and fruitful and in no way is idle. Some are blowers of glass, others make paper, all are at least linen weavers or belong to some craft or other. The lame have theirs, the eunuchs theirs, the blind theirs and not even those whose hands are crippled are idle. Their only god is money and this the Christians, the Jews and in fact all nations adore.[1]

The rustic Thebans must have walked through the streets in wonderment balanced by *brio*, a healthy military pride. Alexandrians respected the army. One of the worst events in the city's history had happened in 38 AD when a Roman general amidst bloody massacres and riots between Greeks and Jews had done the cruellest thing possible – nothing.[2] He ordered his troops to remain in quarters until the savagery exhausted itself in order to teach the public its need for Rome rule.

In 41, and again in 66 and 73, waves of anti-Semitic violence had swept Alexandria, promoted by the first revolt of Israel versus Rome. Greek culture with its reason and rationalization contended for dominance against Jewish faith and morality as it still does. In 115–119, Alexandrian Jews revolted, resulting in the virtual annihilation of their entire community.

A generation previous to the Thebans' visit the plague had occurred, which killed a third of the inhabitants and debilitated a third more.[3] Having no cure, the pagans dared not treat the ill. Terrified and feeling helpless, they were ready to believe that Christians aiding the ill had deliberately caused the epidemic in order to rob the dead. The mob murdered the Christians.

In the cities, not only was there the greatest need felt for a new faith, but it was easier to preach to large numbers of people. Some of the greatest philosophers of the church, including the Gospel writers Mark and Luke, were Alexandrians or had studied there. Most were Hellenized Jews. Clement was alone in encouraging as bishop that converts stay in the army.[4]

As the Thebans chafed at delay after delay and changes in plans, officers might have recollected the words of Petronius, an earlier careerman.

We trained hard … but every time we were beginning to form up into teams we would be reorganized. I realized later in life that we tend to meet any new situation by reorganizing … and a wonderful method it can be for creating the illusion of progress while producing inefficiency and demoralization.[5]

Carus was emperor. He was an affable fellow. It was his custom to wear and sleep in an ordinary soldier's cloak of coarse wool. He dined on cold porridge served in a wooden bowl. Whatever his faults, greed for material possessions was not apparent. Meeting envoys from Persia, he had uncovered his bald head and warned that if he was crossed his troops would despoil Persia and destroy trees until it was as barren as his head.[6]

With approval from the Senate, Carus had left his son Carinus in Rome to attend to the Empire in the West. Setting forth to the East, he was accompanied by another son, Numerian, given administrative control of the East. His intent was to strengthen his family's hold on the Empire, but the practical advantages of the dual arrangement in administration were manifold. Carus' temporary measure was to become policy. It eased many problems, in particular the difficulty of interchanging officials between the Latin-speaking West and the Greek East.

The Theban officers inked records and perhaps wondered if there was a hidden agenda as Rome began stripping Egypt of its native troops and withdrawing all forces from Mauritania Tingitania. The legionnaires were being asked to defend Romans elsewhere while their own homelands were left defenceless.

It took about a week for the news to arrive that Carus was dead. He had been killed by a bolt of lightning while on campaign. Lightning was the awesome vengeance of heaven. Nothing was allowed to be built where it had struck. Those killed by it were buried in a hidden grave at night.

It was all very convenient for some people, Thebans could suspect. It might not be convenient for them.

Rumours soon had it that Numerian might hold the Theban Legion in the East.

Routine demanded regardless of politics. Nothing could be allowed to delay the fleet. The grain warehouses of Rome and other Mediterranean cities were steadily depleting. One ship from Egypt could carry more grain faster than dozens of wagons from the backcountry of European coastal cities. The Thebans would sail with the fleet. Carinus wanted them in Italy.

Probably in the spring of 284, within the shadow of the high tower of Alexandria's Pharos lighthouse, one of the seven wonders of the ancient world, the Thebans boarded the fleet carrying the grain to Rome and received their bread rations.

Final shore leave and, as was the custom, a soldier pays an artist to sketch his portrait. A wooden panel in coloured chalk sealed in hot wax, 'encaustic', is sent home as a souvenir of son, brother and friend, gone except for memory. One by one, anchors were hauled in like happy memories to be stored away as future security. Sails were unfurled.

The average merchant ship of Alexandria, no bigger than a modern seagoing tugboat, was 120 by 30 feet at maximum.[7] Passengers seeking comfort used the few larger vessels of 180 foot length. With narrow low bows and high bulging sterns, the Alexandrians rode the waves like swans, a small mast angled forward at the bow and a tall one amidships carrying a huge square sail. A pair of triangular canvasses topped the mainsail and its ship's emblem upon it.

The fleet leaving port scattered across the crisscrossed chop of waves marching to the horizons. In the sailing season, late spring and summer winds were from Africa, Latin for 'the land from which the breezes blow'. The vessels could hardly make five miles in an hour. Steering depended on handheld oars at each side. It was disconcerting to landlubbers to see that a ship so painstakingly constructed had as typical captain a sun-bronzed old man clad in rags who seemed to make decisions on the basis of a wet thumb stuck into the wind. The greatest danger was not the deep sea but hidden rocks and reefs near shore. By the first nightfall they were far beyond sight of the fire signals of the Pharos.

Most of the fleet carrying grain pushed directly towards Crete. Other ships held eastwards until, about the afternoon of the fifth day, the change of the sea from deep blue to green, shorebirds and landborn clouds revealed the coast of Israel over the sea's rim. Perhaps they stopped at Joppa or Caesaraea Maritima or Antioch where the Theban Legion's officers had received the sacrament of confirmation. Heeling about to starboard, they tacked northwards for a week skirting Cyprus to keep their bearings and reached the Isle of Rhodes, crossroads of routes in every direction. There they could stretch their sealegs and obtain repairs.

In separate ships, families and friends, servants, artisans and merchants would have preceded or followed the legionnaires. The Acts hand down the names of at least three women accompanying the Thebans, by *cognomen*: Ursula the bearwoman, Verna the truthful little one, and Regula the lady.

Sailors regarded women as jinxes. The timbers to build a ship were cut with prayers to the forest wood nymphs. Beautiful but jealous, they might haunt a ship thereafter. A ship was always a she. On board the vessels carrying the Thebans the only females were the small wooden statues, *puppae*, decorating the door of the aft deckhouse, the poop deck, their gaudy colours contrasting with the hull's tarred blackness.

From Rhodes, the ships beat their way to the south of Crete. Within view of that long island's western mountains ships reunited and divided again as ships began the many tacks northwards the length of the Adriatic to Aquileia, the army depot of north-eastern Italy. Farewells signalled, the main group ploughed the seas due west to Sicily. There they would drop anchor and await, with luck, winds from the south to take them through the straits of Messina. If southerly winds were lacking they would have to laboriously make many tacks around Sicily and slowly sail northwards along the Italian coast, wary lest they be blown ashore.

Voyages from Alexandria to Italy straight across the sea out of sight of land for weeks were made but risky. What could be gained in time in good weather could be lost in bad. If they were beaten about in contrary winds or storms, navigating was hopeless until they again identified some coastal site. Most ships with little cargo and many passengers avoided direct passages. The cargo fleet was more willing to hazard them. St Paul two centuries earlier had sailed a merchantman carrying 276 people crowded shoulder to shoulder, the vessel almost empty of cargo as it tried to squeeze in a second run to Rome late in the season.[8] It was wrecked upon Malta as a gale of many days sent the squarerigger crashing ashore. The sailors attempted to save themselves by abandoning their passengers until Paul advised a centurion aboard to cast the boat overboard, knowing that few sailors could swim. No lives were lost.

Roman ships carried a boat on deck. Another often trailed on a line behind the vessel. The two were inadequate to carry half the people on board. The boat trailed astern might help someone who had fallen into the sea but to reverse the ship's direction to rescue a man overboard was tricky, dangerous and likely to be futile by the time the vessel completed the manoeuvre.

Each ship was crowded, with neither privacy nor shelter, save in the hold. Below deck were hundreds of stacked *amphorae* jars the size of barrels. These contained goods ranging from grain to wine, beer, olive oil, colouring dyes made from shellfish, pickled fish and meats and the pie-shaped ryebread scored into eight sections that was the soldier's shipping-out ration. Ships were constructed external hull first, planking mortised and tenoned as if the wall of a house. Thereafter, the inner framework of timber arches, complex but flimsy, was hammered within the hull. Nave meant ship but also was the term for the central corridor of a building with a roof braced by wooden construction identical to a ship's hold upside down. The hold was without watertight compartmentation. Sheets of copper and lead were nailed to the interior of the planking as waterproofing. Despite the cleverly designed pumps, a serious leak courted disaster.

As night fell the ships lost contact. Each dawn those aboard tried to catch sight of one another with less and less success. To witness no sail in sight from one rim of the world's edge to the other had the consolation of making all on board realize that they might share the same fate.

Life settled into routine. They did exercises and received instructions. They learned to speak Latin and Greek and write them as well, washed clothing and cooked. They played the Egyptian ancestors of checkers, chess, backgammon and parcheesi and tossed dice and knucklebones. They talked of many things, religion among them. It was a popular topic in the era. And they listened to military lectures.

The majority of Thebans were archers, the first legion of its kind. The double-curved Asian shortbow backed by horn that they would use could shoot five hundred feet, three times as far as a javelin throw.[9] In battle, bowmen did not aim precisely but, standing close together behind a shieldwall, fired sleets of arrows. The enemy would huddle under shields, unable to strike back. An entire legion had once been caught in the open by Persians in this manner, its men not daring to charge since the archers would simply fall back in good order still shooting arrows, the Romans unable to touch them. They were freed by other units after a week of living on their haunches under shields.[10]

Practice shooting was at narrow poles set in the earth. The deliberate accuracy of Roman bowmen was phenomenal. Defending a fortress, they were practically unassailable. In a civil war four legions had besieged one hundred men holding a small but well-designed stone fortress.

The attackers had fired 140,000 arrows without ousting them.[11]

That the Thebans, many of them Christians in sympathies if not in baptism, were archers was significant. To shoot was not as certainly to kill as stabbing with a sword or spear. Depending upon the design, arrowheads could kill, wound or knock unconscious. Roman warheads in the era were of metal with three small barbs intended to penetrate deeply. At close range they could penetrate a shield and even metal plate.

The men found it discouraging that they earned less than a carpenter or scribe yet had to pay for rations, clothing, armour and weapons, in addition to deductions for pension, official festivals and oiling centurions' palms for good slots on the duty roster. There were no official provisions for family. They would have to find land to farm or engage in some part-time trade in order to manage … or bully civilians into paying graft.

Most Thebans had been raised in extended families where they learned to cooperate. They had entered service among comrades known from youth. They would seek ways to continue relationships with their families.

There was no educational system in the Empire. All schools were small and private. Teachers were little respected. Marc Antony's sardonic reply to a friend's enquiry regarding a mutual acquaintance was 'He is either dead or become a teacher.' Wealthy youngsters had slaves, whipping-boys, who took beatings for them. The martyrs Cassianus and Carterius were stabbed to death by their pupils using iron writing styluses. The feebleness of education made all Roman culture fragile.

The army taught its own, providing the basics of schooling, plus foreign languages and technical skills to impressionable farm boys, gaining loyalty in return. Soldiers learned loyalty to the Empire, not merely their tribe.

A man fingered the cheap metal of lead, bronze and silver of a coin of Alexandria. A soldier was paid in imperial coinage,[12] not Alexandria's debased mintage, but he had saved it as a souvenir since it bore an emblem symbolizing the embarkment of troops for a new legion from the port.

In centuries to come, German legend would claim that Mauricius brought from Jerusalem to Europe an item with strange powers, the lancehead that had pierced the side of Jesus at the crucifixion. This icon, supposedly, made its owner invincible. The supposed Moritz Spear, the so-called Spear of Destiny, is preserved today in the Vienna Kunsthistorisches.[13] The Nazi Party would develop a cult of the 'god-killer' spear in the 1930s.

There is no evidence whatever to prove that the lancehead is linked either to the crucifixion or Mauricius of the Theban Legion. It was forged centuries later.

A shift in the wind as a ship changed tack rocked its round-bottomed hull until passengers sliding on the deck wonder if it might not capsize. Stuck by a sirocco bringing warm fine sand from Africa, the ship crashed into the waves instead of riding bow high over them. Sailors scrambled to spread the foresail and partially haul in the mainsail, leaving the vessel with its bow dangerously high as the stern sank and received the thunder of following seas breaking upon it. The stern was the weakest structure in the ship. Mainsail properly adjusted, the ship achieved proper trim and again surged northwards.

Showers from the north pelted upon men of the Nile who had never experienced rainfall in their entire lives.

In fifty to seventy days the fleet, loaded with some 150,000 tons of grain, arrived at Ostia, the malarial manmade port down river from Rome.

Glad to be ashore, reunited with comrades from the many ships, the Thebans assembled over the course of days until ready to march to Rome. Filled with confidence, probably few suspected that they were entering a web of treachery.

Chapter 13

All Roads Lead to Rome

You gotta stay happy. You owe it to other people.

James Stewart

A century earlier, another Egyptian recruit had written a letter home from Italy as many a Theban must have. The papyrus survives. He had joined Legio Julia Alexandriana.

Apion to Epimachus, his father and lord, very many greetings. Before all else I pray for your health and that you may always be well and prosperous, together with my sister and her daughter and my brother. I thank the lord Serapis that when I was in danger at sea he straightaway saved me. On arriving at Misenum I received from Caesar three gold coins for travelling expenses. And it is well with me. Now I ask you, my lord and father, write me a letter, telling me first of your welfare, secondly of my brother and sisters, and enabling me thirdly to kiss your handwriting because you educated me well and I hope thereby to have quick advancement, if the gods so will. Give my many salutations to Capiton and my brother and sister and Serenilla and my friends. I have sent you by Euctemon a portrait of myself. My name is Antonius Maximus, my company (ship) the Athenonica. I pray for your health.

Sernus son of Agathodaemon salutes you … and Turbo son of Gallonius and …

To Philadelphia to Epimachus from Apion his son. Deliver at the camp of the first cohort of the Apameni [at Alexandria] to Julianus, vice-secretary, this letter to be forwarded to his father Epimachus.[1]

Waiting for ships to arrive, Mauricius may have been troubled by news that troops were being withdrawn from Mauritania Tingitania. Volubilis, the 'city of the winds', if left unguarded might lose its civilian population as well.

Archaeology alone reveals this troop withdrawal.[2] Official historians concealed it.

Rumour had it that a plan was emerging to radically change the tax system of Egypt, which the emperor controlled without need of Senate approval.

The old system taxed farms on the desert's edge less than better land in order to reward the struggle against the desert's expansion. The new system unwisely eliminated differential land taxes. Land that became unprofitable would be yielded to the desert as a result. Knowing that the higher new taxes would be bitterly unpopular, legionnaires may have pondered that they were to defend strangers while their own families could be exploited in their absence.

With troops landed, the Thebans probably marched to Rome to be formally welcomed by the emperor of the West, Carinus. The Acts make no mention of it but politics demanded it.

All milestones for thousands of miles marked the distance to Rome. Eighteen aqueducts brought pure mountain water to it from as far as a hundred miles. Most of its overcrowded people had to carry water many blocks from public fountains. Laws regulated lawsuits by persons struck by slop tossed from upper storeys, differentiating between homes that were privately owned, rented, leased, sublet, etc.[3] Romans with caution stepped on the intermittent stones in the middle of the street, the gutters open sewers. The public baths and court buildings of the capital contained rooms the size of stadiums beneath the arches and domes, the trademark of Roman culture. Grandeur stood alongside squalor.

To despise cities risks despising humanity. Rome was the home of many struggling people, the harmony of most the city's true monument.

Under the Roman forums' triumphal arches the conquering general customarily rode in a chariot in which was hidden a slave whispering 'Remember that thou art but a man.'

Carinus had defeated barbarian raids on the Rhine and Danube – victories but hardly triumphs. He needed a display of power. The city mob was fickle and dangerous. Parades and executions were cheaper than circuses and gladiatorial shows.

The Thebans mingled in the streets with the Praetorian Guard and men of Legio II Parthica stationed near the city.

Carinus[4] seemed intelligent, dapper and diffident. Unusually for a Roman, he sported a thin moustache. The crown had been thrust upon him and his brother Numerian as Carus' sons. He realized that to quit invited death for himself and anyone loyal to him. Men coveting the throne tolerated no potential rivals. Some perceived an air of dissolute pessimism about him, badly concealed by sarcasm, and an inflexibility that served as determination.

Pagan historians described Carinus as a compulsive libertine who seduced the women of his closest associates. It was said that he had nine wives, divorcing them in short order although several were pregnant by him. His coinage honoured a Magnia Urbica and Nigrinian, possibly a wife and child who died soon after he donned the purple robes of imperial power.[5] With his brother marching towards him from the East with what might be hostile intent, his army of dubious loyalty, the odd death of his father suggesting a murder plot, Carinus reacted in accordance with the motto on many a mosaic floor and drinking cup, 'Eat, drink and be lusty for tomorrow we die.'

A sixteenth century account states that the Theban Legion marched through Rome and received the benediction of Marcellinus, the man who became pope in 296.[6] This quite late account is not known from any earlier source. It may be a counter-Reformation effort to boost the prestige of the papacy. That the Thebans landed in Italy is implicit in the Acts. Marcellinus as a priest probably was in Rome at the time.

The Church in Rome was accused of laxity by some Christians living in areas much safer from persecution. Of Rome's first twenty-four bishops, the successors of Peter, at least a quarter were executed. Others spent their offices in hiding, 'white' unbloodied martyrs.

Threatened by persecution, Christians used legal subterfuge, paid pagan protectors or met secretly. Cardinal in Latin was a door hinge, in slang a man with influential connections, who might help members of the unpopular cult of the Nazarene carpenter, for a price or favour or, perhaps, simply friendship – a very Roman value. The underground cemeteries of the catacombs were a refuge when persecution was at its worst. Pagans tended to fear the dead.

In early December of 283 in Rome the young Egyptian (Theban?) Chrysanthus and his wife Daria had been buried alive in a sandpit after being handed over by the tribune Claudius as Christians.[7] A year later, an entire congregation perished when the authorities, having discovered them in a catacomb, walled them in alive. Among the victims was this same Claudius, his wife and sons. Seventy men of his unit were beheaded. To the authorities the most infuriating aspect of the Christians was their willingness to forgive, which could make converts even of their persecutors.

It was obvious that Rome was not a safe place for Christians.

The formal title given the Theban Legion was presumably Legio Augusta Thebeorum. Like Alexandria's marine legion, it probably had no unit number. The shield insignia of Thebeorum units in the *Notitia Dignitatum*, a compilation of Roman army units, was a yellow disk ringed by a red, a yellow and an outer red band. The shields were large, light and circular, to be utilized by infantrymen shielding bowmen behind them. Since Nilotic blacks traditionally placed arrows in their hair, the Thebans can be readily identified in Roman art. An archer with this headdress appears on the shield of an army unit from the Thebaid at a later date.[8]

Rome combined the worst of private ownership and socialism with the better features of neither. Bread, wine, tickets to the games and metal tokens to the whorehouses were provided to the poorest citizens by the government. A third of the city's population was on welfare, another third were slaves, the rest officials or aristocrats paying no taxes or the miserable small businessmen who paid taxes to support all the others.

The welfare system of the city of Rome began not as a handout to the unemployed but as a wage subsidy. Recipients did not get all necessities. They still had to labour to provide for rent, many of the slumlords being senators. The dole was principally food given to the father of the family, a system that did serve to keep families together. Those on the dole had to struggle from day to day to find work at inadequate wages. Most laboured at night to early morning, free by noon to attend the circus and games.[9] They found work through personal *patrones*, the rich they toadied.

There was no danger that the poor, whether slaves or citizens on the dole, might unite for a revolution. Many hated one another. Riots at the public games often occurred. It was *catharsis*, a purging of emotions that would not be tolerated elsewhere. The government pandered and pimped to placate people living in a world of frustration and boredom with no positive outlet. Churchmen would list *accedia* as one of the seven deadly sins. Translated as anger, more properly it was the acid egoism and spiritual sloth and rage of undeveloped minds that sought instant gratification. The mob at the games found torture, blood and death fascinating. There was a perverse satisfaction in knowing that others suffered more. Ovid remarked, 'Girls, if you can get a fellow to play with you while watching the games, he is yours.'[10]

In hundreds of cities, thousands died in the arena every few days to cheers and jeers. Mock cities with real people were stormed and burned to the ground, starving animals were hunted or became the hunters of human flesh, warships battled in flooded stadiums and people died of every variety of weapon, torture and wound.

The games recognized four factions: the reds, whites, blues and greens. Spectators rioted and killed in the stands in imitation of their factions in the area. The colours, apparently, did not represent any particular ethnic or economic group. The factions gave people an illusion of community, freedom and power they did not possess. Pliny remarked that, 'The people know only the colour.'[11] Few could know more since the life of a gladiator in the arena might last no more than a few days. 'In the circus the people are the rulers',[12] a performer had bluntly told the Emperor Augustus, 'Your position depends on how we keep the mob amused.'[13] Occasionally, the government intervened. The Emperor Vitellius had fans killed when they booed his party. Their rivals applauded.

Juvenal observed, 'The people who have conquered the world now have only two interests – bread and circuses.'[14]

Plutarch, Lucian and Seneca deplored the human slaughter. Cicero and Pliny thought the games edifying and appropriate to preserve 'warlike spirit'. Revolted by the bloodshed of the arena, the Emperor Tiberius had been in the habit of turning his eyes from it. The Roman historian Tacitus considered this to be a sign of a serious defect of character. The Emperor Marcus Aurelius thought the games dull and did his clerical chores while attending the show. The mob hated him for it.

There was a grotesqueness to this that worsened with time. Seneca had witnessed the new practice of fights to the death between a man wearing armour and one who had none. The winner was then matched without armour against a man with armour. This continued for hours. He wrote:

> All previous games have been fair. These are murder. The men have no defence, their bodies are exposed to every blow and every attack is bound to be successful. Most spectators prefer this to the regular duels of skill. They would! Protection and training only postpone death, which is what the crowd has come to see.[15]

Gladiators blinded by metal masks fought guided by the spectators' shouted directions or misdirections. Women fought dwarfs as Statius describes: 'It was enough to make Mars and the goddess of bravery split their sides laughing to see them hacking at each other.'[16] Many gladiators were homosexual mates fighting in two–men teams, bodies and minds programmed to serve those in power.[17] The Emperor Trajan had five thousand pairs of gladiators fight to the death in a victory celebration that lasted days.

Not all gladiatorial games were fought to the death. Gladiators were expensive slaves. If a gladiator fought for three years, he became an instructor. After five years of service he was set free, usually to work as a bodyguard or enforcer.

Martial remarked with repugnance that he thought that he had heard of everything until a woman was raped by a bull in the arena to reenact a Greek myth.[18] He quit the city of Rome.

The Emperor Gallienus, Valerian's son, had a jeweller guilty of fraud placed in a cage to await the entry of a wild beast.[19] He whimpered for mercy. The door lifted and the beast entered. It was a chicken. Fraud deserved fraud. A bullfighter who ten times had failed to kill an animal received a wreath from the emperor who remarked that it was no easy task to miss so large a beast. Gallienus fell to an assassin's sword.

With the writing of history and all media crushingly censored, officials hiding bad news from their superiors, people cavilling, wearing many masks, depending upon their audience, Romans were unreflecting or despairing of the Empire's future. Patriotism was becoming compulsory religious devotion, those in power deluded that loyalty could be forced upon people.

The great issues moving the masses were not those of freedom, economic opportunity and human rights, but events in the games where the mob had the illusion of power. Stars of the arena and stage were the peoples' heroes, filling the vacuum of any other sort of representation. Entertainment substituted for politics to the benefit of the ruling class.

Chapter 14

In the Eye of the Storm

Never waste a crisis.

Rahm Emanuel

The Roman public in hundreds of cities enjoyed the violent death of others as public spectacle almost daily, not merely as entertainment but example and morale booster.

The legionnaires would have seen the Circus Maximus, Rome's largest stadium, which could hold 385,000 ecstatic fans, built with the slave labour of Jews after the first revolt and inaugurated in the year 72. The use of Christians as circus victims had been initiated a decade earlier. Tacitus wrote:

> Nero had all admitted Christians seized. These informed on others who were also arrested, not so much for setting fire to the city as for their hatred of mankind. Everything was done to make their deaths humiliating. They were dressed in animal skins and torn to pieces by dogs, crucified, or covered with pitch and used as torches to light the arena after dark. Although as Christians they deserved punishment, still people felt that they were being punished to satisfy the emperor's love of cruelty and not for the good of the nation.[1]

An altar stood in the arena offering Christians the opportunity to recant. Tossing a few grains of incense would immediately save their lives. Few did. Presumably, they would have done so before being thrown into the arena.

The games opened and closed with religious ceremonies.[2] The gladiator incarnated Roman ethos, brutal yet glamorizing violence, disciplined yet profligate, murderous yet masochistic. A great many were volunteers, others prisoners of war or criminals. Graffiti demonstrated the adulation given to the few enduring winners who could become wealthy men. But money was not the attraction, nor the women morbidly and erotically fascinated by the gladiator's situation. Men of every class of society chose the arena, as if escaping life found unbearable in order to seek release by confronting death.[3]

The gladiator typically showed no emotion. His coldness was held inspirational by men as eminent as Cicero.[4] Applauded, cheered and praised by the mob urging him on to die a hero, he rarely disappointed his audience. If visibly frightened or hesitant, the gladiator could trigger a collective rage among the spectators, a social rejection held worse than death.

The martyr, too, fulfilled his role and could inspire his audience but in ways unrecognized and unintended by persecutors. He or she died for being defiant. It was not the lesson taught by the gladiator.

Nine out of ten people in the Empire lived in the countryside where there were no arenas. They laboured to support the way of life of the cities and the circuses. Their labour was despised by the ruling class.

Cicero declared, 'All gains made by hired craftsmen are dishonourable and base for what we buy of them is not their labour but their artistic skill; their success only increases the slavishness of their work.'[5] He begrudged the craftsman's pride in accomplishment. '*Ars gratia artis*,' art is enough for the artist, was his rationale for paying low wages to skilled workers. 'All retailing too belongs in the same category for the dealer gains nothing except by profuse lying ... the work of all skills is shameful. There is nothing ennobling in a workshop.' And Christ was a carpenter.

No banks in the modern sense existed. The purchase of slaves absorbed most money available to be invested. Amidst inflation, profits were more easily gained by producing less to gain a higher price than by producing more.

Chimneys, doors, windows, public toilets, the liberation of slaves, prostitution, burials – almost everything was taxed. The tax in gold and silver collected every five years from great merchants to blind beggars, and the price of the licence to practise their trade, caused men to hide their shops and sell children into slavery to escape it. Free craftsmen fled the cities as if honest labour was a crime.[6]

Members of the upper class were carried through the streets in litters accompanied by servants, gladiator bodyguards and assorted hangers-on. Matrons walked slaves on leashes wearing iron neckbands inscribed with requests to return to the owner in case the banded strayed. A house fortune teller and dream analyzer was usually close at hand. Fate excused people from responsibility they found too much to bear, so they claimed.

Slavery did not make slaves simply victims but moulded many into sly, flattering, sullen, treacherous, two-faced and disassociated personalities. Devious qualities that might aid a slave to survive could make him unfit for freedom. 'So many slaves, so many enemies,' wrote Seneca.[7] 'These people are not enemies we have but those we have created.' He added, 'We must live dependent on those who hate and weep because of us.'

There were Roman virtues worse than vices. A free father by law could beat or kill his wife or offspring or sell his children into slavery, subject only to the interference of in-laws who could legally beat or kill him.[8] For better or worse, the law did not intrude into family matters.

Parents stood at the city gates and market stalls pleading to sell waifs they could not support.

That the declining birthrate and weakening of the empire was the result of ever looser morality was a fallacy. Soldiers and slaves alike had low birthrates. Their lives were not spent in self-indulgence.

Six senatorial families owned most of North Africa. The Senate of Rome was powerless yet had enormous prestige, all that money could buy. Born into senatorial families, or appointed by the emperor, senators were envied and patronized. Generals wanted more than victories; they wanted gold and honours and respectable retirement. The Senate sought men with no scruples in drawing swords to defend it. Shrewdly, it had opened its ranks to all legionary generals, active or retired.

The Senate had the potential to be a true congress of nations but was overwhelmingly Italian. Its members refused to yield place to persons less than fifty years of age or anyone who was not the owner of vast tracts of land. Wealth from trade and industry was detested. The Senate's gift to the public was rhetoric, endless speeches stringing together quotes, mythological allusions, unctuous flattery, diatribes, rantings and logic far removed from reality. Clerks groaned and visiting barbarian chiefs snored loudly. An emperor forbid comedians to wear the violet-bordered toga, the uniform of the Senate, 'lest the public be confused'.

At sundown, the capital of the Empire shuttered and double-bolted its doors, the streets left to the creatures of the night. Few dared walk its tenement canyons unless part of a large group. The rich returned to suburban mansions proceeded by torchbearers as wagons rolled into the city with supplies. No wheeled vehicles were allowed during the day. In the shadows the *fornicari*, the prostitutes of the streets, offered their wares. *Fornus* was the stone foundation of a bridge where their business was conducted. Praetorian guardsmen, paid double a legionnaire's normal salary, staggered down the streets. The *vigiles*, the police of the capital, were not so foolish as to antagonize them.

Reports arrived in Rome that Numerian had called off the Persian campaign and was leading his army back to Europe. Might he challenge Carinus' crown, or was he anxious to find safety nearer his brother? Whatever the case, the Senate would approve the winner. In 218, it had auctioned off the Roman world to the highest bidder, the winner a senator cut to ribbons by the army within a month.[9]

Numerian was a lawyer little attracted to the military. The feeling was mutual. At Antioch, Numerian and a bishop, Babylus, argued in a church doorway.[10]

Christians were growing ever bolder. Often, they bought burial and other licensed societies in order to use them as legal fronts. Archaeology demonstrates that the shrine of the Theban legionnaire Gereon at Cologne, West Germany, had been a temple of the Egyptian goddess Isis before it became a Christian church during the era of persecution.[11] This suggests that Egyptian Christian priests, said by pagans to worship Serapis, may have bought pagan temples to gain their licences to worship.

One does not argue with anyone in a skirt be it a priest, judge or a woman, so goes the proverb. Bishops were ill advised to argue with an emperor. Babylus was executed without trial in violation of his rights as a citizen and his church seized.

The reports were that Numerian's army was steadily marching towards Italy.

To offset the power of the Praetorians, a second officers' training corps, the *promoti*,[12] served as a cavalry bodyguard for the emperor in the field. The Praetorians provided a detachment as infantry bodyguard.

Numerian was losing his sight, having contracted an eye ailment in the East. To conceal his disability, he confined himself to the curtained litter in which he was carried, an unmilitary means of transport. His army arrived in the Balkans unimpressed by their ruler.

The leader of the cavalry guard was an Illyrian, Diocletian. He was intelligent and introspective, with a face as wizened and impassive as an actor's mask. His parents had been imperial slaves, supervisors of the slaves of a palace.[13] Diocletian's mother was a priestess of a Balkan cult. As a young officer in Gaul, a druidess had foretold that he was destined to be emperor, but not until he had killed a boar. *Aper* is the word for a wild hog in Latin.

The commander of Numerian's Praetorians was Arrius Aper.

Aper had been stealing money from the imperial treasury. The penalty was death. Aper was warned that Numerian had learned of his guilt. Fearful of being arrested, Aper murdered the semi-blind prince of the empire. As Numerian rarely left his litter the murder remained undetected until the stink of the corpse revealed it.

On 24 November 284, before the assembled troops, Diocletian confronted Aper on a stage erected for the emperor.[14] Announcing the murder and its motive, he stabbed Aper to death. Moments later, swords clattering upon shields, and the troops hailed Diocletian emperor as he swore innocence of any plot.

That was the official version.

Diocletian swiftly acted to abolish the grain commission, the *frumentari*, the imperial secret agency for cloak and dagger acts, replacing them with his creation, the *agentes rebus*, 'agents for things' – things unmentionable, such as espionage, blackmail, assassination and the like. The Praetorians were oiled, polished, placed on the shelf or eliminated.

Carinus received the news as if anticipated. The only major troop reserves in the Empire were those near the city of Rome and those blocking the southern Alpine passes. Carinus harangued that Diocletian intended to abolish the Praetorians as he had the grain commission. It was a fair statement. The

Praetorians were the Empire's military academy and the emperor's bodyguard, a centre of intrigue and coups, elite, overpaid and arrogant. 'Who guards the guards?' was a bitter Roman saying.

The Thebans received orders to march to northern Italy and await further orders or Diocletian's invasion of Italy through the eastern Alps. Other Acts suggest that other Thebans were arriving at Aquileia on the northern Adriatic by sea. After Diocletian was defeated, they could go over the Alps to their duty station, Britain.

The Thebans realized they soon might be in battle for the first time as a legion. Most soldiers spent their careers without seeing combat. They might soon be warring against fellow legionnaires.

Diocletian, if not innocent of shedding blood, at least had been careful to limit it to a few important victims.

Carinus was legally emperor, coming to power peacefully by inheritance and approved by the Senate.

Diocletian was a *tyrannus*, taking power violently.

The clash of legions would choose between them.

The Theban Legion was inexorably being drawn into a political maelstrom that its members sought to avoid.

Chapter 15

Destination the Saxon Shore

To our country, right or wrong, may it forever be in the right and if not may we correct it.

Stephen Decatur

Hundreds of Roman coin hoards and hundreds of thousands of Roman coins have been discovered in England's soil. Romans squirreled away coins in pottery buried in the earth because banks did not exist and invasion, civil wars, slave revolts and banditry were all too common. For whatever reason, many troves were never recovered by the owners.

In 1908 during excavation for a building on Fetter Lane, London, a few blocks from the Thames, a jar of Roman coins was unearthed.[1] What was unusual about the Fetter Lane hoard was that it was entirely of Alexandrian coins. One other like it is known outside of Egypt and that was found in the Channel Islands.

Alexandria's tetradrachms by the late third century had only 2 per cent of the silver content of centuries earlier.[2] The result was inflation and the tendency to hide away older coinage.

Dozens of Alexandrian tetradrachms have been found singly in Britain in the twentieth century in garden topsoil, on pavements, paths and steel bridge walkways, most of them far from known Roman habitations. These can only be souvenirs lost by modern British tourists or servicemen returning from the Middle East. One single coin of this type was found in Britain among thousands of coins of other types in a Roman army payroll hidden under fire-blackened ruins denoting the violence that had prompted its burial. The coin probably was a souvenir or small change accidentally brought to Roman Britain.

Authentic finds of single Alexandrian tetradrachms deposited in the Roman era are known from eighteen sites in Britain.[3] Some were in Roman ruins, one was in a seashell brought up in a fisherman's net. A dozen hoards of Alexandrian tetradrachms ranging from two to seven coins are recorded, all before 1840 in Britain.[4] Alexandrian tetradrachms were of a denomination that did not exist outside of Egypt and were intended to be of no value elsewhere in the Empire, forcing travellers leaving Egypt to exchange their money, in effect paying a tax. These coins would be useless in Britain unless circulating among a community of immigrants from Egypt.

It can be argued that these coins appear outside of Egypt in the late third century because imperial coinage had become so debased in quality of metal that they had become the equivalent of a tetradrachm's low quality and currency value. If so, one could expect many throughout the Empire mingled with other coins.

The patterns of such findings on the continent, however, is that of hoards exclusively or largely of Alexandrian tetradrachms. All were found along the major routes overland from Italy to Britain, i.e. in Switzerland or along the Rhine or Garonne or on the Channel Isle of Guernsey.[5]

London, Augusta Londinium, was the capital of Roman Britain. The Fetter Lane hoard had been found outside but near to what once had been the south-western Roman city wall. The jar had been given unopened to Mr F.D. Ringrose who did not report the trove until several years later. It contained fifty-six pieces dating from 66 AD to 284, a wide range of dates, typical of hoards found in the villages of the Nile.

The latest year dates the deposit of the treasure trove as 284: the year of the Panopolis papyrus receipt from the Thebaid and the year of Carinus' coin abbreviating Legio Thebeorum. A coincidence?

Mr Ringrose was a builder who made no claim to be a scholar. His credentials were precisely his disinterest in doing what he regarded to be his duty in publicizing the find. The hoard was a minor article in a coin collector's magazine.

The money in the hoard was at least four months' wages for a semi-skilled workman in the Roman era, but a nest egg a peasant would have earned the hard way. That the hoard was misplaced by some Victorian tourist back from Egypt does not explain what it was doing deep under London's streets. Historical hoaxes are usually concocted in the hopes of profit or to promote some cause or theory. Mr Ringrose had no such motive. He simply reported the trove and made no claims for it.

Alexandrian tetradrachms are the most inexpensive of Roman coins for a collector. Rare types among them can bring a good price, nevertheless. Would a merchant sell a jar that by weight and sound was obviously filled with coins or jewellery without opening it? Would the buyer then absentmindedly lose it in the depths of a building excavation? The find won Mr Ringrose neither fame nor fortune and he had not expected them. He had unwittingly invited the ridicule of scholars versed on the subject area. None came forth, however. The find created no stir and was forgotten.

Obviously, the trove had been smuggled out of Alexandria in an attempt to evade the moneychangers. It was a civilian's since soldiers were paid in regular imperial coinage. One explanation is that a legion from Egypt was to be posted in Britain with its entourage of families, servants, craftsmen and tradesmen.

Archaeology indicates that new troop units were planned for Britain at the time.

A network of nine major coastal forts was under construction, matched by others on the coast of Gaul (France and Belgium), the so-called Saxon Shore defences against sea raiders from the Elbe and the Frisian islands.[6] Each would have needed a cohort of five hundred men with the exception of the larger headquarters unit. This presumably involved a new legion in Britain. Coins found in the foundations of the Saxon shore forts in Britain date their construction to 282, the date of the Panopolis papyrus original rations requisition.

The admiral of the Atlantic Fleet was Carausius, a Belgic Celt of the Menapii tribe of what is presently south-western Holland.[7] Menapii were sea rovers ranging as far as Hibernia (Ireland) to trade and settle. The Isle of Man in the Irish Sea, County Fermanagh, Ireland and sites in Wales memorialize their name.

Carausius had been ordered to build a fleet at Boulogne and on the Rhine, according to a Roman writer.[8] This accords well with the building of the coastal forts and ports known as Litus Saxonicum. He '*occupate une legione Romana*,'[9] he seized a Roman legion. This is a curious phrase. Carausius commanded several legions. The comment implies that the legion did not voluntarily join his cause. All legions were Roman. Either *Romana* is redundant or it is in the ablative of separation, signifying a legion from the city of Rome, which fits the Theban Legion's itinerary.

Carausius began his career as a helmsman and pilot. The Channel and North Sea are treacherous waters with tidal differences of as much as forty feet, currents twice as fast as a sailing ship, broad shifting sandbanks, hidden rocks and storms that make the Mediterranean's seem mild. Piloting required extensive knowledge not to be found in any book. Carausius had learned ropes and shoals from boyhood. He was a sailor's salt, barrel-chested, double-chinned, gifted in friendships and popular with all ranks. The success of his strategy versus Saxon raiders won his appointment as admiral.

The Osberg and Nyndam ships uncovered by archaeologists in Denmark and Sweden give direct examples of Saxon-type vessels that were predecessors of the later Viking drakkars.[10] Fabricated of overlapping planks lashed together, averaging sixty feet in length, they were slim light rowing skiffs, mounting small sails if any. Low in the water, sails down, they would be very difficult to sight in daylight and impossible at night. With the attackers' advantage of choosing time and target, they had plundered without check.

Until the new shore forts were ready, Carausius boldly decided to sail for the Saxons' home ports while they were ravaging the channel coasts. His barge-like *biremes*, sailing craft with single banks of oars with two men on each oar, could readily crush the fragile Saxon skiffs if they could come to grips with them. This was exceedingly unlikely on the high seas. When the homecoming raiders had to manoeuvre through the sandbanks and inlets off their native shores, they found Carausius' war vessels waiting for them. The victories won by the Romans stopped the marauders for the next hundred years. They also made Carausius a rich man as the loot aboard the raiders was confiscated. He was accused of deliberately refusing to defend the Roman coasts in order to gain loot from the defeated Saxons who had taken it.

It was an understandable complaint from citizens who felt undefended against the onslaught from the sea, but unwarranted considering that any other strategy would have had quite doubtful chances of success, not that Carausius and his crews objected to their newfound treasure.

The admiral was also credited by the imperial government with victories in Gaul against a new menace by land, the *bagaudae*. The word was coined by their foes, Roman landlords, perhaps from *bucaeda*, a whipped slave, with a pun on *vacuus*, free or idle, and *cauda*, blockhead.

The West had suffered worse than the eastern Roman Empire in the decades after the frontiers had been overrun in 260. The Germanic chief Crocus had devastated Gaul, annihilating entire town populations.[11] The Church recorded thousands as martyrs killed by Crocus, most fugitives seeking safety in churches only to be massacred. Few may have been Christians originally but they had had more trust in the Church than in Roman authorities. Legionary generals in Gaul declared themselves emperors, yet were unable to control their own troops. The auxiliary cavalry from Batavia on the delta of the Rhine had gone beyond extortion; they had laid siege to the second largest city in Gaul, Augustodunum (Autun), and pillaged it in 269. Generals fighting barbarian invaders were overthrown by other generals, until imperial forces from Italy smashed the usurpers. Gaul was reduced to chaos, inflation rampant and taxes exorbitant.

In response, many villagers led herds from abandoned estates to refuge in deep forests and woodland pastures, raising crops in isolated holdings, deserting civilization. Marauders, bullying soldiers and tax collectors could not find them. This was not a revolution but a retrogression by choice. Class struggle was not the issue. The leaders of the *bagaudae* included landlords regarded as chieftains. Runaway slaves, army deserters, barbarians who were more correctly refugees rather than invaders, and people fleeing their over-taxed occupations soon joined the ranks of the rebels.

Tax collectors, their property security for the revenue estimated, ran away and joined them. This more than any external threat demonstrated the decline of the Empire. Civilization was crumbling. The rural population was not unduly alarmed. To many, it seemed a lessening of oppression.

The *bagaudae*[12] were evasive rather than aggressive, a threat not in what they did but what they refused to do. Under the leaders Amandus and Aelius, they had fortified an old walled settlement on a loop of the Marne, today the Parisian neighbourhood of St Maur-des-Fosses. Several rare coin types are recorded minted by Amandus.[13] Poorly equipped and organized, they were no match for legionnaires and they knew it. Soon they scattered and retreated towards the Atlantic coast from Normandy to Brittany, the area in Celtic called Amorica.

The *bagaudae* would be a problem to the Western Empire for centuries to come. Some two centuries later Salvian, a Christian and a Gaul, was to describe these supposed rebels, marked for death in the minds of imperial rulers.

> I must now speak of the *bagaudae*, who, despoiled, afflicted, and murdered by wicked and bloody magistrates after they had lost the rights of Roman citizens, forfeited also the honour of the Roman name. We transform their misfortunes into crime, we brand them with a name that recalls their losses, with a name that we ourselves have contrived for their shame! We call those men rebels and utterly desperate, whom we ourselves have forced into crime. For by what other causes were they made *bagaudae* save by our unjust acts, the wicked decisions of the magistrates, the proscription and extortion of those who have turned the public exactions to the increase of their private fortunes and made the tax indictions their opportunity for plunder?...
>
> How does our present situation differ from theirs? Those who have not before joined the *bagaudae* are now being compelled to join them...Such is the case among all the lower classes...[14]

The sombre picture Salvian paints is complemented by a Roman comic playwright who portrayed *bagaudae* life in the forests of the Valley of the Loire and the Channel seacoast.

> That's where men live by the laws of nature, where there is no rank, where capital sentences are posted upon an oak limb or marked on a man's bones (identification amulet), where peasants make the speeches and ordinary people do the judging, where anything goes![15]

Babolenus, a seventh century abbot, was to record that Amandus, one of the two leaders of the *bagaudae* in 286, was a Christian.[16] It is easy to dismiss this as hearsay until one realizes that Babolenus' monastery was at St Maur-des-Fosses, Paris, the site that had been the *bagaudae* stronghold. The idea of *bagaudae* as Christians was not appealing to secular or ecclesiastic authority in the turbulent Dark Ages. Babolenus presumably put in writing an oral tradition he believed accurate, however disturbing to the establishment.

The *bagaudae* felt little need of civilization. But Roman civilization needed them. Their defection was more dangerous than any invasion. To abolish slavery would be to abolish civilization, totally unacceptable according to Aristotle. Slavery could be abolished and civilization preserved if machines could do the labour of many workers. That, however, would have entailed a social revolution most of the ruling class preferred not to consider.

The legend of Robin Hood who robbed the rich to give to the poor was English but similar to French legends of the *bagaudae* that Alexandre Dumas developed. He drew upon Welsh tales but his chief inspiration was the folklore and legends of the forest glens of the Loire Valley and the Channel coast of France lauding the *bagaudae*. He set his novel *Robin du Bois* in England because of the reactionary politics and censorship of France in his day.

Diocletian's closest subordinate Maximian Herculius, some 1,500 miles from the Channel, declared Carausius a criminal to be punished by death. Carausius, in response, proclaimed himself emperor of Britain. Diocletian thereupon made Maximian his viceroy west of the Alps. Maximian, while always loyal to Diocletian, was not above manipulating him. He may well have made Carausius a rebel in order to be promoted to oppose him. Otherwise, his action appears reckless. He telegraphed his punch.

That the Theban Legion's intended duty station was Britain adds a political dimension to their religious situation, a motive not in the Acts, which make no mention of the Thebans' destination.

The Theban Legion had to be stopped by Maximian from joining forces with Carausius.

Its force could be the balance of power west of the Alps. The pagan foes of the Christians in the army never accused them of intrigue and coups. Meanwhile, Carinus was emperor and the Thebans would support him.

While Diocletian waited with his legions north and east of the Alps, Carinus was marching to Verona, the city dominating the Brenner Pass. The army was convinced that only an able soldier could be an able emperor.

Chapter 16

Contenders for the Crown

We dare risk intelligence.
Unaccepted CIA motto suggested by
Senator Daniel Patrick Moynihan

The general Julianus of Pannonia's (Hungary) grab for the throne delayed the clash of Carinus and Diocletian.[1] Julianus had support of only one or two of the more than thirty-two legions of the Empire. Diocletian's moves had deprived him of most troops of the Danube frontier and the Balkans. That he acted under Diocletian's orders in invading north-eastern Italy is tempting to believe, but the coinage he issued assert his challenge to that wily Illyrian. Nevertheless, he served Diocletian's purposes. Julianus seemed desperate, perhaps caught in double-dealing or with his hand in the treasury's till. Rome's inflexible harshness in these situations repeatedly motivated men in power to worse crimes once they were discovered.

When Romans struggled for the throne, each claimant personally led his army against his rival. One battle usually settled the issue, the legions throughout the Empire accepting the winner. Meanwhile, frontiers were stripped of detachments to form the contesting armies.

Carinus occupied Verona, protected on three sides by the Adige river and by a wall across the neck of the peninsula. Presumably on the basis of records no longer existing, the medieval historian Otto of Freising, crusader and member of the German royal family, related that Theban legionnaires fell at 'Bonn called Verona'.[2] This seems a misreading or typo. No town had both names. The Latin script '*et*' and the abbreviation for '*eadem*' were very similar.[3] Probably, Bonn and Verona were intended. No Theban legionnaires are venerated at Verona, although the tradition of their martyrs at Bonn is long honoured. Possibly, Thebans fell at Verona not as martyrs but killed in the clash between Julianus and Carinus.

Geography must have determined much of the battle. Carinus was well supplied and could wait. Julianus, as an invader coming through the eastern Alps, had to act precipitously. The tactics were the deeply instilled methods of the legions. Thousands of men clad in iron bands and helmets trod rank behind rank towards one another across meadows daubed in wildflowers. Within throwing distance each side halted, shields raised protectively. The executive officer, the *primipilus*, literally the first javelin, tossed his metal-necked spear, joined in an instant by thousands more. The intent was to pin the enemy down, reluctant to move. Trumpets blared and both sides charged, sunlight gleaming on shortsword blades.

Bloody carnage ensued. The word for death in battle, *occidit*, meant literally to be cut to pieces. The soldier was drilled not to slash but stab in a deadly upward thrust. Limbs, being without armour, were most vulnerable. The thrust to the throat could be fatal, regardless of the leather bands and bandana containing a soldier's coins knotted about it. Individual combat was not a duel but a heavyweight slugging contest. No one was expected to be able to endure it for more than twenty minutes. The youngest were the first rank, the next two ranks accordingly by age, older men encouraging those foremost and ready to step in to cover a wounded or exhausted man.

Battle between equally able Roman forces in toe to toe combat was the least preferable of resolutions. The winner might emerge permanently weakened. Strategy sought to avoid equal contest of forces. If Julianus attacked Verona believing that the legionnaires within it lacked confidence in not taking to the field he was in grave error. Men trained as archers were a more effective defence than ordinary infantrymen for a walled and moated city.

There is another way in war. Cloak and dagger could be more effective than armies.

Julianus fell to Carinus' sword or so the winner's account relates. It gives no details of the battle.

Rome expected every enlistee to obey his unit commander. Losing in a coup, they could expect leniency if they had done what was expected of them. To be severe would give the losing side the courage of desperation.

Green grass nourished by the rains of northern Italy's autumn, trampled underfoot, red and slippery with blood, became carpeted with weapons and shields cast down in surrender. Men stood grimly as the victors surveyed the ranks. Some murdered colleagues to settle old grudges and placate the victors. Others handed a sword to a comrade and fatalistically asked to be killed. The defeated survivors were scattered and incorporated into units of proven loyalty.

The situation impressed upon Carinus' forces what they could expect if they lost to Diocletian. Meanwhile, Carinus' seductions of the wives of his most trusted officers stirred resentment.

The Thebans' officers had rejoined the army expecting a purely training function, handing over the legion in Britain to its regular officers, its role strictly defensive. Events put them in hazard of the laws of the Church. Desertion was punishable by death and totally against their conditioning. Their holding together as an effective unit was their best protection come what may.

It would seem wise for them to set the legion's troops marching across the Alps into Gaul at the earliest opportunity as soon as the snows in the mountain passes had melted and the worst dangers of floods and avalanches had passed. The headquarters section would be the rearguard so that most of the troops would be out of harm's way while the unit's commanders might deal with the emperor's appointees, whomever the emperor might be.

Northernmost Italy was cursed and blessed by the ruggedness of its terrain. Its farms were small, accessed by steep paths. The soil was so thin and rocky that not even the greediest of lowland landlords coveted them. Except for Egypt, huge estates were the norm, owned by absent landlords. Increasingly, they were turning to herding because it required far fewer workers and yielded greater profits. Unneeded farmers and their families on the estates were 'liberated' to fend for themselves. Some drifted into the cities, some broke apart, others sought to become rural slaves. In the hill country, small farm owners were poor, but independent and free. They were one of the few recruiting sources for the army away from the frontiers.

Independent small farmers produced a good crop of children, if a bare subsistence otherwise. This was in contrast with the Empire's slave population who were denied a normal family life, and rarely reproduced its numbers. Innumerable gravestone epitaphs attest the lot of most slaves, most of whom were unmarried.

In Rome, events were occurring in the aftermath of the departure of the Thebans from the city.

Sebastian was a baptized 'nobleman' of Milan who came to Rome in 285 to join the army in order to protect his fellow Christians amidst persecution. This was a clear case from the Acts of a Christian joining the army although church law until then had forbidden it.

His Act makes no mention of the Theban Legion.[4] He, apparently, arrived in the city after the Thebans had departed. Meanwhile, Carinus had murdered the commander of the Praetorian Guards and replaced him with an elderly civilian of no military experience, Matronianus, whose chief function was as a procurer of lovers of either sex for Carinus.

Sebastian was possessed of a civility that mollified even his enemies. The Acts declare that Carinus made him second in command of the Praetorians, presumably in order to leave Rome in the care of officers he could trust.

Diocletian sent forces to Rome after Carinus' departure, including a man born in the same town of Diocles as he and bearing the same name who became mayor of Rome. He was said to be a relative of the Bishop of Rome at the time, Marcellinus, another Illyrian.

Sebastian busied himself aiding needy and politically harassed Christians. He preached his faith among the Praetorians. Diocletian, the mayor, repeatedly asked Sebastian to cease his public display of belief, emphasizing that he wished him no ill, but others might. Disobeyed, he had him handed over to be practice target for the archery of the Praetorians. Soldiers were executed by beheading or being clubbed to death according to military law. Officers were not subjected to torture. Wounded, Sebastian was handed over to fellow believers who nursed him back to health, his punishment perhaps a mockery of his desire to be an officer of a unit of bowmen, the Theban Legion.

Healed, Sebastian renewed his activities. He directly approached the mayor to ask for better treatment of arrested Christians. At this point the patience of the mayor snapped. He ordered Sebastian to be clubbed to death. In violation of a citizen's rights under Roman law, the corpse was thrown into a sewer so that it would not become the object of a martyr's cult. Recovered nonetheless, it was buried in the catacombs.

Until the Renaissance, Sebastian was depicted in art not as a youth but as a grey-bearded man in soldier's cloak without armour or weapon. It is hardly likely that a young civilian would have been placed in command over the Praetorians. Probably, Sebastian was another recalled veteran intending to join the Thebans as *campidoctor* (a military retiree recalled to train a newly recruited legion), but accepting command of the Praetorians officers' school instead.

Other victims of the *praepositus cubiculi* Diocletian (in effect, the Mayor of Rome) in Rome were the Armenian brothers Calocerus,[5] a civilian, and the *primicerius* Parthenius. More Armenians were killed with the priest Aemilianus[6] at Trebia twenty miles east of Rome. Their record makes no mention of a legion. *Primicerius*, first among equals in rank, was not a legionary or auxiliary rank at the time but suggests a special status. Mauricius was a *primicerius*. Parthenius was possibly his predecessor over the Thebans or leader of another new legion, the XII Victrix, intended for the continental forts of the Saxon shore. The channel had become a frontier province and Roman frontier provinces each had two legions.[7]

The presence of Armenians martyrs in Italy and Gaul at this time when none appear earlier or later suggests some common cause.

In the winter of late 285, Carinus awaited Diocletian's advance by the Brenner Pass southwards into Italy or by the Via Gemina through the eastern Alps or by pincers utilizing both, as was the case.

Diocletian waited also. It was not simply ambition that impelled him. He wanted to reform the Empire in order to reverse its decline. Every phase of life was to be affected. His solutions would be temporarily effective but brutally totalitarian. Scarcely any ruler previously had ever displayed his administrative zeal and imagination.

Introspective, and aloof yet aware that he needed an alter ego whose qualities balanced his, Diocletian had chosen a general, Maximian to be his deputy.

Diocletian would be emperor, *augustus*, and Maximian would be *caesar*, viceroy. Born on the same day of the year as Diocletian but younger, Maximian was about thirty-five.[8] To believers in horoscopes their common interests were preordained.

A propagandist of Maximian Herculius wrote that he had campaigned earlier in his life as far as the River Hibero, the Habur (Nahr Khabour), the eastern frontier of Roman Mesopotamia.[9] The town of Nicephorium was to be named Maximianopolis after him. Probus had encouraged the career of Diocletian but not Maximian in the East. Maximian might have been present at Carrhae in 276, since Nicephorium was fifty miles south-west of that city on the same river.

Like Diocletian, Maximian was an Illyrian, the son of slaves of the state, managers of other slaves, the first Roman rulers from this background. Brilliant in using unexpected routes to gain the advantage of surprise, Maximian did not lead his men but drove them. He was poorly educated, a crude extrovert with a lust for physical action, and an able, loyal and willing instrument of his patron. Maximian's contemporaries declared him bizarre in his decisions, easily swayed by bad advisers and a remarkably poor judge of men. The pagan Eutropius described him as 'a man inclined to every kind of cruelty and severity, faithless, perverse, utterly devoid of consideration for others, undisguisedly vicious and of a violent temper, showing his disposition in the sternness of his looks.'[10] Another held him 'of a bloodthirsty rashness, foolish in council.'[11]

Maximian was to adopt in 286 the name Herculius. He shared with that demigod muscular strength, brooding vanity, obstinacy, bisexuality and a propensity for suicide. No individual portrait bust of him is known. His lust for physical action complemented Diocletian's chill intellect. He was to become so detested that crowds would shatter every public image of him they could lay their hands on. His portrait survives on coinage and the mosaics of his palace in Sicily.

Carinus was exasperated waiting for Diocletian to move. The winter was mild and the mountain passes were not blocked by snow, prompting him late in 285 to order his army to march into the icy winds funnelling through the Brenner Pass. He would meet his foe deep within the adversary's territory.

The indications are that the Theban Legion remained in north-eastern Italy along the road from the army port of Aquileia to Bergamo. They would guard Carinus' supply route and be his link to Italy and the West. In the meantime, they would be reinforced by more troops arriving at the port of Aquileia in north-eastern Italy and prepare to march over the north-western Alps to the Rhine and passage to Britain in the spring of 286.

At Margus near the Danube Carinus collided with Diocletian's army. He won the battle. According to the official story he was then murdered by an outraged husband among his officers. Or Diocletian's intrigues had proven once again more effective than legions.

Not long after Carinus' death his nephews and niece, Cantius, Cantianus and Cantianilla, were brought to Aquileia by their Christian tutor, Protus.[12] All were martyred. Two years earlier the city's bishop Hilarius[13] and his fellow clergy had been put to the sword there. Why would Protus take his wards to a scene of recent persecution, a great army depot, unless he believed it contained friendly forces? The Theban Legion presumably departed shortly before they arrived.

None of the Acts of Aquileia mention the Theban Legion. Each is very brief and although many martyrs fell the same year they do not refer to one another, the typical problem confronting the historian attempting to reconstruct the events.

Valentinus,[14] a *magister militum* or military instructor fell in 286 about the time of Protus and his wards. Concordius,[15] a navy doctor, and his two sons joined them in martyrdom at Aquileia that year. No other martyrs at Aquileia are known from 286. A motive in killing these individuals may have been to prevent them warning the Thebans that the army of Maximian had arrived through the Eastern Alps and was pursuing them.

An inscription at Aquileia from early 286 honours Diocletian as the sun god Sol and Maximian as Belenus, 'starry eyes', the Danubian Apollo.[16] This was nothing less than the first notice of a revolution in Roman policy. The Senate had declared several emperors, including Probus, to be gods after their deaths, but had never allowed any living person to be worshipped.

Diocletian did not consider himself a god. He did believe that he ruled by divine right – heaven or fate or whatever gods had enabled him to achieve power. Philosophers could argue as to definitions; he saw emperor worship as a shrewd test of loyalty. He had a flair for pageantry but was less interested in principles than results. Maximian, too, would be an object of worship.

Maximian Herculius' insecure personality may have welcomed the idea that he was the embodiment of a demigod. One of his hireling poets wrote that wherever he might retire all lands and seas were full of him.[17]

Maximian's religious enthusiasm was sealed by Diocletian appointing him high priest of the Empire, a sharp break in centuries of custom. The high priest, the *pontifex maximus*, had always been the emperor.[18]

Maximian had a Syrian wife.[19] A pagan gossiped that his official heir, Maxentius, had been sired by another man. Church scribes mention an illegitimate son, Olympius, who was martyred at Antioch.

The gross corpulence of Maximian in his later years is manifest in his image on coinage. His swings in personality from passive obsequiousness to raging violence seem symptomatic of a deeply disturbed nature.

That Maximian later became a eunuch could explain the submissiveness with which he obeyed Diocletian who, like the Persian shahs, introduced to his court an entourage of castrated officials.[20] This was the totalitarian concept of virtue, not freedom but physical constraint. Castration was utterly repugnant to Latin values. It had been illegal. Diocletian's fondness for silk robes contrasted with early republican Rome, which had held it a crime punishable by death for a man to wear silk.

Maximian's extraordinarily rapid rise demanded that he quickly win victories or be sacked or worse. To rule, he thought it essential to inspire fear. Some people could be made examples to impress the rest. Christians as an unpopular minority ideally suited the role.

His career depended on the Theban Legion not arriving at the Channel to join Carausius. And the Thebans were already on the march northwards after wintering at Verona.

Chapter 17

Race Across the Alps

Those who like war rarely fight it and those who fight it rarely like it.

Anonymous

The headquarters unit of the Theban Legion as its rearguard was closest to Maximian's pursuing forces. The rank of its officer, Candidus, *senator militum*, suggests that it numbered about two hundred men.[1]

It was March. The legion was on the march westwards to Forum Augusta Julia (Aosta), staging area for the ascent of the Alps by the Mons Jovis, the Great St Bernard Pass of today. Beyond it, the Rhone flowed northwards through the Valais of Switzerland towards the road to the Rhine and ships to Britain. Octodurnum, atop the pass, the modern Martigny, was some 240 miles from Verona as the crow flew.

The Alps loomed higher daily as they proceeded. Ploughmen stopped in the fields to regard them. Women gazed from doorways. Mail couriers galloped by, annoying packmules and the oxen pulling the wagons. Straggling behind for many miles were relatives, peddlers, craftsmen, and wayfarers of every sort on foot or horseback, the camp followers of the legion.

Forested hillsides began to yield to rocky slopes.

The Theban route from Verona was the Via Postumia, fifteen feet wide on foundations ten feet deep drawn like a surveyor's line from Verona to Brescia. At Bergamo the road turned to the south to avoid the foothills. Heading away from that turn, the Thebans trekked north-westwards.

The towers, walls and huge parade grounds of Aosta's Roman past remain visible today. The town guarded the road winding tortuously up into the Alps. It was five days' difficult uphill march in good weather from Aosta to Martigny. From Aosta the Alps tower to the north a ruddy gold in the sunlight, a jagged mountain wall making men seem like insects on the steps of a cathedral in comparison.

Many of the Thebans had probably already reached the Rhine.

Couriers brought news of Maximian's approach with an army from the east.

The reports abruptly ceased.

Had he halted?

Or had he taken another route? For Maximian, to follow the Thebans up the narrow, steep and winding Great St Bernard Pass was inadvisable. The distance from Verona to Martigny by the Great St Bernard Pass was almost identical by way of the Mons Cimbronius (Simplon) Pass, not a paved road but a smugglers' route plagued by avalanches and ending in the Alps with no route northwards but a road westwards along the River Rhone to Martigny.

The Acts of the Thebans record nothing of the route of Maximian's advance. It can be conjectured that he took the Simplon Pass to gain time and perhaps the advantage of surprise.

A pagan historian cites his crossing the Alps in 286 in the region of the Simplon.[2]

Scattered Acts add background to the momentum of events. Alexander,[3] a centurion at Bergamo, left his post to warn Christian soldiers of an unidentified unit and of approaching danger. Whether he succeeded or not is obscure. Captured and jailed, he managed to escape only to be retaken and killed. Another brief Act relates that Domnio,[4] a high-ranking civilian of Bergamo, confronted Maximian and rebuked him for conducting a persecution. He was executed. These accounts place Maximian at Bergamo, far off the route to the Great St Bernard Pass but on the road to the Simplon Pass. They do not mention the Theban Legion.

The Act of Proculus[5] describes him as a soldier in northern Italy under Diocletian. Alerted to a messenger carrying orders for a persecution, he demanded that the courier give him the document. The messenger refused. Proculus killed him and destroyed the order. Caught by other soldiers he surrendered without a struggle and was put to death. His is the only account of a Christian soldier taking someone's life in the Roman era. Proculus' effort was apparently at least partially effective in preventing a persecution. The only other martyrs in the region besides those of Aquileia were a group led by Donatianus[6] who fled during Diocletian's reign but were trapped and died at Concordia (Venice). They were eighty in number.

Realizing that the Thebans might slip out of his grasp unless he acted urgently, presumably Maximian took a day's passage by water northwards along Lago Maggiore. From there the trail rose to Domodossola and the Simplon Pass scrambling halfway up and along the eastern slopes of a deep canyon forty-one miles to Brix. Today, a railway tunnel provides swift transport for passenger cars under the pass. The Simplon Pass was three thousand feet lower and less steep than the Great St Bernard Pass.[7] From Brix, walled in on three sides by mountains, it was forty-one miles westwards to Martigny along the turbulent white waters of the Rhone in spring flood.

For the Thebans the road from Aosta paralleled the stream of the Buthier and Drance to the village today known as Gignod. Local houses were of stone topped with log upper storeys and roofs of wooden shingle proof against deep winter snows. The road turned westwards and climbed, keeping near the brook but east of it, unlike the modern auto route. Little evidence of the Roman road survives on the southern approaches of the Great St Bernard Pass. Passing through the hamlets, today La Clusa and St Rhemy, the Thebans arrived at Etroubles, the Celtic name unchanging to the present. Here was the commencement of the steep ascent northwards, countless tight curves upwards between sheer precipices and stark drop-offs into misty valleys. The road became a trail twisting along the sole natural route available, widened in places by hammer, chisel, fire and the process of freezing water in cracks until its expansion snapped the stone.

Mules could use the trail, oxen and horses could not. The geographer Strabo called the ascent 'steep and narrow' and 'impassable for wagons'.[8] Much of the road today is tunnelled. To Romans it was essentially a military route. Anyone making the passage had to carry his own rations for a week.

Couriers brought news that *bagaudae* were hailing their chief Amandus emperor while also proclaiming another leader, Aelius. Carausius was massing a fleet at Boulogne having moved his Rhine Legio XXX Victrix to that port, utilizing merchant sea captains and barbarian Franks to bolster his forces. Thus four men, Amandus, Aelius, Carausius and Maximian, were claiming to exclusively rule Gaul. It was politics, no affair for the Thebans. Their orders were clear, to defend Britain from sea raiders.

But how would they find sea transport if Carausius had sailed away with the Rhine fleet?

The nights were bitingly cold and camping space limited. Ice sealed water buckets every dawn. The legionnaires curled up in cloaks of unwashed wool, the grease their only waterproofing. Eight men took turns sleeping in a 'butterfly', a squad tent. The scent of wool, leather, animal dung, woodsmoke and grass was the last consciousness before first light of dawn.

Trumpets sonorously blared, the sky already day but the deep valleys shadowed. Breakfast was porridge with whatever in addition a soldier had been able to purchase. The daily ceremony beginning a day's march repeated. The troops chorused three hurrahs. Trumpets blared. Mauricius ordered the army to march. There was no room for all to take part in the ritual but it did not matter. Those closest to the staff participated.

A Theban gazed in awe at the peaks above him and the first snow he had ever seen. They resumed the upward trek.

The summit of the pass was 8,082 feet high, crowned by a small lake, a temple to Jupiter and a few large stone buildings. At least eight months of the year the lake was frozen solid. The winds and unexpected blizzards at the summit were so furious that Roman engineers carved a two hundred-foot trench to escape the blasts that could send a person tumbling. Below the summit on the northern slope the Roman road, crudely paved, can still be traced by way of the hamlets of Sarraz, Liddes, Orsieres and Sambrancher to Martigny. The Roman Octodurum was divided by the Rhone. Scarcely anything survives of it.

The worst was over Thebans thought as they began the descent. Octodurum came into sight: white walls and red tile roofs set in the bend of a great valley two miles wide, mountains rising steeply to confine it. The Rhone coming from the Simplon in the east turned sharply northwards to carve a slot some thirty miles long straight to Lake Leman. From there, it was five days' march to the Rhine on good roads.

They would rest and give thanks before continuing.

It was about Easter, Sunday, 26 March of the year 286 by the calendar of the Church of Alexandria.[9] Some churches celebrated Easter on the equinox, 22 or 23 March. Others honoured the same date as Passover, which in 286 would be about 7 April. The custom was to baptize initiates at Easter. To pagans, 26 March was an unlucky, 'nefas' day, every month containing one as a holiday and day of rest.

Any oath in Latin was a *sacramentum*. Jesus had warned against oaths. Baptism was taken to be a notable exception, the carefully considered decision to reject evil, a truly free act.

Two pagan festivals overlapped in late March, the *quinquatrus*[10] of the 19th to 23rd and the *megalesia* of the 15th to 27th. The *quinquatrus* was celebrated with gladiatorial games to the death between prisoners and general merrymaking. It was the feast of many trades, including the schools and the military. In the army it involved a ritual washing of weapons and ended with the blessing of trumpets and their call to another campaign season.

The *megalesia* festival worshipped Cybele, mother of the gods, and her son and lover Attis, a self-castrated suicide in repentance for his incest. It was a Middle Eastern cult in origin. A Greek philosopher ribaldly satirized its eunuch clergy. The Christian Arnobius vilified it.[11] The *megalesia* was divided into two parts, the *tristia*, dedicated with fasts and sexual abstinence as madly dancing priests slashed their arms in sacrifice, and the *hilarias*, the masquerade and orgiastic revelry of Attis' resurrection. Typical of many cults in the era, the emphasis was upon experiencing the rawest emotions to the fullest, whether agony or ecstasy.

Attis, Herculius and Mithra were honoured as different aspects of the same deity.

The Acts specifically state that the leaders of the Theban Legion met with Maximian on the occasion of the *hilarias*. This would have coincided with the Alexandrian Easter.

The Thebans rested in the barracks of Octodurum (Martigny). Housing for each squad was a narrow two rooms, tile-roofed, the outer room holding a table, chairs and brazier with double-decker bunks in the room beyond. Windows were at a minimum. Narrow walks separated the barracks.

The legionnaires were at ease yet troubled by reports.

They celebrated Easter, renewing baptismal vows or taking them for the first time.

The sky was cottoned with clouds, snow spraying in wisps from the highest peaks. The movement of the sun cast shadow on the mountain walled north-south axis of the Rhone.

Gleams of light upon metal revealed Maximian's army advancing along the alpine valley from the direction of the rising sun.

His task force would have included detachments of a thousand men each from at least two legions, plus auxiliaries. Carausius' coins honoured detachments of two eastern legions in the West, Legio IV Flavia Pia Fidelis and VII Claudia. The symbol of the fourth legion was a radiate lion with thunderbolts in its jaws, the emblem of one of the higher ranks of the Mithraic order. In the Acts Exsuperius is described telling his comrades that they were indeed like Daniel in the lion's den.

Before Maximian's arrival, Mauricius sent most of the headquarters company on a march to the next overnight stop on the route, sixteen miles north of Martigny at Acaunus (St Maurice-en-Valais).

The monastic accounts give no year for these events but are in accord that Mauricius encountered Maximian during a campaign against the *bagaudae* when the latter was *caesar*. Maximian was *caesar* so briefly that no coins commemorate him by that title.[12] On 1 April 286 he was inaugurated with Diocletian's approval as *augustus*, his co-regent. This and the *hilarias* mentioned date events to the last week of March in 286 or possibly 1 April, April Fool's day, a lingering tradition of the madcap celebration of the *hilarias*.

The earliest Act relates that the clash to occur was occasioned by Maximian's insistence on everyone participating in a pagan rite. A version two centuries more recent states that the issue was a refusal to carry out a persecution of Christians. In either case, Maximian considered his orders to be military. Belief was a matter of indifference to officialdom. It was Christian behaviour that stirred persecution.

Mauricius had already sent most of the legion ahead into Gaul. Many Thebans had already arrived at Argentoratum (Strasbourg), the stone-walled island fortress bridged to the west bank of the Rhine. There they were welcomed by the troops who remained after their comrades had sailed to the channel with Carausius. Every hour of Maximian's delay brought the Thebans on the march closer to safety. Knowing that the Thebans might give lip service to any order, trusting to discretion when free of Maximian's presence, Maximian needed to create an occasion that might incite insubordination.

Within seven years Maximian would have his own *caesar*, Constantius Chlorus, father of the future Emperor Constantine. Whether or not

Constantius was his aide in 286, presumably there were others in the army who shared his views. A Stoic and monotheist, he cared little for rituals. He was to pursue a policy of leniency towards both *bagaudae* and Christians. Constantius bluntly gave his opinion of threatening Christians with death if they did not perform pagan rites. 'Can a man who denies his God be trusted to be loyal to his king?'[13]

Chapter 18

Martyrdom in the Mountain Valley

Courage is a kind of denial.

Anonymous

The *bagaudae* must have been a topic of conversation between Mauricius and Maximian or his officers. To campaign against them seemed questionable. Roman infantry were ill–suited to combat against hit and run tactics. To seek foes hiding in the forests covering most of Gaul would be like trying to put fleas in a sack. An unsuccessful campaign would be worse than none, an exhibition of Roman inadequacy making *bagaudae* morale soar. The rebels were divided. To attack could unite them or prompt them to join Carausius. The chief offence of the *bagaudae* was not paying taxes. Killing them would not resolve it.

The Acts agree on Mauricius' view of the *bagaudae*. They were Romans. His task was to defend them, not kill them. If it was a civil war the Thebans chose neutrality and the preservation of order.

Maximian's staff reiterated the need to crush the upstarts. Unless order was restored the towns would be without food, labour or income. Civilization would wither. There was no need to punish all the rebels. Making examples of the most vulnerable would put fear in the hearts of the rest.

Making examples of scapegoats could be counter-productive. What if they were held as heroes to be imitated in their defiance?

Every rebel to be killed had family, friends and neighbours. All but a few were peaceful or, at worst, reluctant lawbreakers ready to respond to any offer of amnesty. To kill them would antagonize loved ones.

Wars cannot be won by making enemies faster than they can be killed.

The official retort was predictable. The decision had been made. The *bagaudae* would be hunted down and killed in the public arenas to entertain and edify the mobs. The Christians among them, as the least popular, would be the preferred targets. They might escape death by burning incense before the idols. The Thebans would take part actively in the campaign. The difference between an army and a rabble like the *bagaudae* was obedience. If the Theban officers would not cooperate they would be replaced and the *bagaudae* persecuted nonetheless. There was no point in dying for principles. The dead had none. The

Theban officers had a responsibility not to put their men's lives in jeopardy foolishly. After all, the Gauls were not their people.

Some officers may have muttered warnings already obvious. Maximian needed swift victories to seal his political rise. His impatience fuelled his rage, and his rage seemed to have a dimension beyond anything normal.

Mauricius perhaps gave a nod. A commander had ample leeway to follow his own version of policy once he was in the field.

Maximian had an effective way of dealing with potential insubordination. He announced the introduction of a ceremony unheard of in Latin tradition, the *adoratio*, in Greek *proskynesis*, the Persian rite to worship the Shah-I-Shah as a living god adopted as a Roman ritual. A person was to prostrate himself face down before the ruler three times.[1] It was the rite Satan had asked of Jesus in the desert.[2]

Mauricius and his comrades must have been astonished. This was much more objectionable than the usual oath of military loyalty. No living emperor had ever been worshipped. Caligula in the first century had come close to demanding it before being murdered, but was universally regarded as an evil madman.

The Theban commander was reminded that as a soldier he must obey orders. A man's belief was his own affair. How he acted publicly was the business of the Roman state. The Thebans were on special duty assignment. Since they were not regular officers they were exempt from rituals. No matter. Everyone would perform the *adoratio*. It was only a ritual. If the Thebans thought it meaningless, all the more reason not to object to it. But if it was meaningless why demand it?

Obedience was mandatory. Men like Constantius were monotheists, yet they presumably performed the *adoratio*.

Easter and its renewal of baptismal vows was a few days past. The Acts quote Mauricius. 'We have sworn an oath to God. What good a second oath that denies the first?'[3]

Survive. Keep up appearances. Obey, those yielding to Maximian urged.

One version of the Acts states that a *decimatio* was carried out at Martigny, one in every ten men chosen at random executed. Usually, a cohort of a legion was selected for punishment, the other cohorts stoning or clubbing the victims. *Decimatio* was very rare.[4] Roman military law was severe in theory but in practice flexible. Julius Caesar, confronted by insubordination of a legion, listened to its reasonable demands, granted rest and back pay and reorganized and returned the exhausted men to duty months later. The emperors Caligula and Galba had responded with *decimatio* and did not dampen unrest but inflamed it.

Other versions make no mention of a *decimatio* at Martigny. If it happened, the names of those fallen are unknown. They may have been enlisted men, in effect held hostage to their officers.

Meanwhile, those Thebans on the march from Martigny northwards to Acaunus were relieved by the broad level valley before them, unlike the arduous ascent behind them. The cadences of the Latin hymn '*Tantum Ergo Sacramentum*', speaking of pagan and baptismal oaths, may have been borrowed from an army marching song.

> Down in adoration falling
> This great vow we hail
> Over ancient forms of worship
> Newer rites of grace prevail.
> Faith will tell us Christ is present
> When our human senses fail.
>
> To the everlasting Father
> And the Son who made us free
> And the Spirit, God proceeding
> From them each eternally
> Be salvation, honour, blessing
> Might and endless majesty.

To be free was an ironic word in a society in which citizens and slaves were hardly distinguishable in degradation.

Maximian's troops were recovering groggily from days of loud, falling-down-drunk celebration. The troopers probably knew little of the Thebans. It was of no importance to them. They did what they were told. Meanwhile, they suffered the exquisite inconvenience of arising from hangovers to resume the march after days of rest that had made them conscious of every sore and aching muscle they possessed.

In ugly mood, some were ready to take out their frustrations on a scapegoat.

The following morning, Mauricius accompanied Maximian's troops on the march to Acaunus where the Theban headquarters unit awaited them. In Celtic, Acaunus was 'the place of the cliffs' where the precipices to east and west hundreds of feet high stretching some thirty miles parallel to the Rhone came to within a few hundred feet of that swollen creek roaring with melted snow. The site had a slight slope with only a few inches of topsoil above rubble. The Thebans were encamped between the western cliffs and the Rhone, a suitable site for defence. They were a half-mile to the south of the small village and customs station. Above them, a waterfall plummeted down a boulder-strewn gorge, the only break in the wall of cliffs for a day's march in either direction. The steep gorge gave access to the alpine meadows and trails above and escape. It was the season that herds were driven into the uplands.

Maximian's force halted across the Rhone a few hundred feet from the Thebans. The Thebans knew that every minute that they delayed bought distance and safety for comrades to the north and the opportunity for some to escape up the gorge behind them.

Maximian's troops began erecting a wooden platform and a stone altar within sight of the Thebans. Traditionally, the altar would be buried on the spot after the ceremonies were completed. Archaeology may yet yield this 'altar of demons' as the Acts describe it. The hammers of carpenters and stonemasons rang clearly in the mountain air, ticking away moments of dwindling life to the Thebans.

Exsuperius rallied the men around the standards and exhorted them like a commander appealing to his unit before battle. Facing them was a long line of painted leather and wood shields of Maximian's troops, beyond bowshot across the Rhone.

There was a stir as the shieldwall parted and Mauricius appeared, wading his horse through waters white with limestone dust. His grim face was ominous.

If he feared that some might violate their baptismal oaths, Mauricius may have feared more that they would respond as they had been trained, with violence in self-defence, taking a bloody toll of their opponents while retreating up the gorge. As a Roman officer and a Christian he did not want that. Regardless of the military oath, he was loyal. He wanted to de-escalate potential violence.

The Acts describe Mauricius removing his armour and weapons and ordering his men to do likewise. It was the time of the opening of the campaign season celebrated with a *lustrum*, a ritual washing of equipment.[5] The *armalustrum*, closing the season in autumn, was a religious ceremony not dedicated to any specific god but to heaven and peace and the keeping of all vows, contracts and treaties. It was a public assurance to foes that they need fear no attack during winter nor were they justified in launching one. Ritual washings were common on occasions of epidemic disease, panic, impiety, unusual runs of bad luck, or the presence of anything regarded as unjust or unholy. Pilate washing his hands at the trial of Jesus was presiding as a priest-official at a *lustrum*. To a truly devout pagan it was sacrilege to attack self-disarmed men at a *lustrum*.

The occasion was the Thebans' second *lustrum*, the beginning of their second campaign season.[6]

The Acts do not specify a *lustrum* but can be taken to imply some such act. It bought time and lessened the chances of a pitched battle.

Mauricius gathered his men around him and shouted for all, including Maximian's formation, to hear. The speech written three centuries later in the Acts is a monk's idea of what he said.

'To oppose any foe whatsoever we offer our hands, which we hold it impious to stain with the blood of the innocent. Our right hands know how to fight against wicked men and enemies; they do not know how to cut to pieces righteous men and fellow citizens. We remember we took up arms on behalf of the citizens rather than against citizens. We have always fought on behalf of justice, on behalf of the safety of the innocent; up to the present time this has been the reward of our dangers. We have fought on behalf of the faith; and how are we to keep our faith towards you – the words are addressed to the emperor – if we do not show forth faith to God?'

Within hearing Maximian held up his hand and shouted. 'Have you no other answer or shall you be punished?'

'We shall not defend ourselves nor shall we take an oath that violates the oath we have taken to God,' Mauricius shouted back.[7]

The Thebans did not see themselves acting in absolute self-abnegation. They held that the most essential part of their being was something godlike and caring in their humanity that they would not deny.

At the drop of Maximian's hand, horsemen and foot soldiers entered the river and struggled across the swift cold creek, knee deep, ready targets for bowmen.

Emerging from the stream, the legionnaires strode between the lines of the Thebans. There was silence.

An officer, sword drawn, walked down a line, halted, and gestured. Suddenly, the Theban before him was seized from behind and dragged off and bound. He paced off ten men further down the line. Another was seized.

So it continued, until a file of victims stood facing the executioner attached to every legion identifiable by his horned helmet. The stone claimed to be the chopping block is preserved today in the chapel of the convent on the site open to visitors. It is stained with blood from some source.

The victims encouraged one another and sang hymns, ignoring demands that they stop. They eyed the snows of the peaks above them so alien to their faraway homeland.

The officers and men were beheaded.

The singing ceased.

The dead were stripped and tossed into a common grave in the banks of the river. The survivors were divided into groups to be sent in various directions so that weakened in numbers they would be less likely to mutiny, routine procedure in such cases.

Brass and silver gleamed and banners snapped in the wind, bearing the pungent odour of incense and smoke gusting from the altar. The troops stood ready to march. Maximian crossed the stream.

By custom, Maximian may have invited his men to take the belongings of the slain Thebans. Enlistees were poor men. But weren't these dead soldiers like themselves? Hadn't they died rather than take the lives of their executioners?

The dead were dead. What did it matter?

Maximian perhaps repeated his invitation as he walked the riverside to view the corpses. Men stepped out of the ranks to gather the goods of the fallen. Others stolidly ignored them. The superstitious believed such loot cursed. A murmur, a wordless expression rippled through the formation. If Maximian was tempted to rage he hesitated. Someone in command gestured.

Trumpets blared and the units stepped forward to begin the march. Men trudged onwards, glad to leave that place of comrades condemned without just cause.

The waters cascading down from the execution place ran red as they flowed to the Rhone and northwards like a stain pursuing the army.

And a hawk, guardian of souls in ancient Egyptian belief, soaring in spirals through mist draping the mountain heights, climbed the sun's rays as if freed of all worldly care.

Chapter 19

Against the Bagaudae

When men talk about defence, they always claim to be protecting women and children, but they never ask the women and children what they think.

Senator Patricia Schroeder

The Theban headquarters' unit had put up a successful rearguard action, enabling the main body of the legion to reach safety, perhaps some of those at Acaunus to flee and stragglers to be warned.

Otto of Freising in the twelfth century wrote that many Theban legionnaires had escaped.[1] Various Acts yield details.

Victor[2] was a veteran hoping to join the Thebans, travelling with a mule a day or two behind the rear column. Arriving at Acaunus, he learned of the massacre. Although dressed as a civilian and unrecognized as a soldier, he announced that he was a comrade of those who had fallen and was killed on the spot.

Other stragglers never arrived anywhere near Acaunus. A second Exsuperius fell at Vercelli in Italy.[3] At Fidentia near Parma on the Via Aemelia, today the Autostrada del Sol, a fifteen-year-old boy, Donnino,[4] perhaps not a Christian, overhearing the conversation of soldiers sent to seize stragglers of the Thebans, burst into a tavern and gave warning enabling a number to flee. He was soon put to the sword.

Many fled south from the Alps. Bessus[5] died at Ivrea and Innocentius at Gressonary, La Trinité. Maximus[6] was captured at Milan, Octavius,[7] Solutor and Adventor at Turin. Another Moor named Mauricius, George[8] and Tiberius fell at Pinerolo; Alverius[9] and another Sebastian at Fossano; Constantius,[10] Victor and Jofred at Saluzzo and Cherasco. Secundus,[11] a North African and dux (*campidoctor?*), was beheaded at Ventimiglia near Monaco on the Rivera.

Others fled northwards deeper into Switzerland. Martinianus[12] was intercepted and executed at Vils near Sion; Nicasius[13] fell at Schlotz; Felix[14] and his sister Regula were martyred near Zurich; and a Victor and Ursus were killed at Solothurn. Placidius[15] either met his death or his relics were buried at Einsiedeln.

Critics of the Theban Legion's historicity point out that the fourth century church historian Eusebius cites no persecution in the West from 260 to 303. Innumerable acts of military martyrs challenge this. Eusebius perhaps classified

124 Lost Legion Rediscovered

executions for disobeying military orders not persecution per se. He never visited the West. He sought to avoid antagonizing Christian emperors with examples of insubordination by military martyrs, yet had a deep aversion to armed violence even when heroic and defensive. Eusebius nevertheless enigmatically wrote that 'From Egypt at this time some went off to other cities and provinces where they showed their worth by martyrdom. At any rate we know those of them who became shining lights in Palestine, and we know of those at Tyre in Phoenicia...'[16] He describes these martyrs as all young men in prime physical condition. It is puzzling who could these Egyptians be if not soldiers, since natives were not permitted to leave Egypt. Eusebius clearly acknowledged that there were Egyptian martyrs outside of Egypt, Palestine and Phoenicia. Of those killed in Palestine and Phoenicia he gave no details.

Eusebius was Bishop of Caesarea in the Holy Land. A brief church record by another author cites an entire cohort of soldiers led by Nicostratus, a tribune, martyred in that city. Some Church leaders were embarrassed by the martyrs they survived.

All records of Maximian's decrees were to be destroyed by imperial order in 310.[17] His hired propagandist, Mamertinus, speaking of 286, makes no mention of the Thebans, military insubordination or even Carausius, but directly admits omitting many happenings. Of the *bagaudae*, he related that 'Ignorant rustics aspired to soldierly ways, ploughman aped infantryman, the farmer imitated the barbarian enemy and wasted his own land. I pass in haste over that episode, I see that your [Maximian's] goodwill prefers to forget that victory rather than glory in it.'[18] Elsewhere, he remarks 'I pass over your innumerable battles and victories in all the Gauls. What speech could suffice for exploits so many and great?'[19] All the Gauls would include Sequania, Narbonensis, Aquitania, Lugdunensis, Belgica and Germania, the western Rhine Valley. To move efficiently through all these districts from the Alps would have required a clockwise route.

The overlapping sites of martyrs and hoards dated by their most recently minted coin trace the path of Maximian's army after Acaunus.

He detoured. Instead of advancing to Argentoratum (Strasbourg), the nearest legionary fortress on the Rhine, he swerved north-westwards, crossing Lake Leman to Nyon. Many coin hoards have been found near Nyon from 286.[20] There fell some forty martyrs, among them Zoticus,[21] Dinocus, Aquilinus and the women Julia and Ninnita. Their Acts make no mention of the Thebans but no Christian community is known to have existed in the Alps in the era.

From Nyon, Maximian sent a flying column to the great bend of the River Loire in central Gaul near Orleans to secure the area. Another column headed towards Paris, the *bagaudae* stronghold. Viator[22] and Amor, two Theban legionnaires, fell on this path in Cevennes in the foothills of the north-western Alps at the village today bearing St Amor's name. Reine or Regina[23] was killed at Alesia near Vezelay, Petrusius[24] at Nevers, Sabinianus[25] and Potentianus at Sens and Ulphus[26] at Arcis-sur-Aube, all civilians.

Maximian displayed again his genius in using routes to take his victims by surprise.

While one of his columns advanced to the north-west, Maximian followed the Rhone from Geneva southwards to the Mediterranean and Marseilles. At Vienne, two recalled Christian officers refused to serve and were executed,[27] Julianus and the tribune Ferreolus. The latter was thrown alive into a sewer; he managed to enter the Rhone, but was caught again and killed. Genesius,[28] a retired soldier and official scribe at Arles, was ordered to copy a decree of persecution. He refused, tore up the original and had almost swum to freedom across the Rhone until struck by arrows. At Nimes, Baudelius[29] fell. At Cannes the bishop Amandus of Noyon[30] in the Rhone Valley was put to death with three priests in another bishop's territory. Bishops had no jurisdiction outside their district and there was never a council of bishops at Cannes. Amandus was presumably fleeing the army of Maximian.

Still another soldier with the name Victor,[31] first names are all that are recorded in the Acts, is specifically cited as a Theban fugitive in Marseilles. When the army he had fled arrived in that city he disclosed his identify by shattering a sculptor's image of Maximian. Jailed, his guards Adrianus and Felix refused to torture or kill him and the three were executed. Defendens[32] and an uncertain number of comrades described as Theban legionnaires were executed in the outskirts of Marseilles.

Coin hoards of the era dot the way from Nyon to Marseilles. Scholars have theorized that these were the results of massive barbarian raids, but there is no evidence whatever to support this. A barbarian raid down the Rhone would have been reckless, the area populous, prosperous and protected by a garrison at Lyons.

No hoards are found in south-western France for 286 but a considerable number of martyrs. The absence of coin caches along the Garonne to the Atlantic suggests that Maximian's forces at this point were travelling by river with no need and less opportunity to pillage. Florentia[33] died at Beziers, Luperculus at Eauze and Foi, Alberta and Caprasius at Agen,[34] all in the valley of the Garonne. Two young Gallic chiefs and sea captains, Donatianus and Carolus,[35] the sort supporting Carausius, were speared by Maximian's men at Nantes.

Continuing from the Garonne to the Atlantic, troops ascended the Loire as far as navigable to Orleans and disembarked to march to Paris. Ionius was killed at Chartres on the way.[36] As Maximian linked up with his cavalry from Nyon, *bagaudae* resistance evaporated. The sweep became two columns moving clockwise across northern Gaul, the outermost led by Rictovarus, a persecutor mentioned in at least six separate Acts.[37] His title of *praefectus* instead of *vicarius* shows that he was a cavalry leader, the persecution not by civil officials but part of a military campaign. Rictovarus meant 'twisted smile', a unique cognomen symptomatic of lead poisoning.

A father and son, Justus[38] and Justinus, having fled Paris, were intercepted and cut down a day's journey northwards. Lucian,[39] Maximian and Julian fell at Beauvais. Achius and Acheolius, Fuscian[40] and Victoricus, all priests sent to the Morini, the Celtic tribe of the Saxon shore on the continental side of the Channel, died at Amiens. Achius or Askius was a Nilotic Black name, Acheolius probably a kinsman. Fuscian, literally, was the 'swarthy or dark olive complexioned' and Gentian who was executed with him, 'the very dark man'.

Many African priests and two Armenian bishops were martyrs in northern Gaul in 286 or 287. None are known from any other time in Gaul's history. The priest whose life was saved in Britain by that land's first martyr, Albanus,[41] probably belonged to this same missionary group, entering the area in which the Theban Legion had been posted. Alban became a patron saint of soldiers, although his Act makes clear that he was a civilian and not necessarily a Christian.

Maximian's inner column crossed overland between the Seine, Oise, Aisne and Vesle, pathfinding a trail of atrocities. Crispin[42] and Crispinian, nobles who had fled land and high rank to become shoemakers, the rejection of caste typical of *bagaudae*, fell at Soissons. The woman Macra[43] with Maurus, Timothy, Apollinaris and dozens of others, were publicly tortured to death at Reims. Two officers of Maximian's bodyguard, Rufinus[44] and Valerius, disgusted, refused to obey their orders. They acknowledged their Christianity and were beheaded.

Maximian's propagandist states that he arrived in Trier (Germany), the capital of Belgic Gaul, on the Moselle tributary of the Rhine on New Year's day in 287. In that city, in 1072, excavations to enlarge its oldest church unearthed a Roman sarcophagus used as a common cremation grave for eleven men, the sign of a sudden disaster. A lead tablet identified them as the highest civil officials in Belgic Gaul, the proconsul Palmatius,[45] the local senators Maxentius, Constantius, Crescentius, Justinus, Leander, Alexander and Sother and the citizens or soldiers Hormisdas, Papirus, Constans and Jovianus. The tablet did not declare them martyrs nor did any Act, but directly over this tomb in the fourth century the Marien Kirche, later a shrine within the present cathedral of St Paulinus, was built. By the early eighth century the Theban *duces* Bonifatius and Thyrsus[46] were honoured there. No Act survives, if it ever existed, but many documents of local history were lost in the repeated Viking raids on Trier in the tenth century.

Church law required that altars contain martyrs' relics or be built over their graves. That the tablet destroyed in the Reformation was non-committal as to religion, neither pagan nor Christian, and lacked family names was typical of

Christian epitaphs in the age of persecution. All eleven may not have been Christian but they shared the same politics. The claim that hundreds of Thebans fell at Trier arose from the medieval unearthing of the Roman military cemetery under the cathedral and the presumption that all in it were martyrs.

Findings at Trier suggest a change in the popular view of Christians. In the second century they had been despised as foreigners, Jewish and Greek craftsmen and merchants with stubborn alien ways annoying to the natives of Gaul. Many were killed at Lyons in 177 in a persecution incited by popular hatred.[47] By 286, they were admired for defying the state while others feared to do so.

Maximian's propagandist boasted that the *bagaudae* campaign ended with a policy of mercy. The anonymous author of *De Rebus Bellicis* wrote that many harsh and corrupt officials were removed from office in order to check the motivation for revolt.[48]

Within a year of the deaths at Acaunus, the persecutor had yielded to the policy his victims had prescribed.

The first of the seven feats given to the mythical Herculius was to destroy the leaders of Thebes, Egypt. The second task was to kill the African monster Gereon. Gereon was a Theban martyr at Cologne, where the Gereon Kirche remains a landmark. A propagandist hailed Maximian for crushing foes 'like Gereon' in 286.[49] Is this coincidence or was the persecutor attempting to act out the myths of his namesake Herculius?

The roster of imperial offices, civil and military, the *Notitia Dignitatum*, shows two legions in every frontier province.[50] The Saxon Shore, *Litus Saxonicum*, is singular, not plural. The army list of the fourth century affirms about 12,000 troops on the Channel, the strength of two legions divided between Britain and Gaul.

A legionnaire's grave discovered in 1914 at Dachstein, ten miles from Strasbourg near the Rhine, contained the skeleton of a lanky, long-skulled Middle Easterner or Nilotic Black.[51] The grave was roofed with tiles inscribed with the name of an otherwise unknown Legion XII Victrix. The only other legion numbered XII was the XII Fulminata of Cappadocia and Armenia, the one legion in the army held Christian by Christian writers by the end of the second century. The Acts cite the Armenian bishops John and Chrysolius[52] killed in northern Gaul about 287. Is this mere coincidence or were they accompanying Christian Armenian soldiers of Legio XII Victrix, the unit probably intended to be partner of the Theban Legion? Why Maximian took a detour of many months and miles to arrive at the Rhine when he was less than a week's march away from it at Acaunus can be deduced.

Maximian's route clockwise from Lake Leman around Gaul scrupulously avoided Strasbourg, the closest legionary fort on the Rhine to Acaunus. Of the

Roman legionary stations on the Rhine, only Strasbourg suffered no martyrs in the era. If Strasbourg held not only its garrison, Legio XIII Augusta, but also survivors of the Theban Legion and those of a predominantly Christian Legio XII Victrix, the detour is explained. Of the four legionary fortresses on the Rhine, at Mainz the officer Ferrutius illegally quit the army and was executed.[53] Further north at Cologne, fifty Theban legionnaires led by Gereon are honoured.[54] At Xanten, a corruption of *Ad Sanctas*, 'place of the saints,' Thyrsus, Mallosus and Victor perished.[55]

But what of the majority of Thebans, those who survived?

Chapter 20

The Sea King

Rank brings on honour to a man; a man must bring honour to his rank.

Machiavelli

In 287, Maximian, utilizing auxiliary rather than the local legionary forces, drove back the barbaric hordes crossing the Rhine near Strasbourg.[1] A year later, confronted with Frankish invasions prompted by the absence of the legion in the hands of Carausius, Maximian for the first time in Roman history permitted the invaders to remain on Roman soil as armed allies under their Germanic King Gennobaudes.[2] A century and a half later this Frankish presence would determine the fate of Gaul.

Judging from their absence on coinage honouring each of the many legions he claimed loyal to him, neither XII Victrix nor the Theban Legion was under Carausius' command in Britain.

On the Gallic side of the Channel, Carausius had the support of a '*cunei militum peregrinorum interclusis*',[3] an isolated, cut-off or blockaded unit of men not citizens. A *cuneus* was a wedge-shaped battle formation typical of archers. Legally resident aliens, *peregrini* were allowed in Legio Julia Alexandriana, and perhaps other fleet units as well. Carausius also recruited barbarian Frisians, Saxons and Gallic merchants. Both Carausius and Maximian were using the Franks and being manipulated by them.

Carausius' continental holdings were Rouen on the Seine and Boulogne on the Channel. Between 286 and 287, Maximian made a sweep behind the coast in which soldiers from an unidentified unit were martyred, the leader of their group, Terentianus, falling at Douai.[4] The priest Quentin[5] was killed near the town today bearing his name, the Armenian bishop Chrysolius at Tournai. At Xanten, Carausius' headquarters was abandoned when he sailed away to Britain with its troops. The tomb of Mallosus[6] and Victor uncovered beneath St Victor Kirche in the 1930s contained two male skeletons of an age to be father and son. Hacking cuts on the bones of the upper body suggest that both had been sitting at a table when attacked. The elder had worn a soldier's-style cloak. As at Trier and Cologne, Xanten honours hundreds of unnamed military martyrs. Their cathedrals were built over army cemeteries and all the graves discovered in the Middle Ages deemed those of martyrs.

An inscription at Bonn speaks of unnamed martyrs buried there but the precise location of the tombs of Cassius and Florentius remain undiscovered.

A major find of Alexandrian coins from this period was found on Guernsey in the 1930s.[7] A few single imperial coins from the era have been found in Iceland, suggesting that sailors aware of the impending conflict detoured to wait out the struggle.[8]

A medieval chronicle has it that Carausius' fleet arrived near the Scottish border. Enlisting barbarian Picts and Scots, he marched southwards and clashed with the forces of the governor of Britain, Bassianus. Part of the governor's army withdrew without a fight. His opponent dead, Carausius occupied the Saxon Shore forts on the coast and based his fleet at what is today Southampton opposite the Isle of Wight.

Maximian, deprived of the Channel coast by Carausius, was forced to hastily build and man a new fleet on the tributaries of the Rhine to send against Britain. In spring 289, with ill-trained crews commanded by army officers, they set sail.

In the ancient world, naval battles on the high seas were too unpredictable to be risked. The strategy was to trap the enemy close to shore, ideally by an ambush in a strait between an island and the coast from which the foe could not readily break out. The Isle of Wight amply suited the scenario.

Except for stating that they encountered bad weather, Maximian's propagandist is silent concerning the armada's fate. Carausius' coins honour no victory but he consistently posed not as an enemy but a colleague of Diocletian and Maximian and honoured them on his coins. Nevertheless, his Southampton mint in 289 added to the legions on his coins the IV Flavia Felix,[9] a Balkan legion. The invasion was a disaster, some of its ships, storm tossed and handled by inexperienced crews, apparently landing in Britain only to surrender.

Diocletian was not pleased with Carausius' continued resistance nor overjoyed at the yielding of Roman soil to the Frankish chief Gennobaudes. A Roman writer remarked that the Franks 'laugh at treaties broken'. In late 289, Maximian was temporarily stripped of his consular title as demonstrated by coinage.[10] Numerous hoards buried in 289 across a wide area of northern Gaul suggest that he had suffered a defeat, massive desertions or a widescale and almost unopposed wave of Germanic intrusions in one of the 'greatest unrecorded battles in history' according to a British scholar.[11] Whatever the case, the morale of his followers had plummeted.

Summoned to meet Diocletian in Milan in the winter of 289–90, Maximian accepted an uneasy truce with Carausius who busied himself reinforcing his foothold on the continent at Boulogne. Deciding that the task of ruling the Empire was too much for two rulers, Diocletian appointed an assistant to each *augustus*. On 1 March 293, he titled Galerius *caesar* or viceroy in the East and Maximian's aide Constantius viceroy in the West[12] Each was compelled to divorce his wife and marry the daughter of his *augustus* to ensure loyalty and heirs to the throne.

Constantius had met his first wife Helena on an eastern campaign.[13] Tradition has it that she was an innkeeper's daughter. He was derided for having married far beneath his station.

Constantine, his only child by Helena, would transform the Roman and Christian worlds. Divorced, Helena and her son would be palace prisoners for many years to come, hostages to Constantius' love and loyalty. Maximian remained at Trier with Helena and her child while Constantius carefully planned the campaign against Carausius.

Besieging Boulogne by land, Constantius blockaded it from the sea by constructing a jetty of moored boats, barges and piles. He steadfastly tightened the siege as food within the port dwindled. Implacable yet generous in the terms he offered, Constantius won the surrender of Boulogne with minimum of bloodshed. The troops captured were asked to prove their trust by liberating the area between the Scheldt and the Rhine taken by the Franks. These were probably the isolated *peregrini* mentioned by Maximian's propagandist. Otto of Freising's mention of Theban martyrs at Bonn possibly referred to Boulogne, both cities are Bonnonia in Latin.

Maximian was at Cologne when he heard of his son-in-law's victory. Acts declare that in response he executed fifty Moorish soldiers of the Theban Legion led by Gereon and a short time later others led by Gregory the Moor 'returned from the expedition against the Morini', the Celts of the Channel, i.e. the siege of Boulogne.[14]

Some 318 Thebans and sixty additional Moors are honoured as martyrs at Cologne,[15] again probably a fallacious presumption based on the legionary cemeteries under several of the earliest churches. Gregory of Tours in the sixth century mentioned only a group of fifty military martyrs at Cologne. A gravestone of the same century in St Gereon Kirche is inscribed 'near the martyrs'. The crematory sarcophagus presently exhibited bearing the inscription that it contains the remains of fifty Theban legionnaires, opened in 1869, held only the remains of bolts of expensive medieval cloth.

In the middle ages, a common grave was discovered deep under the Cologne cathedral with a stone inscribed X I V.M., eleven virgin martyrs. The M was nevertheless taken as the abbreviation for mille, a thousand, and a fantastic cult arose venerating a supposed 11,000 virgin martyrs 'maidens and princesses from many lands'.[16] Somehow, an Ursula was postulated to be their leader and they were assumed family members of the Theban legionnaires, their chaplain the Armenian bishop John.

The year after the fall of Boulogne, Carausius was assassinated by his treasurer, Allectus, in Britain. The eighteenth century historian William

Stukeley would describe the find about 1751 of a large hoard of Carausian coins in a burial containing several bodies at Amersham in Buckinghamshire. He added that 'the people here have a notion that Carausius was slain near this place in a field called Caversfield, about 4 miles from Newport.'[17]

At Penmachno in Cornwall a cairn tomb, an unusual Celtic archaism from the Roman period, exists with the Latin inscription that it is the burial place of Carausius.[18] The only two instances of this name known are of the Roman admiral and whoever was interred in this tomb.

The Penmachno tomb is Christian. The martyrdoms in Britain in the era, Alban and Aaron and Julius, are attested to by the Anglo–Saxon writer Bede. Thereafter, Britain escaped persecution. Carausius sought to conciliate, not antagonize. He was not a persecutor.

Constantius had taken three years to systematically organize, build ships and train his men for the reconquest of Britain. The invasion plan was simple to avoid confusion yet draw the defenders away from the main landing. Asclepiodotus, unusual in being a Greek given Roman command, a sign of change in policy, sailed from the Seine to southern Britain, while Constantius led a diversion to the north in 296.[19]

As ships crept across the tossing Channel, the invaders were wary of being spotted by the leather–hulled skiffs with sails down and a lookout at the masthead used as scouts by the Channel fleet. Constantius' anxiety was eased by a low fog concealing their approach. If scouts noticed them, their signals were lost in the mist.

Asclepiodotus' troops landed, burned their ships and marched on London. Allectus dropped his efforts to counter Constantius' landing and hastily set out for London with a horde of barbarian mercenaries. Encountering Asclepiodotus, he made no attempt to pull his troops together, use prepared defences or deploy and await reinforcements, but plunged headlong into battle. His army shattered upon the disciplined ranks of the reconquerors who had few casualties. Allectus' Celts fled but his Franks fought to the death. His body was found on the field. Constantius arrived in London in time to stop it from being looted and burned by leaderless bands of Allectus' hirelings.

In the 1920s, construction on the Thames embankment revealed a Roman vessel struck by several large stones hurled by catapults and burned to the waterline, dated by coins aboard to Constantius' liberation of London.[20] In the 1930s, a hoard found near Arras on the French Channel coast included a magnificent gold medallion issued by Constantius to commemorate the saving of London.

Britain was part of the Empire once more.

And the survivors of the Theban Legion, far from vanishing, had been given the most prestigious task in the army by the very men who had persecuted them.

Who else could they trust not to assassinate them?

Chapter 21

Cure Worse than the Illness

From his mouth came a two edged sword ready to smite the nations.
Revelations 19:15

Diocletian was determined to reorganize the army.[1] The legions with their six thousand heavy infantry were too cumbersome to deal with guerrilla warfare by barbarian invaders. Auxiliary cohorts of five hundred men on too many occasions had been overrun. A political motive was involved as well. The legions repeatedly had used their strength to overthrow the throne. Therefore, Diocletian formed many new-style legions, each of one thousand men.[2]

The army was divided into two types of units by Diocletian's reforms: the *numeri*, local defence forces, and the field army that actively moved about the Empire's frontier, the *comitati*. The word literally meant those who ate together, i.e., live in barracks, ancestor to the word 'committee'. The changes were flawed. The *numeri* would tend to be lax, reluctant to defend any area other than their locale. Many units were each of one ethnic group. The previous system had integrated legionnaires of every ethnic origin, transferring them repeatedly to units throughout the Empire. This had inspired an imperial loyalty and high morale. The new policy undermined it.

One of the strongest arguments against the truth of the legend of the Theban Legion was that Roman authorities would not have annihilated an entire old-style legion. The Acts are quite clear that the Thebans numbered about six thousand.

Voltaire in the eighteenth century believed the legend of the Theban Legion to be nonsense. He knew nothing, apparently, of the surviving Roman army list, the *Notitia Dignitatum*.

The *Notitia Dignitatum* lists hundreds of units with their duty stations and their individual shields. It records four Legio Thebeorum.[3] Three are the only legions bearing the names of Diocletian and his viceroys, the I Maximiana Thebeorum,[4] II Flavia Constantia Thebeorum[5] and III Diocletiana Thebeorum.[6] Their consecutive listing and numbering gives evidence that they were a series.

The Act of Maximilian describes him as the son of a centurion, and therefore eligible to directly enter the army as an officer. Diocletian's new policy demanded that he enter the army. In 295, in North Africa, he was brought before a judge for refusing military service. The pagan official is depicted as not hostile to the youth's Christianity but anxious to save Maximilian's life. Maximilian had tossed away his military seal, the lead identification tag worn around the neck. He refers to another seal, undoubtedly his baptism. He was to be an officer and therefore required to take the military oath.

'I will not accept the seal,' he replied. 'I already have the seal of Christ who is my God.'

The judge attempted to make a strong point in rebuttal.

The proconsul Dion said: 'In the sacred bodyguard of our Lords Diocletian and Maximian, Constantius and Maximus (Galerius), there are soldiers who are Christians, and they serve.'

Maximilian replied: 'They know what is best for them. But I am a Christian and can do no wrong.'[7]

The Act of Maximilian cites the bodyguard units of the tetrarchs to be Christian. These by all logic must be the Thebeorum units cited above.

These three units must have been created with a unit later missing from the *Notitia Dignitatum* carrying the name of Galerius, the fourth tetrarch. Becoming a challenger of those succeeding to the emperor's throne, presumably his name was dropped from the unit title. Thus Legio I Flavia Constantia, which shares its shield design with II Flavia Constantia Thebeorum, was originally IV Galeriana Thebeorum.

The Theban Legion was never annihilated. Staff and enlisted men of its headquarters company were martyred and the legion reorganized into the four bodyguard units of the tetrarchs plus two other units.

Most emperors had been killed by their bodyguards. The Thebans had not used violence even in self-defence against their persecutors. The effort would have brought persecution. The worst critics of Christians never accused them of involvement in coups.

That the first of the bodyguard units was named for Maximian supports the Theban legend. Two other units have the same shield design as the I and II Flavia Constantia.[8] These are the Sagittari Nervi[9] and the Leones Seniores.[10] Both were Saxon Shore units, the Nervi composed of archers. The Leones were from Leon in Asturias, Spain. These four are the only identical shields of hundreds in the *Notitia Dignitatum*. The six together had as many men as an old-style legion. The persecutors were to trust their lives to those they persecuted.

The Swiss scholar Van Berchem has argued that the legend of the Theban Legion is false,[11] based on a misunderstanding arising from the transfer to the Alps of the cult of a Mauricius, a tribune put to death with seventy of his men at Apameia, (Homs) Syria, when Galerius passed through that town on a campaign versus Persia. This must have been in 297. But Mauricius of Apameia[12] and his

The Shields of the Six Smaller Units Formed from the Original Theban Legion

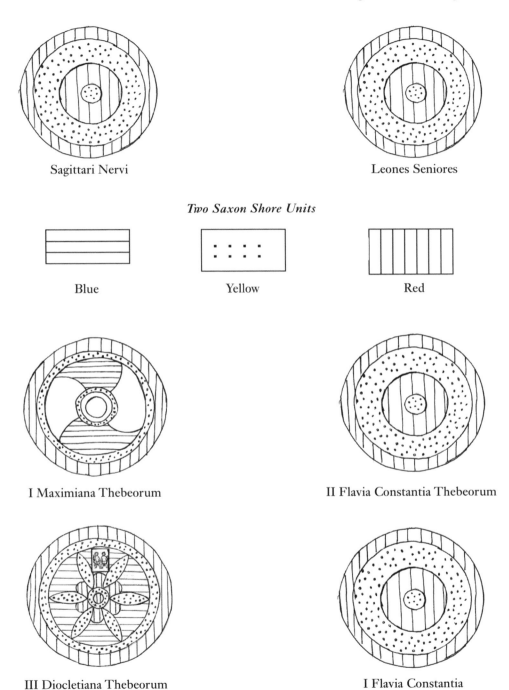

Sagittari Nervi

Leones Seniores

Two Saxon Shore Units

Blue

Yellow

Red

I Maximiana Thebeorum

II Flavia Constantia Thebeorum

III Diocletiana Thebeorum

I Flavia Constantia
(IV Galeriana Thebeorum)

The four Theban bodyguard units of the Tetrarchy

circle died of thirst, exposure and the bites of scorpions after being tied to palm trees. The military rank he possessed was different from that of Mauricius of Acaunus and his Act makes no mention of Thebans. Moreover, the names of the officers accompanying him are entirely different than those of the Thebans at Acaunus. His son was crucified, an event not in the Theban legend.[13]

Galerius began his eastern campaign with his forces caught while crossing the Euphrates and the vanguard badly mauled. Diocletian was so annoyed that he had Galerius run alongside his chariot in humiliation before the army. Galerius was a former wagon driver with a vocabulary suited to the task. Massive and red faced, he had a short temper and a brooding hostility towards those who offended him.[14]

On this campaign against Persia the emperor employed a troop of barbarian cavalry, Sarmatians and Slavs from the great plains north of the Black Sea. The two chief officers of this unit, the Schola Gentilum, the 'band of foreigners', were Sergius and Bacchus.[15] They had the rare honour of being 'friends of *caesar*', a legal rank that allowed them to initiate conversation with the emperor. To Diocletian's dismay, he discovered that both were Christians who refused to worship the idols or take the military oath. Their punishment was to be dressed in women's clothes and forced to run for many miles alongside Galerius' chariot. Thereafter, one was beheaded and the other clubbed to death.

A manuscript by Coptic Christians, the so-called cycle of Basilides,[16] describes events of these years that are not found in Latin and Greek accounts. Not translated until the twentieth century, it has the appearances of a romantic novel, with Basilides the kinsman or friend of the many individual martyrs in the tale. It contains no claims of the miraculous and emphasizes Christian military insubordination and international policy independent of both the Roman and Persian imperial governments. This may have made it an embarrassment to churchmen under Christian emperors, if they knew of it.

After a successful Persian campaign about late 297, Galerius returned to Antioch with hostages. According to the Coptic account, he discovered officers openly preaching Christianity to their troops. A Persian prince, Nicomedes,[17] a hostage allowed to reside at the home of the archbiship of Antioch, escaped. Another hostage, the general Banikarous, had been baptized.

Diocletian demanded that his officers worship the idols. Claudius the Stratelates or general, Justus, Leontius the Syrian, Theodore the Oriental (Armenian) and Anatole the Persian refused. Anatole, a man with high-ranking relatives in the Persian Empire, had been fifteen years in the Roman army.[18] In other words, he entered in 282, the year that Probus had set his project for a Theban Legion into motion.

Hearing of this, the troops of Leontius[19] and Theodore on the River Atoush near Lake Van in the satellite realm of Armenia baptized themselves by the hundreds. Neither bishops nor clergy are mentioned in this action. Diocletian's order to evacuate Armenia in keeping with his treaty with the Shah Narses was disobeyed by these troops, who may have feared to expose Armenian Christians to Persian persecution. Diocletian was moving to declaring Christianity illegal but Armenia as a satellite kingdom, strictly speaking, was not within his Empire.

Diocletian was readily convinced at this point that Armenian nationalists and Christians were conspiring against him. He was aided in this view by the staff officer Veturius[20] and the neo-platonist philosopher Theotecnus[21] whose writings provided the ideological justification for persecution that appealed to Diocletian's intellectual bent.

Eusebius states that a plan was conceived to purge the army of Christians.[22] All were offered immediate discharge, apparently with no loss of pension or veterans' privileges. Those remaining were demoted. None were allowed to be officers. Considering that there may have been pagans glad to receive early discharge before their twenty-five years were completed, this policy could appear to reward Christians for being undesirables. It was a deceit in order to attack those released once they were disarmed and unorganized.

About 298 the troops of Leontius and Andrew in Armenia, according to the Coptic accounts, were no longer invited to retire but ordered to do so. Galerius was instructed to kill them when they arrived on Roman soil. Himes[23] and Philkiades, kinsmen of some of these murdered dischargees, in revenge pulled Diocletian from his horse as he rode through the streets of a town and were killed. For Diocletian, this was full justification for persecution. At Antioch, 2,000 troops led by Fasilidas (Basilides)[24] and 900 led by Anderuna (Andrew) were martyred. Martyr in Greek literally meant witness. Those who survived loss of property, demotion, jail or torture were considered living 'white' martyrs. Not every martyr was necessarily executed. In Cappadocia, Agapitus[25] legally quit the army and was harassed and imprisoned. He survived to become a bishop and die a natural death. Gordius[26] and Seleucus, likewise, retired but their bold admission of faith incurred their executions.

The most famous of soldier saints is George. Miracles and deaths by hideous tortures and as many resurrections abound in the Coptic narratives regarding him, tales that make his dragon-killing pale in comparison. He is not in the Basilides cycle. George's fantasies in 485 were formally condemned by Pope Gelasius and a council of bishops as 'false and unedifying'.[27] Sifting through the Coptic account, objective data are to be found, nonetheless, which stand out from the lurid material, suggesting the hand of a different writer than the pious fantasist. George is declared to have been the son of Anastasius, governor of Melitene, Cappadocia. The account makes no mention of it but this was headquarters of Legio XII Fulminata, the 'Christian legion'. His grandfather had been John, governor of Cappadocia. Justus, the new governor and father of

George's fiancée, appointed him commander of 5,000 men, presumably Legio XII Fulminata. Upon Justus' death, George went to Tyre to ask to be confirmed in his father's rank. Possibly he was seeking a civilian rank in order to evade the army purge of Christians not yet extended to civil offices.

Arriving at Tyre, George found Dadianus (Tatian?) and his officers worshipping Apollo. He left, distributed his goods among the poor, released all but his closest servants and returned to confront Dadianus. Refusing to honour the gods, he was tortured and killed. Some 3,000 of his soldiers were martyrs, either 'red' and executed or 'white', harassed but surviving. Eusebius stated that outright revolt broke out at Melitene under Diocletian's persecution, the only revolt by Christians he records.[28] He gives no details, consistently ignoring the military martyrs.

The effort to oust Christians from the army in its treachery encouraged Christians who were secretly in the army to remain.

Soldiers directly refusing idolatry were not offered an option to quit. In Spain at Leon, the fortress that had sent troops to the Leones Seniores associated by its shield with the Theban Legion, the centurion Marcellus[29] had been baptized with all his family. Possibly he was a veteran who was later recalled. Sent to Tangiers, North Africa, and a detachment of II Traiana, he refused the military oath. The governor ignored it. In October of 298, in the presence of visiting high officials on the anniversary of Maximian's birth, he refused to sacrifice to Hercules and threw down the belt that was the symbol of his office. He was beheaded. Later in Spain more than ten of his sons or godsons were slain.

Eusebius, without mentioning any units by title, wrote that in 298 he had encountered Constantine, the son of Constantius Chlorus, as tribune of Galerius' bodyguard in the Middle East.[30] In context of the *Acta Maximiliani* and the *Notitia Dignitatum*, this means that Constantine began his army career as an officer of survivors of the Theban Legion.

Embarking for Egypt, Diocletian took Claudius[31] and Justus and their families with him as prisoners. The Egyptian soldier Hor[32] and his brother Bhai, 'having left Antioch', were martyred at this time in Alexandria under Diocletian as was John[33], a soldier 'of the emperor's cohort', sent from Antioch. An official papyrus proves that Diocletian's bodyguard, Legio III Diocletiana Thebeorum, was present in Egypt by 300.[34]

In Egypt, Diocletian initiated his reorganization of the Roman world into a rigid totalitarianism, Egypt the property of the emperor unhindered by the Senate.

The legionnaires of Egypt sent elsewhere had been replaced by European troops to avert the army joining with the peasants in opposition to the new laws. Meanwhile, Christianity was accelerating among the population, the Bible translated into the Coptic language appearing in the decade,[35] written not on scrolls but in bound books.

As the *bagaudae* had taken to the forests and meadows in the West, in Egypt thousands of men fled into the desert to escape the increasing oppression. They became hermits and beggars called anchorites, in Greek, 'those who ran away'.[36] The Copts had been a virtual caste society for thousands of years. They had revolted on countless occasions with grim results. But revolt is not revolution. Revolution requires a change in mentality, a new philosophy. The Coptic peasantry had never had this until Christianity offered it to them.

They did not seek violence.[37] Their defiance was thrust upon them, their courage that of peaceful folk, yet it threatened to become a profound upheaval, alarming the government.

Diocletian's perspectives were military, his understanding of economics meagre. In this he was no worse than other thinkers of his day.

Many cities of the East had issued their own coinage alongside the imperial issue, competing in the value of their coinage by avoiding overproduction. Imperial abolition of these local issues in 260 provoked catastrophic inflation as the government, short of silver, debased the coinage with cheaper metal. Deliberate scarcity offered more profit than increased production amidst inflation. Farmers had less incentive to sell with buying power reduced. Estate owners established workshops on their villas to avoid the high prices of city goods as craftsmen fled the high taxes of the cities. Civilization was coming apart. The government, in repairing a system that worked, however inefficiently, was wrecking it.

Diocletian's solution was drastic. All prices and wages were fixed by the government in 303.[38] Marketplace stone walls survive inscribed with Diocletian's prices and wages. Despite the death penalty for violation, the effort quickly failed. It made some goods so underpriced that producers lowered production.

To support the enlargement of the army Diocletian introduced a new system of recruitment.[39] Previously, all soldiers were volunteers with the very rare exceptions of conscriptions in emergencies. The new system demanded landlords and villages provide draftees for the army. It should have been foreseeable that these recruits tended to be people considered good riddance.

The army's numbers increased with the crushing taxes to support them as the economy crumbled. To make matters worse, Diocletian experimented with the conscription of slaves, criminals, gladiators and prisoners of war. The effect on the morale of men of these backgrounds forced into twenty-five years' service should have been obvious but Diocletian's underlings habitually told him what they thought he wished to hear. Roman practicality had become expediency.

In Egypt, in the transition after traditional army units were withdrawn to be replaced by European units, military camps were undermanned, an invitation to revolt.

Alexandria alone had been allowed to continue issuing its own coinage despite the reforms of 260. The abolition of its coinage in 296 had the effect of a high temporary tax as the old money was exchanged for new. Many businessmen were ruined. In response, the director of Alexandria's mint, Domitius Domitianus,[40] known as Achilleus, led the city in revolt and declared himself emperor.

At the same time, farmers upriver, squeezed by landlords living in Alexandria who tried to save themselves at the expense of their tenants, also revolted. Egypt was soon in chaos. Diocletian crushed the revolt in the metropolis seven months after it began. The towns of Busiris and Coptos in southern Egypt were burned to the ground with a savagery rare in Roman warfare, which usually respected Roman towns, the very purpose and justification for Roman rule.

In the army and outside it, many oppressed people had no rallying point, common creed or trust except the Church. Political revolt was given religious ardour by Diocletian's self-defeating intolerance and persecution, yet Christian scribes would ignore any issues involved except religion. History of these events would thus be distorted for ages.

Chapter 22

Agony in Egypt

If I feed the hungry they call me a saint. If I ask why the poor are hungry, they call me a communist.

Dom Helder Camara

The purge of Christian soldiers in the Middle East presumed accomplished, Egypt's native legionary forces largely replaced by Europeans, Diocletian ordered the application of his reforms in Egypt.

The innumerable small farms on the Nile rented from the state, the lack of powerful land owners or local senates, the isolation especially of the Thebaid, and the desert-thwarting guerrilla warfare and revolt, recommended Egypt to be the first province for the new laws to be enforced.

If Roman officials had offered the peasant population a reform of landholdings, eliminating absentee landlords, which would have been readily done legally since all Egypt's farms were state owned and leased, order might have been preserved. If the lower tax rate on poorer farmland on the margins of the desert, vital to holding back the encroaching sands, had been continued, the populace might have had an incentive to obey the new laws. If the government had used the army as had Probus to improve the irrigation systems, the military might have been regarded with favour. As it was, soldiers quite unfamiliar with Egyptian villagers, without consultation or explanation, were suddenly used to enforce crushing new laws.

The Christian Church had never sought conflict with the government. *Caesar* had received from Christians the things of *caesar*. Now, the state singled out Christians as examples to be targeted in order to terrify the general population into obedience to the new laws. Egyptian villagers for ages had lived in a virtual caste system that Diocletian would make empirewide. Local Christian clergy had, in effect, replaced the representatives of the absentee landlords as village headmen, the clergy well organized and popular.

What had been religious was once again made political as in the eras of Decius and Valerian, but this time the government had a hardly hidden economic agenda that every Egyptian farmworker, Christian or pagan, had bitter reason to oppose as taxes soared.

Those in power held militarism to be superior to any effort at democracy.

As *deditici*, Egyptians were without the rights of Roman citizens.[1] Anyone breaking the new decrees would be judged, without the benefit of due process. Christians would be made priority in enforcement. Watching family and friends undergoing torture and death rather than sacrifice to the idols — and the state – Christians, presumably, would yield. Devout individuals might be willing to lose their lives but they could be broken by threatening their loved ones. From their example the pagan peasantry would learn its lesson. The leaders of the churches were removed to weaken their congregations.

The authorities were newly arrived outsiders. Colonialist prejudice influenced their mentality. They had no concept of the emotional wilfulness of the peasants they collectively aroused. The persecutors sought to focus on the middle class of the villages. Because of difficulty identifying these people, anyone who seemed a potential leader was threatened. Many a worker asked to burn incense won popular praise for the first and last occasion in his life by his refusal.

Coptic records honour 20,000 civilian martyrs in Egypt at this time.[2] These were overwhelmingly people tortured and killed, not 'white' martyrs. The peasantry had no land, wealth or rank to lose. The persecution became a frenzy for both victim and victimizer. For four thousand years of stifling repression Egyptian peasants had been denied permission to marry, travel, or assemble without the approval of those in authority. Their only refuge was religion. It had divided them, each village worshipping its own god and feuding with its neighbours. The universal creed of Serapis had countered this but it was created by and pandered to those in power. Christianity had brought populations together. Becoming illegal, it gave peasants an encouragement to defy the state.

Eusebius was an eyewitness to the torment in the Thebaid:

> But words cannot describe the outrageous agonies endured by the martyrs in the Thebaid. They were torn to bits from head to foot with broken pottery like claws till death released them. Women were tied by one foot and hoisted high in the air, head downwards, their bodies completely nude without a scrap of clothing presenting thus the most shameful, brutal and inhuman of all spectacles to everyone watching. Others again were tied to trees and stumps and died horribly; for with the aid of machines they drew together the very stoutest boughs, fastened one of the martyr's legs to each and then let the boughs fly back to their normal position. Thus they tore off the limbs of the victims in a moment. In this they continued not for a few days or weeks but year after year. Sometimes ten or more, sometimes over twenty were put to death, at other times at least thirty and yet at other times not far short of sixty. And there were occasions when on a single day a hundred men as well as women and little children were killed, condemned to a succession of ever changing tortures.

I was in these places and saw many of the executions myself. Some suffered death by beheading, others punishment by fire. So many were killed on a single day that the blunted axe, worn out by the slaughter, broke in pieces while the exhausted executioners had to be periodically relieved. All the time I observed a most wonderful eagerness and a truly divine power and enthusiasm in those who had put their trust in the Christ of God. No sooner had the first group been sentenced than others from every side would jump on the platform in front of the judge and proclaim themselves Christians. They paid no heed to torture in all its terrifying forms but undaunted spoke boldly of their devotion to the God of the universe and with joy, laughter and gaiety received the final sentence of death. They sang and sent up hymns of thanksgiving to the God of the universe till their very last breath.[3]

Eusebius makes no mention of Diocletian's totalitarian new reforms nor the insurrection that had erupted in the same area two years earlier. He would have the reader assume the martyrs completely devoid of political or social motives or involvement. How, despite twice being imprisoned, he evaded torture and death he passes over in silence. The lessons of one of the strangest conflicts in history, a civil disobedience in which all the casualties were on one side and that side refused to kill to defend itself, are obscured.

The authorities did not seem to realize that the faith was no longer that of a small minority but the total population in many villages. The colonialist authorities were undergoing a cultural shock in colliding with people united in a cause they held far greater than themselves.

Unlike Eusebius' account the Coptic accounts tell of families split asunder as spouses, siblings, parents and children denounced one another to the authorities.[4] Eusebius makes no mention of those who yielded under oppression, managed to conceal their faith without violating it, escaped into the desert or bribed their way out. Many martyrs died unrecorded as well.

Witnessing loved ones murdered often provoked not yielding but defiance the persecutors had neither foreseen nor comprehended. This fierce intractability was worsened because they were deprived of bishops, priests and deacons who might have cooled their fanaticism if not their courage.

Church leaders were not entirely united. Bishop Peter of Alexandria and Melitius of Lycopolis,[5] sharing the same cell with other clergy, seriously disagreed over the *lapsi*, those who had yielded in fear. Peter, in accord with the Bishop of Rome, favoured a reasonable leniency towards them. Melitius was adamant that the *lapsi* never be permitted to remain in the Church. Peter drew a curtain across the room and asked the prisoners to choose sides. Thereafter, the two groups refused to speak to one another. Most joined Melitius. Some Christians found it easier to die for their faith than to forgive those who refused to do so. Ironically, Melitius the firebrand survived the persecution. Peter and his fellow bishops and priests were killed. The authorities had acted in their own interest. Peter was more dangerous than Melitius, his policy of forgiveness likely to heal and increase church membership while that of Melitius would reduce it.

Of the army units for centuries on the Nile, judging from the Acts, there were some 400 military martyrs in Egypt during this period. The units of some can be deduced. Forty soldiers at Alexandaria, led by a man simply called 'the Black,'[6] were likely of Legio Julia Alexandriana or the Cohors I Apamenorum.[7] At Thmuis in the Thebaid the dux Melitius[8] and his wife Susanna and 252 men and, in a radical departure in policy, their women and children as well were slaughtered. They were Galatians and must have been from Egypt's only unit from that province, Cohors III Ulpia Galatarum. Fifty fell at Diopolis with the dux Ischyrion of the Rutilian Band.[9] Rutuli was twenty miles south of Ostia, Italy, matching well with the Cohors Scutata Civium Romanorum, Egypt's only Italian force. Forty men led by Philemon,[10] members of the Masturian Band, were of Cohors II Asturum from Asturia, Spain. Menas,[11] of Phrygian ancestry, had served in this unit and then succeeded his father as military governor of Pentapolis, west of Alexandria. Fleeing alone into the desert to escape orders to persecute, he later avowed his family faith before the audience of the circus at Alexandria. Refusing bribes, he was tortured and beheaded. Half a century earlier, Mercurius[12] had been a martyr of the Masturian Band, indicating how Christians tended to congregate in certain units. The names of eighteen other isolated military martyrs are known from eleven locales in Egypt in the era.

Arrianus,[13] the chief civil prosecutor, a lawyer by profession although the persecution flagrantly violated Roman law, found a temple afire when he arrived at Luxor. The soldiers Chanazhoun and Sophronius, non-Latin and probably baptismal names, were accused of arson, tortured and killed. The acts of martyrs neither deny nor affirm their guilt. Pagans were apprehensive that a violent reaction by Christians was beginning, with property but not persons the first target. Months later, amidst a routine day of cruelty and murder, Arrianus astonishingly announced that he would join the martyrs, in an almost gladiatorial gesture of acceptance of death. Arrested with another high-ranking prosecutor who had sickened of his role, Julius of Aqfahs,[14] they were killed at Atripe among a crowd of 1,500 doomed peasants. The victims were being made popular heroes by the cruelty of official policy.

A series of earthquakes disturbed the region not long after, omens of heaven's disfavour to pagans.

While the bloodshed was still underway the military draft was introduced. The draft was rife with contradictions. In Europe, men who had deserted their occupation to volunteer for the army were brought back to their civilian calling in chains while barbarians were recruited. In the Thebaid, Christians and pagans were conscripted. Locked in prisons every night of their procession northwards, jailers for a bribe allowed them gifts from Christians, which included pages of the New Testament recently translated into Coptic.[15] Pagan draftees found common cause with those of the faith.

Beyond Egypt at Tomi (north central Turkey), the soldiers Marcellinus and Narcissus, discovered to be Christians, were executed. Their brother Argeus was flogged and drowned for refusing to enter the army.[16] The scribe recording this took no note of the contradiction in ousting Christians from the army while drafting more. To ban Christian draftees would be to discriminate against pagans.

Many men fled into the desert of the Thebaid to escape the new regime. One of these was Pachomius[17] who, upon receiving baptism, had deserted the army or had been released in a change of policy. He introduced to his anchorite community the military-style organizational structure that would secure monasticism's development. Monk and soldier had much in common – they were celibate, disciplined and dedicated. Yet in the East, monks attracted an element that at time flocked the towns to riot, their beliefs more pagan Egyptian Gnostic and Montanist than Christian; labour, crafts and intellect were scorned. They attempted directly and mystically to reach God. Jerome who translated the Bible into Latin described monks he met in the Holy Land as 'ignorant and filthy louts'.[18]

The Thebaid was the major supplier of grain to Rome and other cities. The persecution was interfering with grain delivery. Policy was altered. The defiant were not to be killed but crippled in one leg and sent for life to the desert mines between the Nile and the Red Sea,[19] one of the hottest and most arid places on earth. Shafts unused for centuries were reopened to provide beautiful marble for Diocletian's extravagant building projects, splendours that belied the wretchedness of those who built them. The followers of the Galilean carpenter carved ankhs, the ancient Egyptian symbol of the resurrection of the blessed to eternal life on the mine walls, symbols noted by archaeologist ages later.[20] The anhk became a Christian symbol.

The massacres in the Thebaid ebbed as the officers of the army awaited further orders from the Emperor Diocletian.

Chapter 23

The Great Persecution

Religion is like a nail. The harder you pound it, the more you drive it in.
Soviet Minister of Education under Stalin

D iocletian transferred his capital from Rome to Nicomedia (today Ismid) on the eastern shore of the Dardanelles across from Byzantium (later Constantinople and Istanbul), a profound change.

A sincere pagan, Diocletian took part in many unofficial private acts of worship. Continually, Galerius, blunt and unanalytical, persuaded him of the perfidy of the Christians. Diocletian was obsessed with the need for discipline.[1] Listening to Galerius' words, he was swayed yet reflected that Galerius' advice had provoked carnage and disorder in Egypt. Galerius' response was that the persecution in Egypt was cut short before it achieved its goals. Galerius was determined to oust all Christians from the army. Despite the privilege of early retirement granted in 298, many had refused to quit the army regardless of demotion.

Increasingly, Christians in the army were baptized despite the Church's ban on baptism for soldiers. One reason was the conscription of baptized Christians.

Roman policy had been tolerant towards religions as long as their devotees worshipped the Roman gods. Few creeds had been declared illegal. One that was was Druidism with its human sacrifices. In 301, Diocletian added Manicheanism to the illegal cults.[2] The emperor may have regarded the world scorning mysticism of Mani as a new branch of Christian belief. Repeatedly, he underestimated and misunderstood the Christian position. Unknown to him, his wife and daughter were Christians, as were many of his retinue. Legend has it that his mistress, Verena, would be a martyr.

At a rite to foretell the future, the emperor was told that the omens could not be read because unbelievers were present. Later in 302, Diocletian ordered that the oracle of the temple of Apollo at Milesia be consulted in regard to Christianity. The guarded reply was taken to be hostile to the Church.[3] On the feast of the Saturnalia, 22 December 302, the emperor presided at a ceremony for the harvests dressed as the goddess Ceres. Zeno,[4] a Christian soldier of the palace guard, laughed at this transvestism in the emperor's presence. His jaw was broken and he was killed within the day.

Galerius seized the occasion. According to the pagan Eutropius, he was 'A man of excellent moral character'[5] whereas he was described by the Christian Lactantius to be 'of a savage intensity alien to the Roman character.'[6] He was convinced that persecution was for the good of the Empire but unenforceable until the army was purged. Aware of the veneration given to their relics, he mandated that the bodies and records of the martyrs be destroyed.

Moved to action, on 23 February 303 Diocletian ordered that the cathedral at Nicomedia[7], situated in full view of the palace, be demolished, the sacred books burned and any goods within the building be given to the mob.

The liturgical calendars of the Catholic and Orthodox rites honour yearly the many who died on this occasion. Christmas was first celebrated in February. Its relaxed and festive air as faithful gathered together was seen as opportune to attack them. At Nicomedia and Nicea, however, the persecutors inciting pagan mobs relented after realizing that Christians were a much larger element in the population than they had assumed.

Diocletian's edict of persecution was extended empirewide.[8] All Christians refusing to sacrifice to the gods were subject to torture and death. A few grains of incense would tip the scales of fate. Christians in civil service were fired. The faithful were forbidden to free slaves, indication from a pagan source that this was a Christian practice. All church members were denied the protection of the laws. Enemies could attack them with impunity. They were, literally, outlaws.[9] Meanwhile, soldiers impressed by the martyrs they imprisoned, Orestes at Sebaste and Victor at Chalcedon, joined them.

Euthetius,[10] a prominent and prosperous citizen of Nicomedia, tore down the posted decree and was roasted alive.

Lightning struck the palace and fires broke out repeatedly. Galerius accused Christians of arson. Several high-ranking eunuch court officials were killed for refusal to worship the idols. The empress Prisca and her daughter Valeria, Galerius' wife, were compelled to do homage.[11] On 28 April, two priests and 268 others were put to death for refusing to recant.[12] Nicetas,[13] an illegitimate son of Galerius, was among the martyrs at Nicomedia that summer.

In new decrees Diocletian ordered the arrest of all Church leaders and their torture until they worshipped the idols.[14]

Meanwhile, the purge of the army became a violent persecution. On the Danube in 292, the soldier martyr Dasius[15] died, at Dorostorum (Silistria). Christian soldiers were few and secretive on those northern borders. In 304, Julius, a veteran, and Ischius and Valentinus fell at Dorostorum, the camp of Legio XI Claudia.[16] In Austria at Lorch, the veteran Florianus[17] was drowned in the Inn after attempting to aid jailed coreligionists.

The tribune Adrianus,[18] son of the Emperor Probus, with Paternus and seventy comrades fell at Nicomedia. Fifty Moorish soldiers led by Callistratus[19] were drowned at Byzance where Acacius[20] and twelve of the palace guard were drowned five weeks later. Those drowned were tied in sacks with scorpions, snakes and dogs, the legal penalty for killing a parent. Memmon,[21] a centurion with an Egyptian name, the priest Severus and thirty-eight enlistees from Plovdiv, Thrace (now Bulgaria), were killed at Byzance the following year. On the other side of the Dardanelles, three Egyptian legionnaires, Solochon,[22] Pamphamer and Pamphalon fell. Cleonicus[23] and more than forty other soldiers and slaves were drowned on the coast of the Black Sea, north-east of the Dardanelles. Many of these soldiers may have been of the Thebeorum bodyguard of the tetrarchs.

The priest Marcus,[24] the brothers and soldiers Alphius, Alexander and Zosimus, and more than thirty comrades were cut down in southern Turkey where Azas who quit the army had evangelized 150 men led by the tribune Aquilinus[25] – all massacred. In Palestine, Nicostratus[26] and most of an unnamed cohort disappeared at Caesarea Philippi (Paneas). Possibly, these were the Egyptians martyred in Palestine mentioned by Eusebius.

Eusebius preferred to overlook these events. He briefly records that a revolt erupted in Cappodocia,[27] the home of the 'Christian legion', the XII Fulminata. A surviving Act gives some details, nonetheless. The *primicerius* Eudoxius,[28] a man with the same rank as Mauricius of Acaunus, senior officer among equals, probably commander of the Fulminata at Melitene after the aforementioned George, refused to worship the gods and cast off his identification tag. Some 1,100 of his men were martyred with him. It is improbable that all the 'Thunderstruck' Legion's men were Christians and not all 'martyrs' were killed, but officers were likely to be.

Hieron and thirty-two other men were killed at Melitene for refusing military service, apparently draftees.[29] At Antioch, Hesychius[30] tossed away his symbol of service and was drowned in the Orontes. In Syria, Laurentinus[31] and more than a thousand of his men were persecuted with the pagan governor Agrippas who disobeyed the decrees.

Judging by the Acts, at least five thousand military were persecuted in the purge. Many, no doubt, were discharged. The two Christian eyewitnesses and historians of the great persecution, Eusebius and Lactantius, certainly ignore the number of military martyred. Lactantius makes no mention of any soldier executed in it, yet cites many men drowned in the Dardanelles without noting that they were soldiers, although Coptic, Greek, Syrian and Latin Acts make it quite clear.[32] Eusebius acknowledges some military martyrs.[33]

Whatever their number, the executions must have been a grave disruption of military order, although the military martyrs under Diocletian were probably less than 2 per cent of army personnel.

Army morale was deteriorating. Battle against an enemy was one thing; to require a man to murder his comrades was something else. Could men who killed their comrades be trusted not to plot against the throne? The logic of drafting slaves, prisoners of war, criminals, gladiators, barbarians and malcontents handed over by landlords as a tax, while killing loyal soldiers whose offence was of religion alone and who were trusted to guard the tetrarchs must have eluded some patriotic pagan serviceman. How long would Christians meekly submit to torture and execution? To the faithful, incitement to violence was a sin and their patience through God's grace endless. Pagans may have thought otherwise. The purge of Christians burdened army discipline when it was more difficult than ever to maintain.

In North Africa, Fabius[34] refused to carry a military standard bearing an idol and Typasius[35], having been paid a bonus in coinage depicting a pagan deity, flung it at the feet of his officers. They were executed. At Algiers, forty soldiers led by Zoticus,[36] Rogatus, Modestus and Castelus are honoured as martyrs.

North Africa had witnessed relatively little persecution in several generations and its churches were less prepared for it than elsewhere. Many recanted or managed to buy their way out.

In North Africa, farmers accused townsmen and their bishops of having lost authority in the church by the yielding of some under persecution, ignoring that persecutors had generally ignored the country folk. This led to the Donatist sect, a political faction, finding points of theology to give ideological fuel to a feud continuing for more than a century[37] thereafter, a pattern repeated elsewhere in the Empire.

In Caesarea, Christians crowded the temples to worship the gods but in Phrygia the entire population of the town of Antandro[38] were executed for their defiant faith.

The entire East was stirring uneasily, the forces of revolt not extinguished but burning underground. Tertullian wrote that the blood of the martyrs was the seed of the church, yet thousands would die for gladiatorial games, witchcraft and banditry, yet not convert millions.

The most winning quality of the martyrs was their goodwill towards their persecutors. The Acts delineate time and again the victim wishing his victimizers well and promising to pray for them with a debonair determination.

Aggravating the tenseness in the East was the news from Armenia, that bone of contention between Rome and Persia. Its Roman-appointed King Tiradates was cooperating with the persecution as many fled to his realm from persecution discovered to their anguish. Among these was a beautiful woman, Hripsimeh,[39] whom Tiradates asked to enter his harem. Her refusal provoked her death and that of some forty other women refugees.

Tiradates was stricken with eriyspelas, his face covered with sores. His doctors of no avail, his sister pleaded with him to seek a cure from Grigor,[40] a Christian missionary he had imprisoned. Grigor was a prince of the royal family that had murdered Tiradates' father. As a young boy he had been brought to

Roman territory, where he had been raised. Cured by Grigor, who made it clear that he had no political pretensions, Tiradates asked to be baptized with most of his court. Armenia became the first officially Christian nation – if any nation can be called Christian.

The troops of Theodore and Leontius who had stayed in Armenia, despite orders to leave it, had served Rome well. During their stay, silver deposits were discovered that would be a boon to the Roman economy. If not for them, the mines might have been seized by Persia.

Continued persecution was becoming a threat to the security of the eastern frontier, the integrity and effectiveness of Legio XII Fulminata among that of units at risk.

In the autumn of 303, Diocletian voyaged to Rome to meet with Maximian. The eternal city had already undergone a baptism of blood. Some 10,000 men and women had been seized. They refused to worship the idols and were forced to labour to build the huge Baths of Diocletian standing today opposite Rome's railroad station. When it was completed, they were taken to the temple of Mars to sacrifice, offered pardon if they did so. Those refusing were killed and buried in the cemetery that bears the name of their spokesman, the tribune Zeno,[41] a site presently occupied by the Church of S. Maria Scala Coeli.

Callistratus[42] died at Rome at this time with forty of his soldiers. Another thirty troopers were killed on the Appian Way[43] and interred on the Via Labicana where ten more were executed.[44] These were probably men of the city of Rome's only legion, II Parthica. The soldiers Papias and Maurus[45] fell on the Via Nomentana. Crescentianus[46] was executed at Tifernum in Perugia after unsuccessfully fleeing there with his parents.

The government systematically destroyed everything in its power to erase from history the memory of the persecution.

Diocletian took no delight in bloodletting. His talent as an administrator made him aware that unwise laws could be counterproductive. Increasingly, he discovered that some of his favourite assistants were Christians as were members of his family, whose forced worship of the idols failed to change their inner beliefs.

Returning from Rome, Diocletian became seriously ill and for months was spasmodically delirious, probably having contracted malaria, endemic around the capital.[47] During his public appearances in the summer of 304, he was so sick as to be almost unrecognizable.

In 305, Galerius successfully pushed the ill emperor to issue the fourth and last decree of persecution. Christians were to burn incense before the idols.[48] The repetition of the previous decrees was an admission of goals unachieved.

Diocletian was emotionally as well as physically exhausted. Let others resolve the dilemmas of dealing with people who multiplied under persecution. He understood the perils of hubris. A month after the fourth decree, at a great military review near Nicomedia, he tearfully declared that he had saved civilization and was about to retire, the first emperor to do so.[49] He made Constantius *augustus*. Maximian, at Milan, begrudgingly followed his example.

Galerius, the only persecutor still wearing a crown, begged his patron to return to power. Diocletian wrote in reply, 'I wish you could go to Salona (the Adriatic seaport his retreat) to see the cabbages I have planted with my own hands. Then you would never tempt me to such an action.'[50]

Christian writers of the era consistently maintained respect for Diocletian, while believing Galerius his instigator to evil. The emperor's boast that he had saved Roman civilization was warranted. His reforms showed a masterful skill and dedication. He succeeded to a degree in his self-appointed mission of freezing the Empire into a little-changing, unprogressing yet prevailing culture in the Greek-speaking East for the next thousand years. The West was not his concern except as a barrier to barbarian invasion. He never visited it except for Italy.

A pagan recorded that Diocletian in retirement complained:

How often it is to the interest of four or five officials to combine together to deceive their sovereign. Secluded from mankind in his exalted dignity, the truth is concealed from his knowledge. He can only see with his eyes; he hears nothing but their misrepresentations. He confers the most important offices upon vice and weakness and disgraces the most virtuous and deserving among his subjects. By such arts the best and wisest of princes are sold to the venal corruption of courtiers.[51]

Galerius, scarcely literate, by decree in 305 sought to reduce all legal process to a dictatorial system, and what little media existed in manuscript publishing to be abolished.

The Christian lawyer Lactantius, unemployed as a result, describes the situation: 'Eloquence was condemned, advocates suppressed; jurists exiled or put to death; letters were regarded as the profession of malefactors and scholars were treated as enemies, crushed and execrated.'

Only Christians dared defy this, as civil administration was militarized and the military was bureaucratized. Yet their opposition was to religious policy. Few dared assert opposition to the destruction of what could have been at least the foundations of a Roman democracy. Drastic measures seemed necessary amidst near collapse. No gentile historian's works survived to record Galerius' traumatic transformation of the Empire into a fascism of sorts. Christians writing of it seemed carefully politically correct, offending no officials beyond the sphere of faith. Thus, historical memory of a turning point in human affairs has been cut short and distorted.

Islamic and Russian cultures through the Greek-speaking Byzantine Empire of the East would inherit the top-heavy state-controlled economies and state-dominated religious models of the heritage of Diocletian and Galerius, surviving by stifling all opposition. Dissent was held treason.

Like other Romans at the time, most Christians desperately sought security, any change from deterioration an apparent progress.

In all but Galerius' eastern provinces, pagans with political power who were friendly, tolerant or bribable by Christians carried the day as persecution waned. Romans turned again to trust in personal relationships rather than ideology.

The Church was gravely disorganized. Bitter feelings erupted over the readmission into the Church of those who had sacrificed to the gods. Marcellinus,[52] the Bishop of Rome, scorned for yielding the holy books to be burned and for allowing *lapsi* to be reinstated after doing penance, confronted riots by *professi* who had honoured the idols but nevertheless suffered at the hands of the imperial authorities. They refused to make any gesture of remorse in the form of good works as penance.

Rome had had forty-six priests and 1,500 widows and distressed persons fifty years earlier.[53]

Some 10,000 were jailed in persecution. Judging from the Acts, these were rarely children or slaves – legally incompetents. The persecutors had succeeded in killing many of the most active and courageous and also the better educated in the Church. From 304 to 308 Rome had no bishop. Marcellus and a Eusebius (not the historian) were the subsequent popes, foreigners called in to fill the void of ecclesiastical leadership. Both were exiled by the state along with the *lapsi* claimant to the papacy, Heraclius.

While the Church was seriously troubled in its succession to leadership, so too was the Empire.

The population anxiously regarded the transition of power from the two *augusti* to their two *caesars*. Many anticipated with dread the usual clash of legions to determine who ruled while the potential for revolution by those deprived of rights by Diocletian had reached a critical mass.

In 306, Galerius, at Diocletian's urgings, appointed Severus *caesar* of the West, a man he privately scorned as 'A dancer who makes his nights days and his days nights.'[54] He was an unsoldierly man of moderate ambition, nonetheless. Constantius made his son Constantine *caesar* of the West.

Persecution of Christians ceased.

It was manifest, however, that Maximian and Galerius plotted intrigue and war against the rulers of the West.

Chapter 24

Politician and Mystic

The greatest evil is to be aware of none.

Voltaire

Constantine's character has fascinated historians for ages. A brutal opportunist and religious mystic, a man of action and a dreamer, he claimed tolerance of all creeds yet initiated legal discrimination against Jews. He was Christian in his fashion yet ever eager to command the Church for his political purposes. He was baptized on his deathbed by a believer in the Arian heresy that believed Jesus to be merely human.

Without Constantine, the Church might have had time to gradually adjust from its status as victim to victor. That a few years later, Christians would thank Constantine for establishing theirs as the favoured official religion was unimagined. There is no evidence that the ramifications of a Christian empire had ever entered the minds of the persecuted.

Ironically, under the caste system Constantine helped introduce, the marriage of his *equites* father to his mother, an innkeeper's daughter, would have been illegal.

Almost as long as he could remember, Constantine had been guest and hostage of Maximian. While respected as a royal heir, he was aware of rivals close at hand who might assassinate him. Three half brothers added to the risk. His mother, Helena, had long awaited the hour of danger and opportunity at the palace at Nicea. It came in early summer of 306. She learned of a letter that Galerius had attempted to conceal, in which her son's father asked that Constantine be sent to visit him in Britain.

At his mother's urging, Constantine feigned a restless boredom and ignorance of his father's request. Knowing Galerius' habit of wining and dining at midday and napping thereafter, he asked his host for written permission to use the horses of the courier service to journey nearby. Galerius signed the note and instructed that no one should disturb him.

Escorted by his most trusted companions, Constantine managed to pass over the Dardanelles by ferry without delay. Arrived in Europe, the riders switched horses at relay stations, hamstringing unused mounts so that none could pursue them. They raced onwards day and night.

The next day, Galerius learned of the ruse and ordered Constantine's arrest. The escaped prince sent decoy riders in several directions and misleading reports. Galerius seemed indecisive. Having no living son, he had persuaded Diocletian to appoint his nephew, Maximian Daia, as *caesar* in the East. Galerius may have considered the empire of the West more trouble than it was worth. He ruled the East, enough for any ruler. Injury to Constantine could have provoked a civil war with his father that Galerius wished to avoid.

Constantine's band continued pellmell down the highways, scarcely stopping for rest until they entered Constantius' territory across the Illyrian border. Thence they continued the pace until they reached Boulogne, just in time to catch the emperor of the West about to sail to Britain. Father and son embraced after twelve years apart.

The riders had travelled 1,600 miles in twenty-eight days.[1] Some 1,500 years later, Europe's postal service was not nearly so swift.

Within a year, Constantius died at York, on 25 July 306, his firstborn son at his bedside.[2] The army of the West proclaimed Constantine emperor.

Galerius, on receiving the news, threw the portrait that accompanied it into a fire. Reconsidering, he promoted Severus to emperor of the West and accepted Constantine as *caesar*. Months passed as Constantine, rejecting any subservient rank, plotted a strategy and organized his forces. By October, with troops from Britain he crossed the Channel and gathered more forces from the Rhine frontier. On the march through Gaul, Constantine and his army witnessed a sundog,[3] a halo around the sun as it cast rays across the sky, as ice crystals at high altitude reflected light. It seemed to be an impressive omen but who should interpret it? Constantine visited an oracular shrine of Apollo in southern Gaul to seek a sign.[4] The message was that other spirits rendered the fortune tellers impotent, the same message Diocletian had received from the Milesian Apollo. Admission of impotence in the presence of Christianity could be taken as hostility to that faith or acknowledgment of its superiority. Meanwhile, the four edicts of persecution were unenforced in the West, while in the East martyrs were still dying.

Maxentius, Maximian's son, an egotistic dullard, 'loved by no one' as a pagan described him,[5] had been passed over in the succession to the throne. At Rome on 27 October 306, encouraged by his father, he declared himself *caesar* of the West, the third claimant to the title. His power base was the Praetorian Guard decreed disbanded by Severus. Refusing to disband, the Guard hacked hundreds of Severus' followers in Rome to death and supported Maxentius. Maximian was delighted when his son gave him military command.

Severus had been appointed by Galerius to be a civil administrator, not a rival. Installing his vanguard at Ravenna in north-western Italy, safely surrounded by swamps, Severus awaited reinforcements. Maximian's envoys arrived and persuaded him that his generals had offered to betray him. Their voracious ambitions made the tale believable. Surrendering Ravenna without a fight, Severus was taken prisoner, well treated, placed in a villa amidst continued discussion of his future rank and, ultimately, given the choice of execution or suicide.[6] Galerius concealed his anger and persuaded Diocletian to return briefly from retirement to attend a conference with Maximian and himself at Carnuntum on the Danube where Mithra was solemnly declared patron deity of the Empire.[7] The General Licinius, hatefully anti-Christian, was made Severus' successor. The absent Constantine was given the hand of Maximian's daughter Fausta in marriage.

The nineteenth century French writer Ernest Renan declared that, if not for Christianity, Mithraism would have become the religion of the Roman Empire. Mithra was the god of warriors, pirates, merchants and public officials. The cult's sacred language was Persian, that of Roman's most powerful foe, yet it would become the secret society and international freemasonry holding the Empire together. More than two hundred of its shrines, *spelae*, literally caverns, have been discovered by archaeologists.

What emperors were its devotees can be known only in a few instances. Mithra, the 'god of ten thousand eyes', i.e. spies, originally gained official favour under Nero. The wall paintings in its shrines depict rituals of seven degrees of initiation. Many involved torture and ceremonies of devotees clad as bears, lions and ravens. The use of narcotics was common.

It has been said that Mithraic moral values, loyalty, courage, obedience, and the like, resembled those 'of a troop of sado-masochistic boy-scouts'. Mithraism, in one of its initiations, offered a member a wreath, the crown of an emperor, on the tip of a sword. It was to be ceremoniously rejected with the words 'I have no crown but Mithra,' a symbolic rejection of involvement in coups to seize the throne.

In another initiation, a worshipper was blindfolded and handed a sword. Told to stretch out his free hand, he felt an unarmoured person standing before him. He was ordered to kill, without question. In fact, no one was intended to be injured in the mock test. Nevertheless, Commodus, the depraved son of the emperor and philosopher Marcus Aurelius, killed a man in the ritual. Commodus was strangled in reaction to his sacrilege.

Renan, who wrote that he detested both Christianity and democracy as faiths for slaves, was wrong. Mithraism was an exceedingly exclusive society that recruited only military and civil officials and powerful merchants. Its shrines were scarcely large enough to hold more than two dozen people. Building these shrines throughout the Empire abruptly ceased within a few years after the Persian capture of the Emperor Valerian, judging from archaeology. A generation later, the first Mithraic burials appear, suggesting a change in its rites or beliefs. Mithraism never had a definite religious doctrine nor are earlier Mithraic graves known.

Until Vatican II's council of bishops in 1962, Catholics in the sacrament of Confirmation received a slap on the cheek with the words, 'You are a warrior of

Jesus Christ.' Religious conversion is rarely ever entirely a one-way street, however subtle or even unconscious the influences.

Mithraism's most sacred rite was the killing of a bull, the *taurobolium*. The initiate in a pit covered by a grating was literally bathed in blood in a symbol of being born again. The word for a bull in Persian also meant a warrior. Mithraism did not condemn killing except, presumably, among its members. It appeased guilt. Mithra was believed by many to be another of the many names of God. Unless directly challenged, it was tolerant of other creeds and indifferent to contradictions between them.

As Mithraism abruptly underwent a crisis after Valerian's capture, its international brotherhood shattered. Christians for the first time attempted to take officers' rank in the army and compete against Mithraic officer candidates. The Mithraic reaction remains hidden. What do people do when their ideological faith vanishes? Among some, ambition becomes more obvious when stripped of ideology. Others may seek a new supportive creed.

The Empire's obvious weakness demanded reforms in policy as pagan emperors, increasingly pessimistic, became increasingly extreme towards a public they felt failed them. Christians were available scapegoats.

At London's Walbrook Mithraeum, a Mithraic shrine, archaeologists have discovered a statue of Serapis, suggesting the presence of Egyptians tending to monotheism among Roman Britain's upper classes. The appeal of Mithraism had been its secrecy, elitism and advantages to career. Made the imperial cult, everyone supposedly a worshipper, the Empire intended to become a caste system, it probably lost more sincere devotees than it gained.

Back again in Rome, Maximian attended a review of its troops. In his son Maxentius' presence he harangued the army to betray his son and restore him to the throne.[8] The soldiers hooted him down. Bewildered, Maximian left the reviewing-stand. He departed for Gaul and the protection of his new son-in-law Constantine who had always shown him patience.

In Gaul, Maximian's insatiable character soon came to view Constantine's hospitality as condescension. He could not live with the idea that he was permanently removed from power. Venturing to Arles in 310, he seized the treasury and told the local garrison that Constantine was dead in order to gain support. With quite unexpected speed, Constantine's vanguard, presumably including his Theban bodyguards, marched from Trier to the Saone at Chalons, thence on to the Rhone to Arles. Maximian fled to Marseilles, where he had once before retreated to avoid a clash with Theban soldiers. He was captured.

Advised by his mother to continue tolerance towards the scheming man who imagined himself Hercules, Constantine brought Maximian back to his palace at Trier as an honoured guest. He remembered more of Maximian in his childhood than he did his father. His reluctance to aggrieve the old soldier may have been as much from sentiment as political considerations. Maximian, true to form, took this goodwill in exchange for treachery to be contemptible weakness. He asked his daughter to let him into Constantine's bedchamber in order to murder him. Fausta informed her husband. Constantine ordered a palace eunuch to sleep in the room in his absence. That night, Maximian stealthily entered and stabbed the sleeping figure to death. Seized, Maximian was given the choice he had given Severus. A Christian writer wrote that he strangled himself to death, a pagan wrote that he was executed.[9]

Constantine formally declared his dead father-in-law *damnatio memoriae*, his statues, decrees and inscriptions to be obliterated.[10] (*Damnatio memoriae* meant that officially all traces of a person's existence were to be destroyed: inscriptions, portraits, documents etc.) Mobs carried out the order with a vengeance.

Galerius heard the news and groaned. He was a dying man suffering from some undiagnosed but agonizing ailment. He drank too much. His son Nicetas, his doctor Pantaleon and friend, secretary and senator, Pancharius, had been among the martyrs, his wife and daughter Christian in sentiments. Renewing Probus' old plan to improve agriculture in the Balkans, he meditated that that good emperor who had recommended him for promotion in his green days had been right in espousing the common good and religious freedom.

With an honest recognition of error very few leaders ever display in public, Galerius had come to recognize that it was wrong to continue to hound Christians. At Milan, he asked Constantine and Licinius to join him in issuing an edict of religious toleration, the world's first.[11] Neither visited Milan at his invitation. A few days later he died.

Christians at the time appreciated freedom of religious conscience as only a persecuted minority could.

The edict freed many of the faithful from prison. In the East, however, Maximin Daia as *augustus* with Licinius his *caesar* ignored it and bitterly revived the persecution, drowning two hundred soldiers at Synope on the southern shores of the Black Sea according to the *Martyrologium Romanum*. No Act of this exists, nevertheless Daia had more motive than other persecutors to purge the army. He was about to plunge into war against Constantine who openly favoured Christians. Licinius exposed forty naked Christian recruits to freezing temperatures until they were dead at Sebaste in Cappadocia.

Maxentius, in Italy, saw no contradiction in promising to raise taxes on the rich and protect the aristocracy, avenge his father and pardon old enemies, control the Church and give it freedom. He stopped persecution, handed over to the Church its confiscated property and exiled the Bishop of Rome. His Praetorians cut to pieces the city's populace who were rioting amidst famine. He was accused of raping senators' wives and daughters and participating in rites of human sacrifice to predict the future.

As his father, Maximian, before him, he could not comprehend why people distrusted him.

Roman coins always showed portraits in profile. Maxentius suffered from crossed eyes. His engraver uniquely depicted him full face, emphasizing the defect.[12] Maxentius seemed unaware of this subtle sedition, like many other signs of his unpopularity.

In response to a flurry of letters from prominent Italians pleading for his intervention, Constantine struck in September of 312.[13] From Arles through the Mount Genevre pass marched the army of the West into Italy. In the van were Theban bodyguards, heavy cavalry and long columns of armoured infantry. They promptly seized the town of Segusio. Constantine's rapid deployment was the harvest of several years' planning; Maxentius' befuddlement at this *blitzkreig* was the culmination of his improvidence. The city of Turin closed its gates to Maxentius' legionnaires as they attempted to find shelter from Constantine's pursuing forces. Turin accepted generous surrender terms from Constantine. Next, Milan yielded. Maxentius fell back to Rome, while Constantine was delayed by the task of taking the city of Verona. Encircled, the troops within broke out and were repulsed, but not before their General Ruricius had escaped southwards to organize a relief column. Coming back with a sizeable army, he was, nevertheless, reluctant to risk a field battle.

Constantine deliberately gave the impression of inadequate numbers by concentrating his personnel. Ruricius took the bait and attacked towards sundown. The wings hidden to the rear of Constantine's army enflanked the attackers. Confused hand-to-hand combat in the moonlight raged all night. Victorious, Constantine wasted no time in speeding southwards by the Roman roads. It was thirty miles to Hostilia, forty more to Bologna, sixty-eight further to Ariminium on the Adriatic and from there along the coast it was twenty-seven miles to Fanum Fortunae. Grizzled Theban veterans may have recognized the route as that by which they had left Rome twenty-seven years previously.

Maxentius' forces in Rome included large numbers of Moorish cavalry, with the Praetorian Guard and Legio II Parthica barracked south of the capital. The total of both sides in the struggle drawing near was perhaps 40,000 men, although ancient writers claimed many more. Pagan and Christian writers agreed that Constantine was greatly outnumbered. Christians in II Parthica had been martyred repeatedly in the prior half century, their numbers increasing nonetheless. Their loyalty to Maxentius was dubious. The graves of a very few Christian Praetorians are known. The Praetorians knew that if they lost their unit would be disbanded.

The battle that emerged would influence western civilization for ages to come. It would be a turning point in history, the culmination of almost three centuries of the issue of Christian soldiers in the Roman military.

Chapter 25

Battle of the Milvian Bridge

Power tends to corrupt and absolute power corrupts absolutely.

Lord Acton

Three miles north of Rome, the Via Flaminia cut a narrow defile through a quarry called the Saxa Rubra, the red rocks. A mile to the west, across rising and broken ground, was the Via Cassia. The roads met a mile southwards within sight of the arches of the Milvian Bridge across the Tiber. The Milvian is still in use to this day. Two miles further south were the walls of Rome. Having occupied the Saxa Rubra, a few days later Constantine's vanguard skirmished against the defending troops and withdrew to the quarry, its terraces ideal for defence by Theban archers.

While Constantine's forces lay largely hidden in their deployment, he benefitted from excellent intelligence, employing leading citizens eager to serve him within Rome, as within every city he had attacked. Maxentius had the unreasonable arrogance and self-isolation of a person unwilling to accept his own limitations or listen to advice.

Maxentius had the reputation of a vain, self-indulgent dullard who overcompensated with a supersensitivity to the demands of the city rabble whose adulation he craved. The population feared a winter siege, and the city's grain supply was inadequate because of troubles in North Africa. Maxentius was openly mocked by the mob, which urged him to do battle outside the city's walls. Consulting the Sibylline oracle, he was told that on 28 October 'the enemy of Rome would perish' – a murky prophecy as usual. He determined to attack rather than await assault and siege.

Constantine's army was badly supplied for a winter of hard labour. Maxentius could have awaited reinforcements arriving with North African grain after the revolt there was crushed. The city's walls of brick erected by Probus against barbarian raids were not intended to withstand assault towers, stone-throwing siege machines, and battering rams. They were more than adequate at the moment, nevertheless. Maxentius seemed more fearful of tensions within the city than the challenger outside it.

A fanciful battle plan was conceived. Alongside the stone Milvian Bridge, a pontoon roadway was constructed. The bridges were defended by numerous towers and turrets. Constantine's forces were to be lured onto them where, confined, they would be slain. The floating bridge was designed to suddenly break apart, drowning Constantine's troops.

Maxentius sent his generals forward outside the walls of Rome with no clear chain of command among men of equal rank, his authority limiting their ability to make decisions in action on the battlefield. All key decisions were to be his, yet he remained miles away behind the walls of Rome.

On the eve of battle Constantine directed his men to paint upon their shields the emblem called the labarum. The word was probably Celtic and survives in Spanish, *labare*, meaning to praise God. Four Christian contemporaries related varying versions of this episode. According to Lactantius, the shields were marked 'with a letter X turned around with a large loop atop', the Latin *'transversa X littera summo capite circumflexo.'*[1] Generally, the labarum has been taken to describe a monogram of the word Christ or Chrestus in Greek, the combined letters chi-ro, XP, equivalent to the Latin CR. But Lactantius, fluent in Greek, does not say that the symbol was a monogram. He mentions the 'chi' but not the 'ro'. Moreover, most of Constantine's army was pagan. Why choose a Christian emblem that might divide his men?

Eusebius insists that the symbol was a monogram but admits that Constantine was so puzzled as to its meaning that he asked that the symbol be explained to him. Constantine certainly knew Greek. If the symbol was a monogram of Christ he would have recognized it.

A Coptic manuscript states that it was an Egyptian soldier, the veteran Aladious,[2] who explained the labarum to Constantine. As a veteran in 312 with twenty-five years' service plus several on recall, he had joined the army about the year of the Theban Legion's departure from Egypt.

The ankh, the cross topped by a loop, is the ancient Egyptian sign of eternal life the Christian author Socrates Scolasticus mentions as used by both devotees of Serapis and Christ in Egypt.

Constantine at the Milvian Bridge was neither a Christian nor the religiously assured leader of later years. He had sought the guidance of Apollo to no avail. He and his men still pondered the strange haloed and beam-crossed sun witnessed months previous.

Constantine's men sensed that he was a force for change, but change towards what? Constantine, perhaps, is most accurately seen as a consummate politician, inspiring not with promises of concrete gain but a symbolic style into which everyone could read what he wished.

Egyptian ankh.

Labarum on Constantine's coins, 316.

The accounts of the battle emphasize the plan to lure Constantine's forces onto a pontoon bridge designed to collapse.

It is difficult to believe that the plot to use the bridge as a trap escaped the notice of Constantine's spies in a city largely hoping for his success. The plan would have necessitated a rapid retreat of part of Maxentius' forces across the stone Milvian Bridge, leaving his two legions in place ready to close in behind Constantine's charge channelled between them. Constantine's battle plan seems to be a direct reaction to such an expected manoeuvre.

War as the extension of politics in the example of the battle of the Milvian Bridge suggests that it was determined as much by the politics within Legio II Parthica as by battlefield tactics alone.

Maxentius' main force on 28 October advanced across the bridges of the city to deploy and meet their foe.

The site chosen for battle left no room for manoeuvre and dangerously separated Maxentius' infantry wings. On the flatlands of the bend of the Tiber on the east, Legio II Parthica, purged of many of its Christian members, formed up screened by lightly armoured Moorish horsemen. The Praetorians deployed southward, confined by steeply higher ground to the west and north.

Maxentius' forces made no effort to seize the Via Cassia, which might have enabled them to move to the north and rear of Constantine's troops.

Maxentius, in setting a trap for his foes, presumed that they would do precisely what he hoped. He, apparently, neither scouted his enemy's forces nor prepared any alternative plans in case of surprise. His strategy was essentially passive. His enemy would be allowed to come to him. Nevertheless, he did not give his troops the advantage of fighting from within Rome's walls.

Between the Praetorians and II Parthica was a gap giving their cavalry access to screen the field before them. Their reserves would have been tightly formed on the road southwards, cut through another ravine like the Saxa Rubra.

Constantine's memorial arch, built in Rome a few years after the battle of the Milvian Bridge, shows him in the middle of the struggle directing his troops. A hands–on commander who kept close to the action, he was not foolhardy. He is depicted not on horseback but in a large wagon, well defended and mobile.

Chi Ro monogram.

After hours of anxious waiting for Constantine's forces out of sight north of the quarry, they suddenly appeared led by a charging column of horsemen, Constantine among them. With the momentum of depth and speed, the column struck the heavily armoured horses and men of the *cataphracti*. Without room to counter the charge as Constantine advanced, Maxentius' cavalry turned in retreat, breaking up lines of their own infantry. Retreat had been part of Maxentius' plan, but not like this.

Maxentius' centre swiftly broke shieldwall ranks and turned its back to the foe to flee towards the bridges, expecting to be pursued by a carefully advancing shieldwall at slower pace. Constantine, instead, sent after them his cavalry, followed by Theban archers unencumbered by armour and racing forwards. The plotted rapid fallback of Maxentius' centre became a panicked rout. His two legions stood divided by the collapsing centre. They failed to close behind Constantine's advance columns.

The unarmoured Theban archers, protected by spearmen upholding round shields, ran behind the cavalry column. Constantine's infantry issued forth from the road defile. His heavy infantry, with rectangular shields, deployed to centre and east.

The task of the Theban was not primarily to keep Maxentius' infantry hunkered down under a sheet of arrows, but to wreak chaos among his cavalry. An armoured and shielded legionnaire could withstand a clout of arrows, most of them missing. A horse as target was much more easily hit and likely to soon panic. Moreover, the Thebans could provide cover for Constantine's cavalry if hard pressed, their racing shieldwall leaving the enemy no opportunity to regroup.

With the advantages of surprise and momentum, Constantine's cavalry forced back Maxentius as Constantine's heavy infantry advanced, armed, according to Aurelius Victor, with 'staves,'[3] probably long lances intended to fend off Maxentius' cavalry.

As long as Maxentius' cavalry fought he had a chance at victory, according to the pagan Roman historian Zosimus. He described Maxentius' Italian troops (Legio II Parthica) as 'reluctant to venture into danger, wishing as they did to find release from bitter tyranny. However, of the other soldiers (the Praetorians) an untold multitude fell ...'[4] Hundreds of martyrs from II Parthica had fallen in previous generations, he might have added.

Maxentius' cavalry, with no room to manoeuvre or regroup, broke and raced through the gap in their own infantry lines.

Usually, cavalry would retreat from position as a frontal screen by way of the flanks of the troops defended. Horses are nervous animals. They instinctively avoid anything they see that might attack their underbellies. A shieldwall of disciplined infantry could generally defeat a frontal cavalry charge but a cavalry

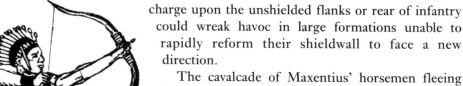

charge upon the unshielded flanks or rear of infantry could wreak havoc in large formations unable to rapidly reform their shieldwall to face a new direction.

The cavalcade of Maxentius' horsemen fleeing through the middle of his infantry, separating II Parthica from the Praetorians, was probably part of his plan. They were to seize the permanent structure of the Milvian Bridge so that Constantine's forces would take to the pontoon bridge that was built to collapse. All depended on surprise, yet constructing a bridge was hardly secret and any skilled workmen might nave noted the hidden agenda in its design.

The battle could still have been won by Maxentius if the Praetorians of his western flank had swung eastwards, but they lacked enough room to form a line and move on the crowded ground where Constantine's cavalry and Theban archers advanced.

Theban archer as on Constantine's Arch, Rome.

Constantine's cavalry, in pursuit, broke into the flanks of their infantry foes. Those of whom who could, fell back southwards. Constantine's vanguard, however, reached the Milvian Bridge and seized it. On his arch in Rome commemorating the battle, Theban archers are depicted firing arrows at cavalrymen on the pontoon bridge below them falling into the River Tiber.

The retreating centre of Maxentius' line, increasingly disorganized amidst a cavalcade of horsemen, both friends and foes, collapsed.

Hearing of the battle underway, Maxentius, in armour resplendent in jewels, left the city to lead his legions ... too late.

He ordered the pontoon bridge to be broken open behind him.[5]

Only the Praetorians courageously stood their ground in their final battle. The labarum-marked vanguard reached the bridge, while Maxentius' men were still hurrying across. Bowmen in their towers, dominating the roadway, could not fire without hitting their own men.

From this higher position Theban archers rained arrows upon their foes until, in the

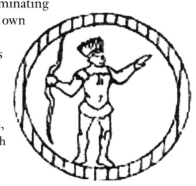

The shield of Legio Felices Valentiniensis Thebeorum, created in the late fourth century. Note the archer with feathered arrow headress.

The red (vertical lines) and yellow (dots) shield of Legio Thebeorum Palatini of Constantine, replacing the Praetorian Guard of Rome.

confusion, the floats were uncoupled as Maxentius had schemed. He fell in the river and drowned, victim of his own trap.

It was barely two months since the vanguard of Thebans had entered Italy.

Constantine's decisiveness was the result of excellent intelligence gathering, planning and training, his swiftness emerging as if by surprise from many months of seeming quietude.

The crucial role that Thebans played in the campaign is unmistakably evident on the triumphal arch completed at Rome three years later, the Thebans readily identified by their headdress of arrows. Four ancient authors cite this as distinctive of Nilotic Black warriors.[6] The unit shield of Legio II Valentiniensis Theboram, created several generations later, depicts just such an archer.[7]

Constantine disbanded the surviving Praetorians. He replaced them as the elite garrison of Rome with a new legion, the Thebei Palatini, the Theban palaceguards, the only eastern troops in the West thereafter.

In Rome, a colossal statue of Constantine bearing the labarum was erected at his orders. The head survives. Eusebius, who never visited Rome, gave a description. He stated that the emblem carried 'beneath' the hand of the statue was 'a crossbarred shaft topped by a loop', i.e. an ankh. He specifically called it a phylacterion, an amulet worn on an arm or carried in the hand as Egyptian art usually depicts the ankh hanging from the wrist of the gods.[8] A Christian inscription in the era from North Africa includes both ankh and monogram chi-ro, together symbolizing resurrection in Christ.

For the original recruits of the Theban Legion, after almost thirty years of service, adventure and sacrifice, it was time to give thanks, celebrate and retire.

Chapter 26

Epitaph for Acaunus

Prayer is God within us and we outside ourselves.

Augustine of Hippo

The emperor did not worship the God of Christians until years after the victory for which he later claimed divine predestination and nor did his mother, Helena.[1]

Enemies claimed Helena to have been an innkeeper's daughter of dubious reputation. Sensitive to the issue, Constantine forbid the prostitution of inn servants, seduction of slaves and concubinage.[2] These were the first occasions of Roman law intervening on behalf of women not of the upper class who previously had no protection, except in cases of rape of a slave by her master if the woman dared press charges before the usual slave-owning judge. Ironically, under the caste system he introduced, the marriage of Constantine's father to his mother would have been illegal.

If there was goodwill, there was also misguided zeal in the emperor's efforts to coerce people to be 'good'. Jesus had rejected political power.[3] To make people 'good' from fear of the state was not the moral freedom taught by Christ. The woman taken in adultery in the Gospels legally was to be stoned to death. Jesus enabled her to escape punishment.[4]

Meanwhile, Maximin Daia in the East violated his promise of religious toleration and commenced a persecution, implicitly a challenge to Constantine. A burial inscription in Greek gives insight into this oppression.

I, Marcus Julius Eugenius served in the army of Pisidia (southern Turkey) as a member of the forces of Cyrillus Celer the senator: I was the husband of Julia Flaviana, daughter of the senator Caius Nestorianus, and I completed my military service with honour. Then Maximin (Daia) issued an order compelling Christians to do sacrifice but without abandoning their service in the army; and having suffered many annoyances from the General Diogenes, I resigned my military commission, holding fast to the Christian faith. After dwelling for a short time at Laodicea, I was by the will of God made bishop, and for twenty years I laboured in the episcopate with the forecourts, the paintings, the sculptures, the font, the vestibule, etc. And having completed all this I renounced the life of man and wrought myself a marble sepulchre. And it was ordered that the aforesaid be inscribed on the tomb built for myself and my issue.[5]

Presumably, Marcus Julius Eugenius was baptized upon retirement. Exactly how he was able to retire is unclear. Maximin Daia's army policy was that officers were to sacrifice or accept demotion to enlisted rank. His policy was a change from Galerius' effort to prematurely retire all Christian soldiers. Daia's refusal to let Christians leave the army demonstrates that their military competence was not questioned and the failure and contradiction of his persecution policy.

Many officers become Christians and on retirement became clergy. Marcus Julius Eugenius almost directly became a bishop. Customarily, he would then, if married, separate from his wife by mutual consent. Ex-officers and officials in the clergy brought efficiency and discipline at times tinged with a materialistic pride as in the inscription above where the episcopate has become not the Christian community but a building of stone.

In 314 Constantine married his half-sister to Licinius who returned to the East to defeat Maximin Daia. The two rulers, Constantine and Licinus, uneasily divided the Empire between them. They wrote one another diplomatic pleasantries and prepared for war.

Constantine's admission of Greeks into the army and civil service revitalized the Eastern Empire. His laws discriminating against Jews revitalized old prejudices dating back to before the time of the pre-Christian Maccabees. Some who had risked persecution, placed in power, discriminated not against former oppressors but a third party, the Jews.[6] But most Christians in Constantine's era continued to avoid government service, civil or military.

The re-emerging political power of the Greeks paralleled the growth of their intellectual influence within the Church. Many theological disputes stirring friction among Christians for centuries thereafter could hardly be followed except in Greek.

Constantine revised the military oath and ceremonies honouring the emperor to make them acceptable to Christians.[7] These matters had long obscured the basic issue of the morality of military violence.

In 314 he ordered the bishops of Gaul and Britain to assemble at Arles to improve church administration. Civil war had erupted between Constantine and Licinius, resulting in an impasse, but it was obvious that East and West would clash again. Many Christians were quitting the army and others dodged the draft. The Eemperor Constantine sought the help of the Church in stemming this flow.

Constantine abolished government support for the old imperial cult, gave Christians exclusive privileges, and handed over to them pagan temples and tax monies paid by pagans.[8] His summoning of the bishops to Arles implied his leadership of the Church. The bishop of Rome, the North African Miltiades, opposed this bid for power and did not appear at Arles. It was clear to him that Church and state could be united only at risk of government domination of the church. A successor, Celestine,[9] wrote in reaction to clergy borrowing the regalia of the old imperial cult, that they should be distinguished from the laity in no way save their learning and exemplary lives.

The decisions of the bishops at Arles were approved by the bishop of Rome.

The council at Arles responded to Constantine's need of Christian military in its third canon: '*De his qui arma prociunt in pace placiut abstineri eose a cummunione.*' — Whoever lays down his weapons in peace, reconcile to be separated from those in communion.[10]

For three centuries the Church had strongly discouraged Christians from joining the army. The time had come that it was threatening soldiers for quitting the army in peacetime with excommunication, although the wording seems hesitant to directly condemn. Perhaps what was most significant was what the Council of Arles failed to say. It did not threaten with excommunication a soldier laying down his weapons in time of war. That was apparently left to the particular situation, the individual's conscience and the discipline of the army and the state.

A few years later, Constantine exempted from military conscription anyone becoming a monk.[11] Joining the clergy became almost the only way of changing one's caste. Monasticism in the East enormously increased, redirecting impulses that might have led to political protest or violent revolt.

The powers of Roman judges were given to bishops if both parties in a case agreed, although they had no armed force to enforce their legal decisions.[12] In the West, increased corruption turned people to the institutional church and a withering away of the state. In the East, the larger population and percentage of church membership sustained the state.

In all the research thus far on the Theban Legion a critical point remains. That a legion was recruited in the Egyptian Thebaid to serve in Britain and that Theban soldiers identified by pagans as Christians became bodyguards of the tetrarchs has been demonstrated. What remains lacking is evidence that Thebans had been martyred at Acaunus, the event of the legend.

In France, the author visited Autun, the Roman Augustodunum, once the second largest city in Roman Gaul. Knowing that burial inscriptions of Roman veterans were common in major cities of the Empire, the thought occurred that a Theban veteran might have left an inscription at Autun.

This led to the monumental collection of Roman inscriptions made in the nineteenth century by German scholars, the *Corpus Inscriptionum Latinarum*. Turning the pages to Augustodunum, at first glance its meagre pages seemed unpromising. Inspection a moment later riveted attention to one word chiselled upon stone seventeen centuries ago. It was the name of the tiny Alpine village and Roman customs station where the Thebans had fallen in 286, Acaunus (Acaunensium, Agaunus).

What would the name of that insignificant hamlet be doing on an inscription in central France?

The inscribed stone had been discovered and recorded in the seventeenth century.[13] It has since disappeared. It had never been debated by scholars. Thin and relatively small, it was not a gravestone but presumably a wall plaque. It reads:

ME. M E M
G V S T A T H
L . VIVI M I
C S C C A VNE
N V S A N
R. M . LVIII
G. P. F. C C C
D V L C I SSI

The right and left margins were both vertically aligned but the left edge of the tablet was missing. Scholars are reluctant to decipher a broken inscription. The inscription's finders nevertheless hazarded a translation, despite several puzzling aspects of the message.

The abbreviated first line, undoubtedly, was a common memorial to the dead but lacked any of the usual religious phrases, pagan or Christian. Abbreviations are typical of Roman memorials but the tablet was more abbreviated than most, as if intended to be understood by only a few.

Because an army unit is with certainty mentioned in the sixth and seventh lines (LVIII G.P.F.), the seventeenth century translators took the word auGVSTA to be the name of a soldier's widow and the inscription a personal epitaph. But no husband's name is mentioned. Would a soldier's unit but not his name be inscribed on his or his widow's epitaph? Moreover, Augusta was not a Roman personal name. It meant royal, the title of an empress or an imperial institution such as an army unit or a city granted the honourable title. London, for example, had been the Roman Augusta Londinium.

The tablet was a memorial to the dead but contains no personal names, or family names or the, usually included, age of the deceased. Curious.

The army unit cited in the sixth and seventh lines, LVIII G.P.F. was accepted by its discoverers to be Legio VIII Augusta Pia Fidelis. This was the garrison of Argentoratum, modern Strasbourg, so carefully avoided by Maximian in his retreat and detour from AcVNENVSAN, the official name for Acaunus, spelled with a corrupt ending on the stone.

The word following auGVSTA is abbreviated TH, a sound that did not exist in Latin save for those words borrowed from Greek. It could not signify a family name as all soldiers by law were required to use a Latin tribal name for that of their family. Could auGVSTA THebeorum thus be intended in line two?

The letters CCC in the seventh line are a date.[14] Commonly, CC represented two *caesars*. Three *caesars* shared power only one year in the history of the Empire, Constantine's sons Constantinus and Crispus, and Licinius the Younger, the son of the ruler of the East, Licinius. This was in the year 317, the very year in which Constantine acknowledged himself to be a monotheist, dropping all official trappings of polytheism. It was a year of rejoicing for Christians.

Normally, the title of a legion in inscriptions is preceded by L or LEG and the unit's number. But the marine and fleet unit Legio Julia Alexandriana had never had a number, nor did the many legions of Diocletian's reforms.

VIVI is not an abbreviation as the spacing clearly indicates. VIVI means 'to be lived', a peculiar phrase. It can refer to the memory or example of a person or group. MI is a common Latin shortening for military service. The tablet thus can be read:

MEmini MEMoriae auGVSTA THebeorum Legionaria VIVI MIlitabant
ConSCissa aCAVNENSAM. Reliqui Militabant Legionis VIII auGusta
Pia Fidelis. CCC. DVLCISSImae.

Remember the example to be lived of the legionnaires of the Augusta Thebeorum torn apart on military duty at Acaunus. The survivors served in Legio VIII Augusta Pia Fidelis. Year of the three *caesars*. They were most gentle men.

As mentioned, the fortress of the Legio VIII Augusta Pia Fidelis was the only legionary station on the Rhine without military martyrs in 286. Moreover, two inscriptions of uncertain date from a Mithraic shrine at Strasbourg cite an otherwise unknown Legio VIII Avgusta Alexandrianae[15] – a unit from Alexandria. The Saxon Shore was a frontier province, each of which would have had two legions, in this case one on each side of the channel.

The phrase 'most gentle' was a common Christian usage in epitaphs and was used as often to refer to men as to women. It was rarely, if ever, used to refer to men in pagan epitaphs.[16]

The translation is supported as relating to the Thebans by the remarkable situation at Autun at the time of the installation of the tablet. The bishop in 317 was Rheticius[17] who was invited to Autun and won ecclesiastical permission for a coregent bishop to serve with him, Cassianus,[18] an Alexandrian by birth,

Bishop of Horta (Hor, the modern Zagazig) in Egypt. The transfer of a bishop to another episcopacy was forbidden by Church law; nevertheless, exceptions were very rarely allowed if there was opportunity for 'spiritual gain in saving souls'. Transfer required the approval of many bishops. The transfer of an Egyptian bishop to serve in Western Europe in the district of another bishop was unique. The purpose for it is inexplicable unless an Egyptian colony existed at Autun – veterans of the Theban Legion?

If this interpretation of the Autun tablet is wrong, then it remains a mystery, a memorial to army dead bearing no personal name but clearly citing the small village of Acaunus.

Epilogue

If a long period gives authority to a religious custom, we ought to keep faith with
so many centuries and follow our ancestors as they happily followed theirs.

Symmachus

C onstantine would become a saint of the Orthodox Christian churches but
not of Catholics or Protestants, wary of his efforts to control not
theology but the organized church.

Christians before Constantine had never imagined their faith would become
a privileged part of the government establishment. The military task of
defending a Christian empire had been unthinkable.[1] Christianity had been a
freely chosen and dangerously disadvantaged commitment, not a creed
privileged by the state.

Christians purged from the army within the generation.[2] In 320 veteran
soldiers addressed Constantine as a pagan. Nevertheless, he attempted to restore
Christians to the army by promotion and other rewards. In 325, summoning the
bishops of the Empire to Nicea, he manoeuvred again to dominate the Church
through the support of Arian bishops.[3] Arius was a bishop who believed Jesus to
be the son of God but not eternal, contrary to the creed adopted at Nicea. The
Council approved those books known today as the New Testament. The Bishop
of Rome affirmed the works of the Council but refused to attend it. To the
emperor's chagrin, most bishops challenged Constantine's intentions. Canon 12
of the Council excommunicated any Christian soldier returning to the army after
being ousted from it, likening them to 'dogs returning to their own vomit'.[4] The
emperor, nonetheless, provided Christian army chaplains and altered the
military oath to make it acceptable to believers in the crucified Nazarene.[5]

Constantine exempted Christian clergy from hereditary army or civil duty.
The great ecclesiastical leaders during the decline of the Empire, Augustine,
Hilary of Poitiers, Athanasius of Alexandria, Cyril of Jerusalem, Jerome,
Germanus and Patrick, etc., as sons of officers or officials, were thus legal draft–
evaders. An exception was the North African Bishop Synesius, who was so
disappointed in the troops sent at his request, Germanic refugees who had been
drafted (poorly trained, poorly equipped and of woefully slack morale), that he
wrote that no one who was blond should be given Roman authority. He created
a militia among his tribesman.

Roman policy believed the best soldiers to be the sons of soldiers but reforms denied the *comitati* a normal family life. Constantine withdrew troops from the frontiers to establish *numeri* as town defenders while the *comitati* took the field. It was a change in strategy worse than what it sought to repair, the *numeri* of little use in the field.

In tactics, leather jerkin, long sword, battleaxe and loose formations replaced the traditional heavy armour, short sword and tight shieldwall. The 1,000-men reform legions lacked the staying power of the older 6,000-men units and cooperated less effectively. Rome's cavalry remained too few and too scattered to resist massive mobile forces.

The Roman army, once composed entirely of volunteers, had become a motley assortment of draftees, many barbarians. The bloated imperial civil service recruited many who might have become soldiers. Meanwhile, the Church was providing services the state never attempted, in particular aid for refugees from frontiers, towns and villas. The monasteries that were developing would become a new economy, although they were never designed to be a transformation of society.

Gibbons' monumental opus held Rome's decline the triumph of Christianity and barbarism, yet it was the most Christian part of the Empire, the Byzantine East, which would survive for another thousand years, revived by recruitment of Greeks for imperial service.

In the West, the Empire withdrew its forces from Britain in 365.

Barbarian raiders had repeatedly evaded the forces on the frontier and struck at the towns within the Empire. Constantine unwisely carried out a reform, worsening matters.

The pagan Zosimus noted Constantine's shift in policy.

Constantine abolished security by removing the greater part of the soldiery from the frontiers to cities that needed no additional forces. He thus deprived of help the people who were harassed by the barbarians and burdened tranquil cities with the pest of the military, so that some were soon deserted. Moreover he softened the soldiers, who treated themselves to shows and luxuries. Indeed to put it bluntly he personally planted the seeds of our present devastated state of affairs.[6]

Manning defences with locally recruited forces weakened willingness to reinforce other areas. Troops were boarded in homes and inns. Officers extorted from civilians more fearful of them than of the barbarians. Landlords bribed troops to serve as virtual private armies looting their neighbours. Social and economic status was reduced to caste.

Eusebius of Caesarea had warned against disputes over abstract issues of creed that provoked more heat than light. Faith was trust in things unproven. It could not be imposed unless lip service was the unmentionable goal.

Eusebius wrote of people eager to enter the Church because they feared the emperor's disfavour if they did not. Meanwhile, Constantine threatened to arrest any bishop denying a person baptism. He scorned theology but sought unity, which to him meant a superficial conformity. His successors went further, stripping of power anyone not claiming their interpretation of theology. Obedience to the emperor became obedience to God, creedal slogans more important than behaviour.

With an established Church, with only one denomination supported by government funds, political parties became identified with particular sects. Civil dissent became civil war and holy war, as Shia versus Sunni in Islam.

The moral issues of military service seem to have disappeared amidst conscription and caste. Volunteers for the army became a small minority. Morality demanded freedom. That was in ever shorter supply.

By 350, a rebellious commander in Gaul clashed with Constantine II (r. 337–362) in a battle in which most of the soldiers on both sides were casualties. Meanwhile, the northern Rhine frontier had been abandoned. Barbarians occupied the area without opposition. Adding appeasement to weakness, authorities hired many of the invaders as soldiers.

By 360, the sole emperor was Julian called the Apostate (r. 360–363), although he had never been a Christian. He forbid Christians from entering the army or being lawyers or teachers. Attending Christian ceremonies with the army in Gaul of political necessity,[7] a few months later in the East he boasted that his army for the Persian campaign was pagan. About this time the centurions Bonosus and Maximian at Antioch[8] refused to exchange the labarum for a pagan ensign and were tortured and beheaded according to their Acts.

Julian urged the pagan priesthood of the imperial cult to aid the poor, realizing it to be one of the Church's strengths. It was an appeal to an aristocratic clergy that had neither the inclination nor the organization to achieve his hopes.

Julian wrote of the Christian soldiers accompanying him that 'the only thing they did well was pray'. Disturbed by the sullenness of the Germanic troops he was leading to sweep the northern Rhine, he offered them a gold coin for every barbarian head they handed over. Returning in a manic mood of victory, Romans locked town gates against them, convinced that they were invading bezerks, not disciplined Roman legionnaires.

Julian had written that you could tell who was a Christian 'by the way they loved one another'. Later, he wrote that they could be recognized by the hatred they displayed towards one another over theology. The more abstract the issue, apparently, the more bitter the dispute.

He received a fatal wound in a cavalry clash at Marenga near Ctesiphon as one version of his death relates.[9] His officers chose Salutius to be commander who protested that he was an inappropriate choice as a Christian to command a pagan force. The officers who had officiated at pagan rites not long before, declared that no problem existed since they, too, were Christians.[10] Salutius' protest was ruse, his motives puzzling. He was a sincere polytheist renowned for honesty and fair policy. He was one of two consuls of the Empire and Prefect of the East. Julian's general and successor, Jovian, chose him to negotiate a peace treaty with Persia. His protest was perhaps a test to see how much religion affected politics. Julian had expressly denied donatives to Christians among his troops at Antioch, proof that he kept them in the army, knowing who they were. Jovian was favourable to Christians but quite tolerant of pagans.

By multiplying and selling tax-collection offices and allowing the death penalty for arrears, the Emperor Valentian (r. 364–375) created a swarm of rapacious officials, further demoralizing the population and ruining the economy.[11] He forbid selling slaves apart from the land. Slavery became serfdom. This was intended as a social reform. The dark ages were on the horizon but at the time some may have hoped barbarian invasion to be a liberation.

Christians are estimated to have been roughly a fifth of the populace of the Eastern Empire and a tenth of the West's at the end of the third century.[12]

Within a few years, hordes of Germanic peoples fleeing the Huns were granted permission to cross the Danube to find sanctuary on Roman soil.[13] They were refugees, not invaders. Exploited, starving, without shelter and threatened with slavery, they ran amok. When they offered to negotiate, the Romans unsuccessfully tried to massacre their leaders under a flag of truce. The refugees became an invading flood. On a day of sweltering heat Valens, choosing not to wait for Gratian's nearby forces to join him, fell with his army before the Gothic cavalry at Adrianople in 378.[14] Valens had been chosen co-emperor by the army at Jovian's death. He ruled the Eastern Empire. Gratian ruled the West. By 375 Gratian proclaimed his son Valentinian II emperor of the East. Gratian, burdened by putting down revolts and political machinations, arrived too late. Or were political motives involved on both sides?

Gratian's response was to decree that the unfit not be drafted and to execute many Goths in the Roman army despite their proven loyalty. Germanic tribesmen loyally serving Rome in response to the dearth of Roman manpower were massacred repeatedly when their victories for Rome and numbers became ominous to Roman leaders.[15] Most of the Roman army was barbarian by the fifth century,[16] with morale ever sinking.

The upper and middle classes continued to dwindle as taxes soared to support the ever increasing army and the bureaucracy as civilization crumbled. 'What are empires but groups of bandits grown large?' Augustine observed.[17] It was hardly encouraging to the Empire's defenders.

In the Roman Republic before the time of Jesus, Romans, with a population of some seven million, had repeatedly suffered losses in battle and shipwrecked fleets of 50,000 men at a time. More than five centuries later, with an imperial population of probably well over forty million, the Romans could not recover their losses at Adrianople. Family life had greatly weakened. The Church's advocacy of celibacy endorsed what pagan Romans of the Republic had regarded as narcissism. The influences of Greek scepticism and Montanism and Gnosticism, labels for a profound world weariness, seeped through all society.

Mobs were asserting power. In Rome, Damasus became bishop after thugs beat to death in the streets the emperor's nominee. He was soon overshadowed in influence by Ambrosius, a popular civil official of Milan, the Western Empire's new capital. A mob breaking into a cathedral had successfully demanded that he be made bishop although he was not yet baptized.

Gratian, emperor of the Western Empire, appointed Theodosius emperor of the Greek East. He soon regretted his naiveté. To retain predominance, he ordered all bishops of the Empire to council at Aquileia in 381. Only ten Italians attended. State and Church vied for dominance, each regarding the other as the aggressor.

Theodosius, without consulting Senate or Church council that year, ordered all bishops not adhering to the creed of the council of Nicea to be ousted. Construction of new church buildings by non-Nicean bishops was made illegal. The state, losing its grip on society, grappled with what it recognized increasingly as its replacement, the authority of the Church.

Damasus, bishop of Rome, as his predecessors, avoided any Church council summoned by the government. He invited all bishops to gather in Rome in 382. Only three easterners attended. Theodosius held a council in Constantinople in 383, inviting only his supporters. Damasus approved state suppression of the Arians as Arians had supported state suppression of the Nicenes. Meanwhile, Ambrosius won Theodosius' public penance for a massacre of 7,000 civilians by the army at a circus and forbid the emperor to allow the reconstruction of a Gnostic church and a synagogue destroyed by mobs.

Social responsibility plunged as the Eastern and Western Empires divided more widely. In the East, eunuchs became generals and high officials, a practice that had been punishable by death in the Roman Republic and that remained abhorrent in the West.

Gratian was regarded as incompetent, his court grossly corrupt. His effort to correct it without consulting any assembly was seen as an example of arrogance. In January 383, Theodosius ousted him. Theodosius was now the sole emperor. That summer the governor of Britain claimed the throne and entered Gaul with an army. Gratian, now a military commander, appealed to Theodosius for troops.

He received none. Marching to meet the usurper, most of Gratian's army deserted. With the frontiers collapsing, civil war seemed pointless and wrong to many.

In 383, all traces of paganism were removed from the Roman state by Theodosius. The army oath became exclusively Nicene Christian, all pagans and heretics ousted.

It was in 383 that Eucherius of Lyon sermonized on the Theban Legion, the earliest record of it.

The pagan Symmachus, a senator of Rome, eloquently pleaded for religious tolerance. He intended to keep Christianity and paganism distinct but his argument that all the names for the gods were names for the one contradicted. He was promoted to consul, now a powerless rank, and shelved. His senatorial colleagues in faith yielded without protest.

Nor did the pagan public fight to keep open their temples. The pendulum of public opinion had swung from readiness to believe everything to unwillingness to defend anything in particular. The gods committed murder, rape, robbery, incest and adultery, but no one any longer believed the myths. Christian mobs at times attacked pagan sites, brutally killing a priestess of Isis in Alexandria whom Jerome, the translator of the Bible into Latin, mourned as a brilliant mind and friend.

Arian Christians depended almost completely on the state for income, and lacked independent organization. Gradually losing favour among Romans, they succeeded in the first mission to the Goths led by Ulfilas who omitted the Book of the Maccabees from his Bible because it might encourage rebellion. The association of Arians with the barbarians did not endear them to many Romans.

Tertullian had been right. 'What has Athens to do with Jerusalem?' The ideological issues obsessing Christians in the fourth century were far removed from the mentality of the apostles. The faithful hotly argued over issues beyond reason. Theology obsessed all ranks of society while social justice eroded.

Two years after Theodosius ended religious tolerance Arbogast, a Frank of high rank in the army, and a pagan, declared Euginius, a senator of the city of Rome, nominal emperor. Euginius ordered all Christians to leave the army. Presumably he thought them to be a small minority.

The armies of Arbogast and Theodosius clashed at Frigidus in northern Italy, a direct combat of pagan against trinitarian Christians. Theodosius won, boasting that he had defeated two enemies at once by using his Goths in the front line of battle where they suffered horrific losses.

Analysis of the *Notitia Dignitatum* reveals that under the ill-fated reign of the Emperor Honorius (r. 395–423) almost half the units of Roman army were replaced, twenty-one of thirty-seven in Gaul. It is doubtful that all the losses were in battle against invaders. Civil war, purges, desertion and units cashiered took their toll.

The Eastern Empire chose to send no aid to save the West after countless invaders walked across the frozen Rhine in the winter of 407–408. The Western Empire's last great general, Stilicho, son of a Goth father and Roman mother, employed barbarians as temporary allies. As if jealous of his success he was executed by Byzantines in 408. Two years later, foe and ally Alaric and his Visigoths, exasperated by broken promises, sacked the city of Rome. An Arian Christian, Alaric wrote to the Bishop of Rome apologizing for his undisciplined tribesmen violating a truce allowing looting but not violence. He ignored the enfeebled Roman government of the West. The eastern Greek-speaking Empire, Byzantium, would survive until 1457. Byzantium would acquire a reputation for intrigue, spy craft, bribery, blackmail, and manipulation of one foe against another. Ironically, this seeming amorality was initially, perhaps, motivated by a Christian desire to avoid unnecessary bloodletting in war.

By the sixth century, on the frontier against Persia, Byzantine bishops were military-governors and rack-rent landlords. In the East, military martyrs who had died for disobeying immoral orders became crusading heroes to Orthodox Christians, Church and state united in a fashion never fully accepted by western churchmen opposing domination by the state.

Soviet autocracy, fixed prices and militarism would be the heirs of Byzantium.

Afterword

There can be no progress unless people demand it. Those in power have never yielded it otherwise and never will.

                                                                    Frederick Douglass

In the Empire's fall Athanasius declared 'It is not right to kill, yet in war it is lawful to destroy the enemy.'[1] Augustine approved the soldier killing to defend civilians, but condemned citizens killing in self-defence,[2] a reflection of Roman ruling caste values viewing ordinary citizens to be more dangerous than any invader. Augustine justified the soldier obeying immoral orders since they were legal, a far cry from the early Church's view.[3] Unintentionally, he opened the door to the 'I was only obeying my orders' rationale for war crimes. The failure of the Empire to establish any short term of service discouraged voluntary enlistment in the military. Rome had no shorter term of enlistment because it feared having many of the populace trained for war – or revolt. Meanwhile, Germanic peoples expected all able men to assemble yearly with their weapons. Among Romans, rank had become caste, whereas among barbarians talent and character could still earn promotion.

No Christian military gravestones are known from the fourth century except those of soldiers of the Sagittari Nervi and the Leones,[4] both units sharing the shield design of the original Theban Legion.

By 416, no pagans were allowed to enter the army,[5] evidence that earlier decrees had failed. The typical Roman soldier had become an unlettered barbarian indifferently respectful to any creed of convenience required of him. Augustine declared 'We are defended by heretics and barbarians.'[6] He wrote of his region of North Africa but the statement was generally true empire-wide.

The Roman Empire in Western Europe and North Africa collapsed when its forces were strongest in number and tax support in the Empire's history. Many things undermined it but militarism was the most harmful. Rome could defeat the barbarians, relatively few and poorly organized as they were. It could not check the *bagaudae* who held Roman ruin to be a liberation.

The collapse of the Soviet Union with its enormous military budget is a modern example of horrendous military expenditures ruining economy and society.

Is it coincidence that Eucherius, Bishop of Lyon, in 383 wrote the first known mention of the Theban Legion, the year that Theodosius purged the army of all but Nicene Christians? His account can be taken as honouring Christian soldiers as defenders of the public or warning that military authority must not supersede God and conscience. It accepts Christians as military without blindly idolizing the state. There is no mention of the theology of Theban creed. Eucherius praises Theban loyalty to the Senate and the people of Rome, a concept echoing the virtues of the Roman Republic, not the empire that had suffocated them. The Senate, by 383, was the last centre of paganism as exemplified by Symmachus, whose priority was not paganism but religious freedom.

Significantly, the Eastern Church, Orthodox Christianity, never recognized the Theban legionnaires in its calendar of saints, as their insubordination was viewed as anathema.

Within a generation, Augustine of Hippo would approve Christian soldiers waging 'just wars'. Machiavelli more than a thousand years later would simplify Augustine, declaring that a morally just war was a necessary war. While pagans declared that the Empire's sharp decline was due to abandonment of the imperial cult, Augustine argued that under paganism Rome had suffered many defeats and yet recovered. He wrote that while barbarians were besieging the walls of his city, most of the citizens were attending the racetrack.

During the US war in Vietnam, candidates for military conscription could appeal to a draft board for exemption on grounds of conscientious objection. Those declaring themselves absolute pacifists who would not use violence even to save a loved one from a madman intending to reduce them to chicken salad, were, generally, successful. Those appealing according to Augustine's view, that some wars were just and others not (i.e., that a person morally has the right and obligation to choose the war to fight, they would fight against Hitler but not against Ho Chi Minh) received five years in a federal penitentiary. That, in effect, was religious discrimination by the US government.

War is the extension – and the failure – of politics, the military the link between them. The Theban legionnaires made no effort to overthrow government, unlike many before them. They did not seek political power. They sought to peacefully influence events to preserve Roman law and order.

Political leaders ordering war without respecting the input of the military on countless occasions has brought disaster. Perhaps worst of all is the blind obedience of professional military to the politicians. Silence gives consent and much of the media confirms it.

The thrust of organized violence is powerful, but deterrence once triggered into action escalates violence. International police action may serve as a brake upon putting massive armed forces into action. There is no need to destroy a criminal's neighbourhood or nation in order to stop him. Police action is preferable to war.

Killing enemies in large numbers does not guarantee victory – the First World War an example. Wars cannot be won by making enemies faster than they can be killed. Killing can be counterproductive because it promotes the opposition of loved ones, neighbours and compatriots and the previously neutral. To refuse to negotiate is both immoral and historically stupid.

Diplomacy and deterrence, peaceful protest and potential disorder function each as the blade of a pair of scissors, the cutting edges of progress. War is the failure to employ them. Peace and development must be offered.

The moral priority of the Gospels is the de-escalation of violence. To turn the other cheek to insult, to return good for evil, to love one's enemies, to carry the shield a mile more than demanded – all are intended to de-escalate violence. In a world of atomic, bacteriological and chemical weapons, the priority is all the greater. ABC weapons could be the XYZ of mankind.

More so than ever before, a thoroughly professional military is required, yet this risks militarism. Most dictatorships are military. Requiring every male citizen to serve one to two years in the military or community service lessens the danger of Praetorianism and the belligerence of civilians who have never served a day in the armed forces. Effective potential deterrence should not be overdone lest it create a paranoiac arms race.

To believe that no military or police are necessary is surely unsupported by history. Morality deals with what could or should be. It is intended to change human behaviour. It is future oriented, but often not given the generations in time needed for good example to be effective and imitated. It is not immediately realistic. It is revolutionary. Morals are ideals and as such they do not change. Thou shalt not kill is non-negotiable. But unwillingness and unreadiness to fight can invite attack. Most wars begin with misunderstanding by one side or the other.

The individual, in order to have a morality that can effectively influence society, needs an organized community of shared belief, *consciencia*, in the original Latin meaning of the word. Pacifism risks passivity, like Pilate's washing his hands of responsibility. The peace movement during the war in Vietnam abruptly ended with the end of military conscription in the US, an ambiguous legacy. Were people protesting the war or the chance of being drafted?

If all decent folk avoid military service, they yield the military to those of ill-will. How best influence any institution, from within or from outside?

A true pacifist must be as willing to risk his life as much as a soldier. Every situation differs. Every individual has a distinct temperament, upbringing and vocation to fulfil.

Example convinces better than words. The Theban legionnaires gave such example.

It can be argued that the evidence of the Theban Legion is purely coincidental. How much coincidence is needed as proof? Only the veracity of the Theban Legion's legend can explain them all, whether a papyrus receipt for shipping out rations, coinage, the relationship of army units in the *Notitia Dignitatum*, martyrs' Acts, London's Fetter Lane coin hoard, or the Autun inscription etc., all fit the irregular pattern that like a key only the legend can satisfy.

The Theban legionnaires were citizen–soldiers who forced authority to change unjust policies later acknowledged as counterproductive. They did not desert or mutiny. Their discipline was extraordinary.

They successfully de-escalated violence, as must we all.

Notes

Abbreviations

AA	Acts of the Apostles
AB	*Analecta Bollandiana*
AM	Ammianus Marcellinus
AVE	Aurelius Victor: *Epitomes*
AVC	Aurelis Victor: *De Caesaritus*
BHG	Aegyptische Urkunden aus den Museen zu Berlin
BMC	British Museum Collection
CIL	*Corpus Inscriptionum Latinarum*
DC	Dio Cassius
EHE	Eusebius: *Historia Ecclesia*
Eutr	Eutropius
EVC	Eusebius: *Vita Constantini*
HR	Herodian
JRS	*Journal of Roman Studies*
LMP	Lactantius: *De Mortius de Persecutum*
MGH	*Monumenta Germanicorum Historia*
MPG	Migne: *Patrologia Graecae*
MPL	Migne: *Patrologia Latini*
ND	*Notitia Dignitatum*
PB	Petit Bollandists
PL	Galletier: *Panegyriques Latini*
PROS	M.LH. Jones: *Prosographia Romanorum*
PWK	Pauly-Wilsowa-Kroll: *Real Encylopaedia*
RM	*Martyrologium Romanum*
SAN	*Journal of the Society for Ancient Numismatics*
SHA	Vopiscus: *Scriptores Historia Augusta*
SS	Sancti Sanctorum
SU	Suetonius
TA	Tacitus: *Annales*
TER	Tertullian
ZON	Zonaras
ZOS	Zosimus

Foreword

1. Mt 22:15:22; Mk 12:13–17; Lk 20:20–26.
2. Josephus: *Antiquities of the Jews* 14:10, 6 & 12.
3. G. Cheesman: *Auxiliaries of the Roman Army*, rp Chicago, 1975.
4. Cicero: *De Divinatione and De Natura Erorum* 1:2–4. Cicero believed in ghosts but not the gods.
5. In *Catilinam* 4:6, 12 and *Ad Familia* 4:12, 3. Pliny over a century later describes a similar massacre of slaves in *Epistolae* 3:14, 25.

6. In F. Cowell: *Cicero and the Roman Republic*, New York, 1948, p. 277.
7. Jn. 16.
8. G.R. Driver: *The Judaean Scrolls*, New York, 1965, p. 199.
9. J.P. Balsdon: 'The Salii and Campaigning in March and October', *Classical Review*, London, June 1966, pp. 146–147.
10. LRE, p. 614.
11. Mt 5:39, Lk 6:29.
12. M. Aurelius 6:6. Another seemingly Christian sentiment of Aurelius was that 'It is man's peculiar duty to love even those who wrong him.' 7:22.
13. A.M. Duff: *The Freedmen in the Early Roman Empire*, New York, 1958, p. 24.
14. Lk 22:36. Mt 26:51.

Introduction
1. H. Delehaye: *Legends of the Saints*, New York, 1961, is a general critique.
2. L. Dupraz: *Les Passions de St Maurice d'Agaune*, Fribourg, 1961.
3. F.H. Cramer: 'Book Burning and Censorship in Ancient Rome', *Journal of the History of Ideas*, New York, 1945, gives many examples.
4. Eusebius: *Historia Ecclesia*.
5. Lactantius: *Divine Institutes VI, XX*, 15–16.
6. D. O'Leary: *The Saints of Egypt*, London, 1937.

Chapter 1
1. A.S. Hunt & C.C. Edgar: *Select Papyri*, London, 1995, rp 1934, II 426 pp. 581–583 and 237, pp. 141–143. P. Parsons: *City of the Sharp-Nosed Fish* (Oxyrhinchus), London, 2007.
2. Juv 16.
3. N. Lewis: *Life in Egypt Under Roman Rule*, New York, 1985, p. 5455.
4. Juv II.
5. H.I. Bell: *Cults and Creeds in Greco-Roman Egypt*, New York, 1953, p. 20.
6. Parker Legions 163, ILS 2288 & BGU I, 140.
7. Dio Cassius LXXVII, 22–23. HR 6:4, 7.
8. J.G. Milne: *History of Egypt Under Roman Rule*, Chicago, 1992, pp. 63, 165–166.
9. Ibid, p. 306 n 21.
10. Ibid, p. 63.
11. P. Geiss 40, M. Car. 377, in Abbott p. 548 and p. 93.
12. Ibid. p. 57.
13. Ibid. p. 297 n 35.
14. Ibid. p. 547–550.
15. SHA Probus 9.
16. W.A. Fairservis: *Ancient Kingdoms of the Nile*, New York, 1962, pp. 192–194.
17. SHA Probus 17.
18. Milne, p. 79.
19. Fairservis, pp. 14 & 46.
20. G. Webster: *Roman Imperial Army*, New York, 1994, p. 165. Citizenship was received at discharge.
21. Y.L. Bohec: *The Imperial Roman Army*, New York, 1994, pp. 101–102. Webster, p. 41 n 2.
22. Hunt, P. Oxyrynchus 1115 now in Brussels Museum as B11-E6009.
23. R. MacMullen: *Soldier & Civilian in the Later Roman Empire*, Cambridge, 1967, 4 n 8. A legion consumed 500 bushels of wheat a week. On the size of the Modius, A.H.M. Jones: *Decline of the Ancient World*, London, 1966, Appendix III, and R.P. Duncan-Jones: *Size of the Modius Castrensis, Zeitschrift Papyrologie Epigraphik*, XXI, 1976,

pp. 53–6. The modius measured volume. As a ration of bread rather than loose wheat it was a larger quantity. C. Clark: *Starvation or Plenty?*, New York, 1970, p. 19 on nutritional needs.

24. P. Oxyrynchus 1412 in Hunt pp. 140–43.
25. J.G. Milne: *Catalogue of Alexandrian Coins*, Oxford 1971, pp. 112–113. 4674–4682, 4690–4696, 4710–4718, 4728–4730, in the BMC British Museum Catalogue these parallel 4675, 4679, 4693, 4728, 5597, 2463, 2472–2473, 5604–5605. Keith Emmett: *Alexandrian Coins*, Lodi Wisc., 2001, pp. 205–06, 4005 + 4018. The American Numismatic Association has several of 283/284 with the more common abbreviation for Oxyrynchus, a dot within a circle and a circle, the Greek omikron and psi on the banners. Milne, Addenda.
26. D. O'Reilly: SAN 8:1976.

Ruler	Legion	
Trajan	II Traiana	BMC Lycaonia 1.
Trajan	XX Ulpia	E.A. Sydenham, *Coinage of Caesaria in Cappadocia*, London, 1933 #225.
Marcus Aurelius	II and/or III	Italica BMC Alexandria, 277.
Lucius Verus	II and/or III	Italica G. Dattari, Numi Augustorum Alexandrini, Cairo 1901, 3415–76, 3695–96.
Commodus	Nova Classis	Libica BMC Alexandria 1367 V
Commodus	II Parthica	BMC Phrygia 3 T.
Septimius Severus	II Parthica	BMC Alexandria 1462 V.
Septimius Severus	II Parthica	BMC Phrygia 49.
Caracalla	II Parthica	Ibid 56.
Caracalla	II Parthica	BMC Galatia 30 and 31
Geta	II Parthica	BMC Phrygia 53, 55 and 57.
Julia Domma	Julia Alexandria	J.W. Curtis, *Tetradrachms of Roman Egypt*, Chicago, 1969, 912.
Severus Alexander	IV Italica	Sydenham, 565.
Gordian III	I, II and III Isaura	A. Krzyanowska, *Mormaies Coloniales d'Antioche de Pisidie*, Warsaw, 1930, Av. II, Rv. 9.
Philip I	I, II and III Isaura	Ibid. Av. II Rv. 1, Av IV Rv 6.
Philip II	I, II and III Isaura	BMC Lycia 122.
Trajan Decius	I, II and III Isaura	Ibid. 126.
Trajan Decius	I, II and III Isaura	BMC Arabia 34–36.
Volusian	I, II and III Isaura	Krzyanowska Av II, Rv 3–4, Av IV, Rv 10, 12.
Claudius II	IV Martia	G. MacDonald, *Catalogue of Greek Coins in the Hunterian Collection*, Glasgow, 1905, Vol. III, Alexandria 992.
Aurelian	I Illyricorum	BMC Alexandria 2370–73.
Carus	The Theban Legion	Ibid. 2442–44 v.
Carinus	The Theban Legion	Ibid. 2448–51, 4460–61, 3351.
Numerian	The Theban Legion	Ibid. 2463, 2470–73.
Diocletian	The Theban Legion	Ibid. 2538–39.
Diocletian	I Armeniaca	J.G. Milne, *Alexandrian Coins in the Ashmolean Museum*, London, 1933, p. 2531.
Maximian	II Armeniaca	Ibid. 2536.
Maximian	IV Parthica	Ibid. 5117.
Diocletian	V Parthica	Dattari 5815.
Constantius	I Pontica	BMC Alexandria 2539.

Galerius V	I Parthica	Dattari 6108.
Maxentius	Ioviani	RIC Vol. VI. 345–52.
Domitius		
Alexander	Flavia Victrix	Ibid. 72 (Carthage).
	Constantiniana	
Constantine	Herculiani	Ibid. 69, 94–99 (Ostia).
Licinius	Herculiani	Ibid. 95b, 97b.
Maximian	Herculiani	Ibid. 95a, 97a, 99.
Licinius	Herculiani	Ibid. 95b, 97b.
Maximian	Herculiani	Ibid. 95a, 97a, 99.

For Trajan's new legions see PWK XIII c1483, XII c1821. For Marcus Aurelius' legions see c. 1409, and 1465. For Septimius Severus' legions see c1435, 1475, and 1542. For Severus Alexander's legions see c1407, 1468, and 1532. For Philip I's legions see SHA Probus 16:5 and 17:1. For Claudius Gothicus' legions see PWK c1406. For Diocletian's legions see Ritterling PWK 12 (1925) 1491.

27. Musurillo.
28. Milne, Catalogue 4742–4745 and 4747.
29. Ibid. p. 126.

Chapter 2

1. Cornish, *Concise Dictionary of Greek and Roman Antiquities*, Lonon, 1898, 5766.
2. N. Barbour: Morocco, New York, 1966, pp. 33–39. J. Willard: *The Great Sahara*, New York, 1978. Ch. 3.
3. F. Snowdon: *Blacks in Antiquity*, Cambridge, 1970, p. 242.
4. SHA: Severus 18.
5. J. Abun-Nasr: *History of the Mahgrib*, London, 1971, p. 19.
6. Augustine.
7. Abun-Nasr, p. 25.
8. S. Raven: *Rome in Africa*, New York 1993, p. 83.
9. Ibid.
10. Abun-Nasr.
11. D.C. Den Boer: *Lusius Quietus*, Mnemosyne 1959, Fasc. 3 & 4.
12. SHA Pescennius, Hr 2.
13. Willard.
14. Ter Apol 38:3.
15. Ter Ad Scap 2.
16. Cyprian: Epistolae 55:9.
17. Raven, p. 168.
18. SHA Gordian, Zos I, Zon XII.
19. Parker, *History*, p. 148.
20. Parker, ibid, ILS 531.
21. Webster, p. 87.
22. Parker, *History*, p. 179.
23. Venatus Fortunatus 14.
24. DC 5:3 & 74:7. Probus was once commander of I Gallica Felix. SHA Probus 5:4.

Chapter 3

1. Apocryphal Gospel of Nicodemus.
2. SS 2 Mar, pp. 384–386.
3. Petrus de Natalibus, Catalogus Sanctorum, Vincentia 1493, XII 6:41.
4. Juvenal 14:86–106.

5. TA XV:45 46. Su VII:7–10.
6. Su Domitian 12:2.
7. M. Sordi: *Christians and the Roman Empire*, Norman 1986, pp. 47–8.
8. DC 68:1,2.
9. Su 10:4. TA, Agricola 45.
10. Sordi, pp. 43–40.
11. SS 3 May, Maro and two other guards died with them.
12. AB XVII, p. 172.
13. SS Sept VI (1757) pp. 123–135, p. 105, pp. 376–417.
14. SS 11 Jun, pp. 265–266.
15. SS 3 Mar, p. 80,004. Among thousands of soldiers' epitaphs in L.R. Dean: *Cognomina of Soldiers in the Legions*, Princeton, 1916, there is no Zoticus, Irenaeus or Hyacinth.
16. SS 2 Sept.
17. SS 27 Jul.
18. SS 2 Sept., pp. 511–517.
19. Pliny, Epistolae X:96.
20. Sordi, pp. 59–78.
21. Ibid.
22. Ibid pp. 66–7. DAG XXII:5,3.
23. HMD Parker, *History of the Roman World*, pp. 22–3.
24. DC LXXI, pp. 8–10, SHA: Marcus Aurelius.
25. EHE XV, pp. 1–2. SS Apr. 3, pp. 564–565.
26. Ter Apologia V:6.
27. Dupraz, pp. 232–235.
28. Ter Apologia XXXVII:4,5.
29. C.S. Welles: *Immunitas of Roman Legionaries in Egypt*, JRS XXVIII, p. 193 and WRS pp. 75–7.
30. H. Musurillo, Acts of the Christian Martyrs, London 1972, p. 261.
31. Hippolytus: *Apostolic Constitution* XVI:17–19.
32. Ter De Corona 1:4–5.
33. Ibid.
34. Ibid 15.
35. DC 71:28. SHA Marcus Aurelius 25, 4 & 26, 1.
36. L. Wooley: *Rome Beyond the Frontiers*, New York 1950, p. 87.
37. Sordi, p. 73 n 35.
38. SHA Severus Alexander 22:4, 24:2, 43:6, 45:6, 49:6, 51:7.
39. A. Quacqarelli: *Note Siigli Edifici di Culto Primo di Constantino Vetera Christianorum*, p. 14, Rome, 1977.
40. Cyriacus Aug. 23 HL.
41. Clement: *Propreticus* X,10.
42. The Apostolic Constitution forbade catechumens to become soldiers. Book VIII:32 reads: 'The soldier who presents himself for baptism is to be instructed that he must do violence to no man, and be content with his hire (Lk 3:14). If he promises to observe this rule he is to be accepted; if he refuses he is to be rejected.' This can be taken to imply military service is permitted to enlisted man with *immunitas*. The Testament of the Lord, a document from Syria, reads: 'But if soldiers wish to be baptized to the Lord, let them quit military service or the position of authority or else let them not be accepted.' Canon 28 from Egypt states: 'They shall not receive into the Church one of the emperor's soldiers. If they have received him he shall refuse to kill if commanded to do so. If he does not refrain he shall be rejected.' This affirms that some enlisted men were baptized, the Church's objection to killing, not military service *per se*. Cited in J. Ferguson: *The Politics of Love, the New Testament and Non-Violent Revolution*, New York 1975, p. 64.

43. EHE 6:28, HR 8:1, SHA Maximini, Zon XII:19, EHE.
44. RIC Philip.
45. Origen: Contra Celsus IV:52.
46. Frend 468 n 17.
47. EHE VII:15, 1.
48. Ter: De Idolatria XIX:49.
49. Commodianus: *Carmen Apologeticum* 826 ff, Cyprian: *Ad Demetrianum*.
50. Ibid, EHE VI:41.

Chapter 4
1. H. Zilliacos: *Sylloge Inscriptionum Christianarum Veterum*, Vatican, 1963. G. Snyder: *Ante Pacem, Archeological Evidence of Christian Life Before Constantine*, Chelsea, 1985. Of 164 surviving epitaphs of Jews at Rome, sixty-five are of children less than ten years of age. H.J. Leon: *Jews of Ancient Rome*, Philadelphia, 1960, p. 229. T.J. Parkin: *Demography and Roman Society*, Baltimore, 1992, presents the many approaches to population studies.
2. *L'Année Epigraphique* (1973) #235.
3. EHE 6:41, 1.
4. De Ruggiero: *Dizionario Epigrafico*, Rome, 1924, VI:1 p. 813ff. From Egypt 43 *libelli* survive, not all Christian.
5. Frend, pp. 301–303.
6. V. Giovardi, 'Acta Passionis et Translationis', *SSMM Mercuri ac XII Fratrum*, Rome, 1730.
7. RM 10 Dec.
8. SS 11 Oct.
9. SS 1 Jun., pp. 25–30.
10. EHE VI:42–52.
11. RM 7 Dec.
12. EHE VI:41–7 and 42–52.
13. Gregory of Tours, *In Gloria Martyrum*, p. 101, 15 May.
14. SS 2 Sept.
15. P. Maltzew: *Menologium der Orthodox Katholischen Kirche des Morganlandes*, Berlin, 1900. 17 Apr.
16. SS 30 Jun.
17. EHE.
18. EHE VII:15.1. Sordi 110.
19. Cyprian: Epistolae 55,9.
20. Zos 1:23, Zon XII:21.
21. Zos 1:37, AVC 30, Eutr IX:5.
22. EHE VI Zon, ibid, Cyprian Epistolae LIX:6.
23. SS Jul VI.
24. Zos 1:28, Eutr, AVC 31, Zon.
25. Zos 1:4 SHA Gallienus 13:6–8.
26. Ter Apologia 40.
27. Petrus 4 Dec., & 26 Jul.
28. EHE VII:10.
29. Frend p. 316–321, Cyprian 76 & 79.
30. Sordi 120 n 13.
31. Bibl. Cassino III ff 49–54, 2 Jan.
32. SS Feb. II 651–652. Gregory Gloria p. 102.
33. SHA Valerian, Zos 1:36, Zon 12:23; Eutro 8:7.
34. EHE VII:23,4.
35. Ibid.

188 Lost Legion Rediscovered

36. Zos 1:41, SHA Gallienus 14.
37. SS 3 Mar., 800–804.
38. HL 25 Oct.
39. HL 4 May.
40. AS 15 Jul.
41. SHA Aurelian 25:6, 28:5, 35:3.
42. RM 8 Jul.
43. RM 25 Oct.
44. RM 8 Jul.

Chapter 5

1. Archelaus: 'Acts of the Disputation with the Heresiarch Mani', tr. Salmond in A. Roberts & J. Donaldson: *Ante-Nicene Fathers*, New York, 1945, VI p. 175–181 and Chapter 37 K. Bihlmeyer & H. Tuchle: *Church History*, Paderborn, 1958, 1 pp. 143–44, 163–64, 247.
2. Kas and Kasr derive from the Latin *castra*, a fort. Thus Castra Carrhae became Caschar. W. Smith: *Dictionary of Greek and Roman Geography*, New York, 1966. Zos 3:13 cites Carrhae as the border bastion.
3. Plutarch: *Crassus*, DC 40:15.
4. Archelaus.
5. Ibid.
6. Ibid.
7. Ibid.
8. Ibid.

Chapter 6

1. Archelaus. A modern traveller's description of the region is F. Stark: *Rome on the Euphrates*, New York, 1966.
2. Archelaus, Introduction.
3. K. Baus: *From the Apostolic Community to Constantine*, New York, 1965, 154 ff.
4. Archelaus, ch. 37. Cyril of Jerusalem: *Catechesia VI*, p. 140 and Eusebius: *Chronicon, Lib. Post.* p. 177 agree with this dating.
5. J. Le Breton and J. Zeiller: *Triumph of Christianity*, New York, 1962, pp. 115–123 holds that Mani never visited the Roman Empire and died in 272 but makes no mention of Archelaus. J. Neusner: *History of the Jews in Babylonia*, Leiden, 1968, III, p. 7 places Mani's death in 277. Cyril of Jerusalem, *Catechesia VI*, 104. Eusebius: *Chronicon*, Lib. Post, p. 177 supports this.
6. *Prosographia Latini Marcellinus 1*, p. 544. Zos 1:60.
7. SHA The 30 Pretenders 30:24–27 & 27–28.
8. Zos 1:59.
9. Archelaus.
10. Cornish, p. 576.
11. Ibid, p. 556.
12. Cato: *De Agricultura* 2:5–7 & 56. Plutarch: *Cato the Elder*.
13. Cornish, p. 556.
14. Horace: *Epistles* Bk. 11:1.
15. Epistle of Paul to Philemon.
16. SHA Aurelius 31:5–10.
17. WRS p. 108.
18. Archelaus.
19. Lk 3:14.
20. A. Alston: *Soldier and Society in Roman Egypt*, London, 1995, pp. 105–108.
21. SHA Aurelian XXXI.

22. Gratian: *Concordia Discordantum Canonum Decretum* 1:4, 7.
23. Vincent of Beauvais: *Speculum Mundi* XIII:II.

Chapter 7
  1. Justin: *Apology* 1, 39 and *Dialogue* 110.
  2. Tatian: *Oratian* 11.
  3. Athenagoras: *Plea for Christians* 35.
  4. Origin: *Against Celsus* VIII:68.
  5. Lactantius.
  6. Deuteronomy, 30:5–7.
  7. Ruderman: 'Peace in Jewish Law', Fellowship, Nyak 1:976, 42 p. 10 citing Tosefta, Sotah 7:14.
  8. Deuteronomy. Nevertheless 20:15–18 approves genocide.
  9. Josephus, *Antiquities of the Jews*, 14:10,6.
 10. M. Burrows ed. *The Dead Sea Scrolls*, New York, 1955, p. 257. Driver, p. 197.
 11. Watson, p. 31.
 12. Josephus, XIII, 9:1.
 13. Josephus, XIII, 11:3.
 14. Josephus, XIII, 15–4.
 15. Josephus, XIV, 15:2.
 16. N.J. McEleney: 'Conversion, Circumcision and the Law', *Testamentum*, London, 1974, XX p. 323 and 443–44.
 17. Josephus, *Wars of the Jews*, 1, 20:3.
 18. Josephus, Ant. XIX, 9:1–2.
 19. Josephus, ibid.
 20. B. Porter: *Archives from Elephantine, Life of and Ancient Jewish Military Colony*, Berkeley, 1968.
 21. Josephus, Ant. XVII, 2,1.
 22. Josephus, ibid XVIII: 3,5, Tacitus Annals 11 85, Su Tiberius 36.
 23. Josephus.
 24. Ibid, E.I. Merrill: 'Expulsion of Jews from Rome under Tiberius', *Classical Philology*, 14:365–72 (1919).
 25. Lk 3:12–14.
 26. Mt 21:12, MkII: 15–17, Lk 19:45, Jn 2:14–17.
 27. Lk 22:36.
 28. J.L. McKenzie: *Dictionary of the Bible*, Milwaukee, 1965, p. 403.
 29. A. Nolan: *Jesus Before Christianity*, New York, 1976, pp. 114–116.
 30. Mt 26:52.
 31. Mt 27:11, MK 15:2, Lk 23:3.
 32. Mt 23:37, Lk 13:34.
 33. Acts 1:6–7.
 34. G.L. Cheesman: *The Auxilia of the Roman Army*, Chicago, 1975.
 35. Ibid, Appendix II, Palestine.
 36. A.H.M. Jones: *The Herods of Judaea*, Oxford, 1967, p. 170.
 37. T.R.S. Broughton: 'The Roman Army' in F.F. Foakes-Jackson and E. Lake, eds *Beginnings of Christianity*, London, 1933, Part I, Vol. 5, p. 421.
 38. AA 10, 1–11, 18.
 39. Jones.
 40. WRS 87 & 153. DC XXV:6.
 41. H.M.D. Parker: *The Roman Legions*, New York, 1971, pp. 185–86.
 42. AA 22:25.
 43. AA 23:17.

44. AA 27:1.
45. Cheesman, Appendix I.

Chapter 8

1. J.T. Milik: *Revue Biblique* RB 60 (1953) 276ff, J.J. Rabinowitz RB 61 (1954), 191–192 and F.M. Cross RB 63 (1956) 47–48. A letter of Bar Kochba discovered in the 1950s refers with hostility to Galileans, perhaps Christians.
2. Y. Yadin: *Bar-Kokhba*, New York, 1971, pp. 19–23.
3. Babylonian Talmud Berakoth XXIXA. Epiphanius: Medicine Box XXIX.9.2. In W.H.C. Frend: *The Rise of Christianity*, Philadelphia, 1984, p. 126. G. Dix: *Jew and Greek*, London, 1967, p. 63. Jn. 9:22 & 12:42 speaks of expulsion from the synagogues. J.D.G. Dunn ed., *Jews and Christians: the parting of the ways A.D. 70 to 135*, Cambridge, 1992.
4. L. Kadman: *Coins of Aelia Capitolina*, Jerusalem, 1956, Serapis types 39–42. Nemisis, an Egyptian Goddess, is another common image on Aelia's coins. Y. Meshorer: *The Coinage of Aelia Capitolina*, Jerusalem, 1989, p. 32. Veterans were also retired to Sebaste, Neapolis and Caesarea in Samaria, Ptolemais in Galilea and Bostra, Sidon, Tyre, Damascus, Beirut and Antioch. Stevenson, p. 228
5. *Archaeology*, Jerusalem, 1974 p. 138.
6. T. Kollek & M. Pearlman: *Jerusalem*, New York, 1968, p. 138.
7. K. Bihlmeyer & H. Tuchle: *Church History*, Paderborn, 1958, I 143–144, pp. 163–64, 247.
8. Ibid. Frend: *Martyrdom*, pp. 170–74.
9. P. Vitz: *Faith of the Fatherless*, New York, 1999, p. 14.
10. Mt. 16:25, Mk. 8:35, Lk 9:24.
11. Mt. 8:8–9. Lk 7:6–8.
12. Mt. 6:14, Mk 11:25, Lk 17:3.
13. Galatians 2:28.
14. Julian: Letter to a Priest 305B.
15. Bihlmeyer, pp. 155–157, K. Baus: *From the Apostolic Community to Constantine*, Stuttgart, 1955, pp. 261–8, 490–492.
16. B. Altemeyer and B. Hunsberger: *Amazing Conversions*, Amherst, New York, 1997, pp. 251–252. This surveys 2,000 Canadian college students.
17. R. Stark: *Rise of Christianity*, New York, 1997, pp. 14–15.
18. Ibid, p. 113–114.
19. Ibid, p. 91–92. Histories 5:5.
20. Stark.
21. Catullus.
22. 1 Cor 7:12–16.
23. 1 Cor 12:13, Gal 3:28, Col 3:11.
24. Plutarch: *Superstitione IV*.
25. M.L.W. Laistner: *Christianity and Pagan Culture in the Later Roman Empire*, Ithaca, 1967, p. 38. C. Munier: *Concilia Gallia*, Turin 1963. In Gaul two years was customary. Hippolytus in Italy speaks of three years' probation.

Chapter 9

1. Polybius 6:56.
2. Ibid 18:35.
3. 1 6:45 & 11:43.
4. F.O. Copley: *Lucretius*, New York, 1977, VIII.
5. F. Cramer: *Astrology in Roman Law and Politics* Philadelphia, 1959, p. 248.
6. Celsus IV, 81.
7. Ibid, 23.

8. Ibid, 111:65.
9. Ibid, V, 34.
10. Ibid, V, 41.
11. Ibid, III, 55, VIII, 41.
12. OAA 2:4.
13. Seneca: *Ad Lucillus* 47:1.
14. Galen: *De Animi Rebus.*
15. Seneca 47:19.
16. Petronius: *Satyricon* 75.
17. Juv III:74.
18. Martial 5.
19. Galen cited in M.P. Charlesworth: *The Roman Empire*, New York, 1968, p. 48.

Chapter 10
1. Epictectus: 'Discourses III-7' in J. Bonforte: *Epictectus*, New York, 1974, p. 104.
2. Archelaus.
3. Cyprian: *Ad Demetrianum.*
4. Ibid.
5. S.C. Gilfillan: *Rome's Ruin by Lead Poison*, Long Beach, 1990.
6. B. Flower and E. Rosenbaum: *The Roman Cookery Book*, New York 1980, p. 96. J. Niragu: 'Saturnine Gout Among Roman Aristocrats, Did Lead Poisoning Cause the Fall of the Empire?', *New England Journal of Medicine* 308:11, Mar. 17, 1983, pp. 660–663. For critique, C.R. Phillips III: 'Old Wine in New Lead Bottles', *Classical World*, 78, 1984, pp. 29–33.
7. Jn 15:13.
8. Jn 4:20.
9. Dean.
10. AB (1933) citing Nicephorus 8-:1, 773. Mombritius: *Sanctuarium*, Milan – 1480, I:7–12. L. Surius: *De Probatis Sanctorum Historiis*, Cologne, 1574, p. 123–131.
11. SHA Probus 23.
12. Ibid.
13. Ibid.
14. Vegetius 1:13 & 2:23, CRE p. 634, DAG 10:1357.
15. Eucherius of Lyon in Dupraz, *Manuscript d'Couvent Einseideln* 256 (461) folio 374. *Campidoctor* was a duty status. An officer also had a title and a rank. Mauricius is cited as a *primicerius*, senior officer among equals in rank. A legion commander under Commodus was both *campidoctor* and in title *praepositus* or general. CIL II 4083 & ILS 2416. Exsuperius is cited as *signifer*. By deduction Candidus was *princeps*, second in command.

Chapter 11
1. H.M.D. Parker, *History of the Roman World*, London 1963, 2nd ed, p. 333, note 55.
2. Hunt, p. 134.
3. Ibid, p. 50 n.a.
4. W. Westermann: *Coptic Egypt*, New York, 1944 p. 12.
5. A. Paul: *History of the Beja Tribes*, London, 1971, p. 20 ff.
6. SHA Probus 14 and 20:1–2, 21:1–3.
7. Cheesman. WRS pp. 38–42.
8. Watson.
9. G. Rickman: *The Corn Supply of Ancient Rome*, New York, 1966.
10. Breasted: *Development of Religion and Thought in Ancient Egypt*, New York, 1959, rp. 1912, p. 602–603.
11. SHA Probus 20.

Chapter 12
1. SHA Firmus 8:17.
2. Philo: *Contra Flaccus* and *Legation Ad Gaius*.
3. EHE 7:22.
4. Clement: 'Exhortation' 10 and 'Instructor' 2:11.
5. Petronius in L.J. Peter: *Peter's Quotations*, p. 83.
6. SHA Carus 6:1. Carus punished the killers of Probus and, reconsidering, sought to remove Carinus from power, pp. 7 and 17.
7. L. Casson: *The Ancient Mariners*, New York, 1959.
8. AA 27.
9. J. Coles: *Archaeology by Experiment*, New York, 1973, pp. 123–26.
10. A. Hirtus: *De Bello Civile* 3:68.
11. Appian: *Historia Roma* 2:60. Every man in the fort had been wounded, several losing an eye. A centurion's shield had been hit 150 times.
12. Milne Catalogue XVI, 4. Alston.
13. T. Ravenscraft: *Spear of Destiny*, New York, 1973. H. Rachlin: *Lucy's Bones, Sacred Stones and Einstein's Brain*, New York, 1996, pp. 70–75.

Chapter 13
1. BGU 423 in Hunt I pp. 304–307. Another papyrus revealed Antoninus Maximus was married with two children on duty in Europe.
2. R. Thouvenot: *Volubilis*, Paris, 1949, p. 18.
3. Ulpian: *Digest* 9:3,5.
4. SHA 16 ff.
5. Madden: *Handbook of Roman Numismatics*, London, 1861, p. 166 pl. 3:2.
6. J. Kelly: *Oxford Dictionary of the Popes*, London, 1986.
7. SS 3 Feb, 62–65 and 2 Aug, 631–32. SS 11 Oct, 469–84. Hilari, his wife and sons, Maurus and Jason, died with Claudius. These were until recently the only married couples in the calendar of the saints.
8. ND OC:V:60 Legio Felices Valentinianenses.
9. J. Carcopino: *Daily Life in Ancient Rome*, New Haven, 1958, p. 210. J. Balsdon: *Life and Leisure in Ancient Rome*, London, 1969. The dole was grain and at times basic foods distributed monthly. Aurelian made it a daily ration of free grain, meat, oil and salt. SHA Aurelian 35:1 and 48:1, Zos 1:61, Hydatius 1:148 A.D. 354.
10. OAA 1:135–64.
11. Pliny: Panegyric 33.
12. DC 54:17.
13. Su: Augustus 4S and Su. Vitellius 7:1 and D 6S.
14. Juv 10. Cicero Tusculum 2 and Pliny 33. Aurelius 1:5 and SHA M. Aurelius 11:4.
15. Seneca 7:4.
16. Statius 1:6, pp. 51–64.
17. Martial: *Liber Spectaculorum*.
18. Martial: *Epigrams* 5.
19. SHA: *The Two Gallieni* 12:2.

Chapter 14
1. TA 15.
2. Cicero: *De Officiis* 1:150.
3. C.A. Barton: *The Sorrows of the Ancient Romans, the Gladiator and the Monster*, Princeton, 1993, p. 25.
4. *Tusculanae Disputationes* 2.17.41.
5. J.P. Levy: *The Economic Life of the Ancient World*, Chicago, 1967, p. 58.

6. Ibid, p. 82.
7. Seneca 47:5.
8. J. Crook: *Laws and Life of Rome*, Ithaca, 1967, pp. 107–110.
9. DC 73:11, Hr 2:6.
10. MPG p. 114, 968–981.
11. H. Signon: *Die Romer in Koln*, Frankfurt, 1972, pp. 166 and 171.
12. LRE pp. 57–8.
13. AVE 39.
14. SHA: Carus 12 and 13, Eutr 9:20, Zon 12:31. Diocletian swore innocence of Numerian's death in an oath to the sun god.

Chapter 15
1. F.D. Ringrose: 'Find of Alexandrian coins in London', *Numismatic Chronicle*, London, 1911, pp. 357–538. The latest is the type with a variant having the Theban monogram.
2. J.G. Milne: *Finds of Greek Coins in the British Isles*, London, 1948, p. 32.
3. Ibid, Appendix 11.
4. Ibid.
5. A. Blanchet: *Les Tresors de Monnaies Romanies et les Invasions Germaniques*, Paris, 1900. Blanchet cites several large hoards of Alexandrian coins that were found in Switzerland. Tracking hoards of Carinus, Maximian and Diocletian from Nyon on Lake Leman into France towards Marseilles are 825, 831, 195, 193, 212, 213, 214, 216. A thrust westwards from Nyon towards River Cher is revealed by hoards 297, 307, 286, 274, 564. A thrust northwards by Maximian's troops who had arrived at Nantes on the Loire by way of the Garonne from Marseilles is indicated by 18, 22, 365, 398, 477, 63, 77, 78, 667 and 693. Rictovarius' column from the Belgian border eastwards to meet the column advancing from Nevers to Trier is revealed by 244, 245, 249, 157, 146, 153, 784, 797 and 798. These are congruent with sites of martyrdoms in or about 286: Aquilinus, Dinocus, Valerianus, Dubanus, Ferreolus, Genesius, Baudelius, Defendens, Adrianus, Victor, Florentina, Maxima, Amandus. Maximian's movement from Marseilles to the Loire parallels Florentia, Vincent, Genesius, Luperculus, Foi, Caprasius, Donatianus, Clarus, Maxima, and Nicasius. Rictovarius' path overlaps the sites of Justus, Lucian, Achius, Fuscian, Terentianus, Quentin, Piat, Rufinus, Crispin, Macra, Maurus, Timothy, Agricius, Palmatuis, Maxentius and Thyrsus, Amor, Regina, Petrusius, Sabinianus and Ulphus.
6. S. Johnson: *Roman Forts of the Saxon Shore*, London, 1976, pp. 112–113. D. White: *Litus Saxonicum*, Madison 1961.
7. N. Shiel: *The Episode of Carausius and Allectus*, London, 1977. AVE 39, Eutr 9:21, Orosius 7:25. Orosius states that Maximian was promoted to Augustus specifically to deal with Carausius. J. Anderson: 'Notes on the Survival of Pagan Customs in Christian Burials, Proceedings of the Society of Antiquaries of Scotland XI', p. 367 in Shiel p. 3435.
8. AVE XXXIX.
9. PI Constantio Caesari Dictus V: *Numismatic Chronicle XIX*, 1939, p. 291, cites a unique coin of Carausius found at Magna Castra farm, Kentchester, its reverse VOT SVSC _ _ _ AVG IIII. C.H. Sutherland held the missing three spaces to be numbers and AVG IIII to be read as AVG IMP. 'Vows undertaken' VOT SVSC is usually followed by X or XX, representing ten or twenty years. This would leave one missing space unaccounted. AVG IMP never appears on Carausius' coin issues. To read the inscription as VOT SVSC LEG AVG THB, commemorating oaths of the inauguration of the Theban legion, can be posited as no less plausible.
10. P.H. Sawyer: *Age of the Vikings*, London, 1962, pp. 66–68 and J. Haywood: *Dark Age Naval Power*, New York, 1991, p. 270.
11. Gregory of Tours: *History of the Franks* 1:32–34.

12. A. Giardina: *Banditi a e santi, Athenaeum* 61:374–79, Rome, 1983, pp. 383–385. R. Van Dam: *Leadership and Community in late antique Gaul*, Berkeley, 1985, p. 54. E. Barza: *The Bacaudae, Dissertation*, University of Chicago, 1962. Eutr 9:20, Zon 12:31, PI 10:4, 2–3 and 7:8, 3.
13. S. Stevenson: *Dictionary of Roman Coins*, London, 1964, p. 40. RIC 595.
14. Salvian: *De Gubernatione Dei* 5:7–8.
15. MacMullen p. 211 and n.22 p. 357 citing the fifth century poem 'Querolum' tr. L. Herman in *Grognon*, 1957, p. 58.
16. Duchesne: *Scriptores Rerum Francarium I*, p. 662.

Chapter 16
1. AVE 38:6, AVH 39:9–10.
2. Otto of Freising: *The Two Cities*, New York, 1928, 111 p. 43.
3. A. Cappelli: *Dizionario de Abbreviature Latine ed Italiane*, Milan, 1967, p. 125.
4. MPL XVII 1021–58.
5. SS 4 May, p. 302–304.
6. *Bibliotheca Casiensis*, Cassino c. 1888 III. Thrason was a high-ranking officer in Rome secretly helping the persecuted. He was not a martyr. Pros.1.
7. PI 3:1,2 and 3:7, 6–7.
8. Smith, Maximianopolis. Nicephorium, the usual name, was to become headquarters for the Dux of Mesopotamia.
9. Eutr 10:20.
10. AVE 40:10.
11. SS Mai 7, pp. 428–430.
12. SS Nov pp. 626–629.
13. Ibid.
14. SS 2 Jun, pp. 461–462.
15. Calderini: *Aquileia Romana*, Milan, 1930, p. 67 n.5 citing CIL V 732, ILS 625.
16. PI 9:14.
17. Z. Klawans: *Reading and Dating Roman Coins*, Racine, 1959, p. 118.
18. AVE 39.
19. EVC 3:52.
20. Su: Domitian 15; Codex Justiniana 48:8, 4, 2.

Chapter 17
1. P. Southern and K. Drion: *The Late Roman Army*, London, 1996, p. 61.
2. Eutropius 9:20 states that Maximian Herculius crossed the Alpis Poenina, the Rhone Alps, in 286. The Rhone begins at the northern end of the Simplon Pass. W.W. Hyde: *Roman Alpina Routes*, Philadelphia, 1935, p. 2.
3. SS 5 Aug, pp. 803–805.
4. Ibid.
5. G. Finazzi: *Atti dei SS Firmo e Rustico*, Bergamo, 1852, pp. 2–28.
6. SS 5 May, p. 380–381.
7. F. Ferrero: *Valley of Aosta*, New York, 1910, and Hyde, pp. 70–73.
8. Strabo 4:6.
9. Bihlmeyer, pp. 131–134.
10. Balsdon Sali, and J. Gilliam: 'Roman Military Feriale', *Harvard Theological Review*, Boston, 1959.
11. Ibid, Arnobius 4:35.
12. PWH p. 355, n 8. The earliest evidence of Maximian's imperial rank are two Egyptian papyri of spring 286 indicating another ruler who could only have been Maximian sharing Diocletian's power. *Aegyptische Urkunden aus den Museem Zu Berlin*, Berlin,

1920, pp. 1090 and 922, O.A. n 8. A.Chastignol: 'Les Années Régnales de Maximian Hercule', *Revue Numismatique*, Paris, 1968, p. 69. Hydatius cites Maximian *caesar*, 1 April 286, and Augustus in September. W. Ensslin, PWK V 2490 argues that he became *augustus* on 1 April 286. W. Seston: *Jovius and Herculius, Historia*, Weisbaden, 1950, agrees. Maximian began his *bagaudae* campaign as Caesar. PL 2:4, Vol. I p. 27.
13. Soz 1:4,3 and 1:4,1.

Chapter 18
1. Livy 5:11; 9:8 and 30:16. Su: Vitellius 2.
2. Lk 7:20.
3. Eucherius of Lyon in Dupraz.
4. WRS pp. 119–121, TA 3:21; TH 1:31, Su: Caligula 48:1; Galba 12:2.
5. Cornish, p. 398.
6. Eucherius.
7. Ibid.

Chapter 19
1. Otto.
2. Dupraz, fol. 367–77, 390–81.
3. HL 21 Feb.
4. SS 4 Oct., pp. 991.
5. HL 1 Dec.
6. SS 13 Oct., pp. 319–324.
7. SS 2 Feb., p. 658.
8. Holweck, *Liturgy of Diocese of Pinerolo*.
9. HL 22 Sept.
10. HL 18 Sept.
11. SS 5 Aug., pp. 795–797.
12. P3 9 Dec.
13. SS 22 Sept.
14. SS 3 Sept., pp. 772–773.
15. Holweck, *Liturgy of Einseideln*.
16. EHE 7.
17. PWH p. 247, LMP 42:1, EVC 1:47.
18. PL 2:1 Vol. I, p. 28.
19. E. Galletier, ed.: *Panegyriques Latins*, Paris, 1949, I. Mamartinius II, VI:1 p. 29.
20. Blanchet.
21. PB 4 Jun.
22. PB 9 Aug.
23. SS 3 Oct., p. 2425.
24. PB 12 Nov.
25. MPL pp. 142, 783–785.
26. PB 22 Jan.
27. SS 5 Sept., pp. 764–765.
28. SS 5 Aug., p. 135.
29. SS 5 May, pp. 196–196.
30. PB 5 Jun.
31. SS 5 Jul., pp. 143–147.
32. PB 25 Sept.
33. Petrus de Natalibus: *Catalogus Sanctorum*, Venice, 1493, XII.
34. SS 3 Oct., pp. 288–289.
35. SS 5 May, p. 280–281.
36. PB 22 Sept.

37. Pros.
38. SS 8 Oct., pp. 338–339.
39. MPL 124, pp. 1111–1126.
40. SS 1 Jan., p. 704 n. 6.
41. Bede: *Historia Ecclesia* 1:6–7.
42. SS 11 Oct., pp. 535–537.
43. SS 1 Jan., pp. 325–326.
44. SS 2 Jun., pp. 796–797.
45. F.E. Schneider: *Die Krypta von St Paulin zu Trier*, Bonner Jahrbuch 1884, pp. 167–198. MPL 154, p. 116–163.
46. SS 2 Oct., p. 351 n. 80–82.
47. E. Griffe: *La Gaule Chretienne*, Paris, 1964, 1 Ch. 1.
48. E.A. Thompson: *A Roman Reformer and Inventor*, Oxford, 1952.
49. PL 11:2.
50. E. Nischer: *Army Reforms of Diocletian*, JRS 1923, p. 8.
51. 'Forrer Anzeiger fur Elsass', *Altertumst Bd 2*, pp. 1913–17, p. 513–520 mit abb 110.
52. SS 2 Feb., pp. 11–12.
53. SS 12 Oct., pp. 538–542.
54. MPL 212, p. 763 ff.
55. Ibid.

Chapter 20

1. PI 10:5 and 11:7.
2. Ibid 6:10 and 10:10.
3. PL 4, 1 p. 91. The other possibility is that the cohort of Frisian *peregrini* on the Scottish border had been moved to Boulogne.
4. HL 26 Jun.
5. SS 13 Oct., pp. 781–787.
6. Gregory of Tours: *In Gloria Martyrium* 62.
7. E.S.G. Robinson, 'Hoard of Alexandrine Coins From Guernsey', *Numismatic Chronicle*, 5 Sept. XVII, pp. 135–38, London, 1937. Guernsey was on the mainland, not an island, in the Roman era, the Channel deepening from the second century AD.
8. H. Shetelig: 'Roman Coins Found in Iceland', *Antiquity*, London, Sept. 1949, pp. 161–63 and F.M. Heichelheim: *Antiquity*, Mar. 1952. H. Holst: 'Mynter Norske Funn', *Nordisk Numismatisk Arsskrift*, Oslo, 1943, pp. 56–101.
9. PL 10:12.
10. RIC V Par 2, p. 441.
11. E. Bickerman: *Chronology of the Ancient World*, Ithaca, 1968, p. 191.
12. LMP 18–19; Eutr 9; AVE 39–40.
13. AVE 39; Eutr; Zon 12–13; Zos 2:8–9.
14. PI 6:5 and 8:6.
15. SS 5 Oct., pp. 36–40; MPL 212, pp. 759–72. Evaluated in W. Levison: 'Uber die Passio Gereonis', *Festschrift A. Breckmann*, Bonn, 1931, p. 43.
16. SS 9 Oct., pp. 154–155, 164–172, 207–209. *Fruchristliches Koln*, Koln, 1965, pp. 59–60.
17. W. Stukeley: *Letters and Diaries II*, p. 9.
18. Ibid.
19. D. Eicholz: 'Constantius Chlorus', *Invasion of Britain*, JRS 43:41–46.
20. J. Mothersole: *The Saxon Shore*, London, 1924, pp. 34–35.

Chapter 21

1. Van Berchem, *L'Armée*.
2. LRE III p. 182 n. 6.

3. ND Oc. V:11, p. 154 and Oc. VII:29. The II Felix Valentis Thebeorum was created in the late fourth century. Or VII:11,46.
4. Ibid Or VIII:4,36.
5. Ibid Or VII:10,45 and Or XXXI:32.
6. Ibid Or VIII:5 Or XXVIII:18.
7. ND Or VII:9,24.
8. Ibid, Oc V:26,171.
9. Ibid, Oc XL:21.
10. AM 1731.
11. D. Van Berchem: *Le Martyr de la Légion Thébaine*, Basle, 1956.
12. MPG 115, pp. 356–72.
13. Ibid.
14. LMP; Eutr.
15. SS 3 Oct., p. 863–869. E. Moore: *Some Soldier Martyrs of the Early Church*, Beirut, 1964.
16. O'Leary.
17. Ibid and H. Hyvernat: *Actes des Martyrs de l'Egypte*, pp. 1–39.
18. Codices Coptici in Vatican Library Borgia collection 16,109. G. Zoega: *Catalogus, Roma 1810*, 59:13 and John Rylands Library, Manchester p. 422 (7).
19. O'Leary, p. 178.
20. Ibid, pp. 264–265; Zoega, pp. 148–49; Hyvernat, 1:34.
21. EHE 8:4.
22. EHE 7:10. H. Delehaye: *La Persécution dans l'Armée sous Diocletian*, Académie Royale de Belgique, Brussels 1921, pp. 150–166.
23. O'Leary. D.H. Kerler: *Die Patronate der Heiligen*, Ulm, 1905, Orient 14 Aug.
24. Ibid.
25. MPG 115, pp. 596–609.
26. Analecta Bollandiana 75, p. 68–69. SS 3 Apr., p. 101.
27. E. Wallis-Budge: *George of Lydda*, London, 1930, p. 57.
28. EHE 8:14, SS 13 Oct., p. 281.
29. Musurillo, p. 259.
30. Eusebius: *De Vita Constantini* 1:19. Lactantius also describes Constantine as a young officer of Diocletian's guard. LMP 18:10.
31. O'Leary p. 262.
32. Ibid.
33. Ibid.
34. T.C. Skeat: *Papyri from Panopolis*, Dublin, 1964, papyrus 2, XXVII. British Museum Papyrus 5; T.T. Crum: *Catalog of Coptic Manuscripts in British Museum* p. 338.
35. Westermann.
36. L. Lacarriére: *Men Possessed by God*, New York, 1964, pp. 51–67.
37. PWH p. 367, n. 66.
38. Johnson pp. 142–43.
39. LMP 7, ILS p. 642. Eutro IX:23, AVC 39:23, Epit 39:3, PI VIII 5, Zon XII:31.
40. Van Berchem: *L'Armée*, E.C. Nischer: 'The Army Reforms of Diocletian and Constantine', JRS 13, 1–55.

Chapter 22
1. PWH 71:7, 76.
2. Malalas XII:308.
3. EHE 8:19.
4. O'Leary, p. 231.
5. Eusebius: *Martyrs of Palestine* 3:1.
6. O'Leary.

7. Cheesman.
8. SS 6 Aug., pp. 14–15.
9. Full office in Coptic rites, 29 Dec.. Ischyrion was killed with supposedly 8,140 others at Ichmin then Panopolis.
10. SS 1 Mar., pp. 751–755.
11. MPL 173, pp. 989–92.
12. O'Leary, p. 201.
13. O'Leary, pp. 174–175.
14. *Revue de l'Orient Chrétien*, Paris, 1910, pp. 301–306.
15. LRE I p. 618.
16. Jzn. 2.
17. J. Cerny: *Ancient Egyptian Religion*, London, p. 149.
18. J. Lacarriére.
19. Jerome: Letter XVII:2.
20. J.G. Davis: 'Condemnation to the Mines', *University of Birmingham Historical Journal* 1978, pp. 99–107.

Chapter 23
1. AVE 39.
2. Edict de Maleficiis et Manichaeis, Gregorian Code 14;4.
3. LMP 10; EHE 8:4.
4. HL 6 Sept.
5. Eutr 10:2, Epit. Caes. 40:15.
6. LMP 9.2.
7. EHE 8:2, LMP 12:12.
8. EMP 11:3.
9. EMP 1.4, EHE 8:3.
10. MPG 116, p. 1037–1081.
11. LMP 15:1.
12. MPG 116.
13. A. Ehrhard: *Hagiographischen*, Leipzig, 1880, 111 p. 296.
14. LMP 15, EHE 8:4.
15. F. Cumont: 'Le Tombeau de S. Dasius de Durostorum', *Analecta Bollandiana* 27, pp. 369–373 and Musurillo, pp. 272–279.
16. SS 6 May, pp. 654–665.
17. PB 4 May.
18. SS 3 Sept., p. 2188–2130.
19. SS 5 Aug., (1741) pp. 810–811.
20. PG 115, pp. 881–900.
21. PG 115, pp. 217–40.
22. H. Delahaye, AB (1912) pp. 192–194.
23. HL 28 Sept.
24. H. Delahaye: *Légendes Grecques des Saints Militaires*, Paris, 1909, pp. 202–03.
25. PG 136, pp. 264–84.
26. Ehrhard I, p. 479. RM May 21, MGR.
27. EHE 8:6.
28. PG 115, pp. 617–633.
29. PG 116, pp. 109–120.
30. RM Jn 15.
31. 'Le Martyrologe de Rabban Sliba' in AB 27, 1908.
32. LMP 15:3.
33. EHE 8:5.

34. AB IX, pp. 123–134.
35. AB IX, pp. 116–123.
36. RM 12 Jan.
37. Frend, pp. 371–375.
38. HL 21 Oct.
39. Ter: Apol. 50:13.
40. V.M. Kurkjian: *History of Armenia*, New York, 1964, pp. 114–118.
41. PG 115, p. 964.
42. RM 9 Jul., F. Krauss: *Roma Sotteranea Die Romischen Katakomben*, Freiburg, 1879, p. 523. G. Schmid: *Roma Das Unterirdische*, Brixen, 1908, p. 316. MPG 115, pp. 881–900.
43. PG 115, pp. 881–900.
44. RM 10 Feb.
45. RM 29 Jan.
46. With Marcellus, SS Jan. II pp. 5–9 and PL CLXXXIX pp. 993–998.
47. SS 1 Jun., pp. 60–61.
48. LMP 17:8–9.
49. LMP pp. 21–23, EHE 8:13.
50. LMP 19.
51. AVC 39 and Eutr IX:16.
52. SS 2 Jan., pp. 5–9, PL CCLXXXIX, pp. 993–98.
53. EHE 6:43 as translated by G.A. Williamsons, New York, 1965, p. 282, n. 2. This is a basis of estimates that there were 30,000 to 50,000 Christians in Rome.
54. LMP 18:12.

Chapter 24
1. LMP 24.
2. AVC 40; AVE 41; Zos 2:8.
3. EVC 1:28.
4. PI 6:21,4.
5. LMP 26.
6. Zos 2:10; AVE 39; LMP 29.
7. LMP 18; AVC 40; Eutr 10; Zos 2:9 and PL 9:4.
8. PI 6:16–20; LMP 29:'4 and 30:5, Eutr 10:3; AVE 40.
9. LMP 42; EVC 1:47.
10. EHE 9:9.
11. O. Seeck: 'Das Sogenannte Edikt von Mailand', *Zeitschrift fur Kirchengeschichte*, Gotha, c. 1884.
12. RIC VII Ostia 1–5.
13. PI 4:22; 12:5.

Chapter 25
1. Soc 12; EVC 1:28–32; DAC 3:3122.
2. H. A. Deake: *In Praise of Constantine*, Berkeley, 1975, pp. 72–74. H. Marrou: *Autour de Monogramme Constantinien in Melanges*, E. Gilson, Paris 1959, pp. 403–414. *Labare* is a Spanish word. The Spanish priest Hosius accompanied Constantine in 313.
3. AVC 40.
4. Zos 2:16.
5. LMP 45:9, Eutr 10:4.
6. B. Berenson: *Arch of Constantine*, London, 1954, p. 27. H.P.L. Orange Maurische Auxilien and H.P. L'Orange: 'Una strana Testimonianza fin ora Inosservato nei Rilievi dell Arco de Constantino', *Revista de Studi*, Rome, 1936, pp. 218–219, citing Heliodorus: *Aethiopica* 9:16,19. Lucian: *De Saltatione* 18. Claudian: *Nilus* 20–23 and *De Tertio*

Consulatu Honorii Augustus pp. 20–21. Roman arrows were in two parts, probably as few long shafts were straight. The Theban headdress utilized only the feathered end shafts. R. Mynor: *XII Panegyrici Latini*, Oxford 1964 XI 17,4 is addressed to Maximian.
7. ND OC:V:60.
8. Eusebius: *De Vita Constantini* I:XL. Socrates Scholasticus: *Ecclesiastical History XVII*, states that the ankh symbolized 'life to come.'

Chapter 26
1. SS 3 Aug., pp. 580–599.
2. LMP 36:4; EHE 8:14 and 9:4.
3. Jn: 6:15, Jn: 18, 36.
4. Jn: 8, 1–11.
5. O. Marucchi: *Christian Epigraphy*, Chicago, 1974, p. 322 citing S. Scaglia: *Notiones Archeologia Christiana* n.d., II Pt 1, p. 271.
6. J.M. Parkes: *Jews and Christians in the Roman Era*, London, 1964. A.M. Jones: *Constantine and the Conversion of Europe*, London, 1948, p. 220.
7. EVC 3:48.
8. EHE 10:6 and 10:7.
9. Y. Congar: *Power and Poverty in the Church*, New York, 1964. The occasion was adoption of a monastic uniform nonetheless.
10. Munier, Canon 3, pp. 5 and 9 noting different versions.
11. CT 12:1; 16:2; 313:2; 313:7 and 330. LMP 1:10; EHE 10:7. Decurions could not legally become clergy. Nevertheless, St Patrick's grandfather was Decurion and priest.
12. CT 1:27. Both parties had to agree to have clergy as judges.
13. CIL VIII pt. 1 fasc. 1, p. 2668 citing I. Gruterius: *Inscriptiones Antiquae Totius Orbis Romani*, Amsterdam, 1707 rp of Heidelberg 1603, 1139 6 *Ae Gillotti Schedis*. The present whereabouts of the tablet is unknown.
14. Cappelli CC and Bickerman p. 146.
15. An otherwise unknown Legio VIII Augusta Alexandrinianae appears on inscriptions in a Mithraic shrine at Strasbourg. CIL III pt. 4 11608 and 11609, the era uncertain.
16. Marucchi 19, 56, 137, 145, 258, 262, 283, 372 are masculine; 60, 61, 79, 123, 223, 257, 320 are feminine.
17. Gregory of Tours: *In Gloria Martyrum* 74 (75).
18. PB IX 319 citing Dinet: *Legendaire d'Autun* by Pequequot. MPL 71, p. 881–882. The earliest known mention of Cassianus as an Egyptian is of the ninth century, G. Mathon: *Bibliotheca Sanctorum*, Rome, 1963, 3:908. Soc 7:36 mentions several transferred bishops. The practice was later forbidden. W. Smith and S. Cheetham: *Dictionary of Christian Antiquities*, Hartford, 1880, pp. 225–226. CIL XII pt 6, 12766, 129970–13000, 13002, 13005, 13007–08 are the only known roof tiles from Roman Gaul with pictorial brandmarks, the face of a black person with a feathered headdress. Theban retirees at Autun and Lyon become tilemakers?

Epilogue
1. CT 7:20.
2. S. Barr: *The Mask of Jove*, New York, 1966, p. 573 n. 1067.
3. Bihlmeyer, pp. 246–250.
4. Munier.
5. Soz 1:8.
6. Zos 2:34.
7. R. Browning: *The Emperor Julian*, Los Angeles, 1976, p. 135.
8. SS 4 Aug., pp. 430–432.
9. AM 25:3.

10. Browning.
11. Bihlmeyer, p. 250–252.
12. AM 30.
13. Zos 4:20.
14. AM 31:11–16; Zos 4:20–24.
15. Ferrill: *Fall of the Roman Empire: The Military Explanation*, New York, 1988, Ch. 3.
16. AM 30:4.
17. Ibid 27.

Afterword
1. Athanasius' Letter to Amun 48.
2. Augustine: *The City of God* IV:4.
3. H. Deane: *The Political and Social Ideas of St Augustine*, New York, 1963, p. 163.
4. DAC 2:1174.
5. CT 16:5; 16:10.
6. Aug: Letters XX. C. Murphy: *Are We Rome?*, New York, 2006.

Select Bibliography

The earliest manuscript Acts of the Theban Legion are analyzed in L. Dupraz: *Les Passions de St Maurice d'Agaune*, Fribourg, 1961, and are criticized in D. Van Berchem: *Le Martyre de la Légion Thébaine*, Basle, 1956. They are also recorded in *MGH III* (Monumenta Historica Germanicarum)p. 32–41.

The basic data is in D. O'Reilly: 'Eagle Between Banners on Roman Coinage', *SAN* 8:1976; 'Maximian's Bagaudae Campaign of 286', *SAN* 8:1977 and 'The Mystery of London's Fetter Lane Hoard', *SAN* 9:1978. Part of the evidence is brought together in D. O'Reilly: 'The Theban Legion of St Maurice', *Vigiliae Christianae*, Leiden 1977. For analysis of the Autun inscription, see D. O'Reilly: 'An Autun Inscription to the Theban Legion's Martyrs at Acaunus', *The Ancient World*, Chicago, 1978.

For chronology H.M.D. Parker: *History of the Roman World 137–338 A.D.*, N.Y. 1958 is followed. On the army G. Watson: The *Roman Soldier* (GRS), Ithaca 1969 serves as guide. Also recommended are Y. Le Bohec: *The Imperial Roman Army*, N.Y. 1990; M. Grant: *The Army of the Caesars*, London 1992 and G. Webster: *The Roman Imperial Army*, N.Y. 1984. The period in focus is in D. Van Berchem: *L Armée de Diocletian et la reforme Constantinienne*, Paris 1952.

A conflict of moral loyalties is described in J. Helgeland: *Christians and the Roman Army, Church History*, Chicago 1974. The view that pagan rites and not bloodshed caused Christian avoidance of the military is that of E.A. Ryan: 'Rejection of Military Service by Early Christians', *Theological Studies*, Washington, D.C. 1952. C.J. Cadoux: *The Early Christian Attitude Towards War*, N.Y. 1982 rp of 1912 is a classic. L.J. Swift: *The Early Fathers on War and Military Service*, Wilmington 1983 concisely surveys newer research.

W.H.C. Frend: *Martyrdom and Persecution in the Early Church*, N.Y. 1967 surveys events and the same author's *The Rise of Christianity* covers the social and philosophical struggles. M. Sordi: *The Christians and the Roman Empire*, Norman 1986 analyzes the changes in Roman religious policy with objective perspectives not found elsewhere. The pagan and stoic background is presented in R.L. Fox: *Pagans and Christians*, N.Y. 1986 and T.R. Glover: *The Conflict of Religions in the Early Roman Empire*, N.U. 1975 rp of 1909 quotes many pagan criticisms of Christianity at length.

F.G. Holweck: *Biographical Dictionary of the Saints*, Detroit 1969 is a starting point for hagiography. F. Halkin, *Bibliotheca Hagiographica Latina* 1949 and the same editor's *Bibliotheca Hagiographica Graeca* 1957 published by the Bollandists at Brussels are key to the earliest sources. These collections begun in the seventeenth century containing complete Acts by feast days in the Church calendar now date several weeks in error because of changes from the Julian to the Gregorian calendar. The *Analecta Bollandiana* (AB) begun in 1882 analyzes the material.

The 222 volumes of J.P. Migne, *Patrologiae Cursus Completus, Serie Graeca* (MPG) and 168 volumes of J.P. Migne, *Patrologiae Cursus Completus, Serie Latini* (MPL) reprinted in 1979 are the most extensive source collection.

Index